IF JESUS WERE MAYOR

How Your Local Church Can Transform Your Community

Bob Moffitt calls the church to action to fulfill Christ's command, "Go and make disciples of all nations." Be prepared to be challenged and changed.

Loren Cunningham, Founder
Youth With A Mission

Bob Moffitt raises an intriguing question: "What would Jesus do if He were Mayor of your community?" His reply comes in the form of a book, fully documented biblically, with illustrations and lessons, making a case for the local church as an agent of transformation.

Tetsunao Yamamori, International Director
Lausanne Committee for World Evangelization

Bob Moffitt has captured the very essence of what ministry entails. I highly recommend this book!

Ralph Neighbour, President
Touch Glocal Training Center, USA

The Lord intends for His church to thrive and grow as self-sufficient and abundantly provided for. This conviction has gripped and led Bob Moffitt to develop down-to-earth teaching material which has now been used around the world to bless the church. Having used it in India and seen its value, I commend this work to churches, that they may realize a healthy future in an age of many challenges.

Siga Arles, Dean
Consortium for Indian Missiological Education

Other works by Bob Moffitt and Harvest:

BASICS Wholistic Discipleship
 Book 1: Jesus the King
 Book 2: The Image of God
 Book 3: The Church

Wholistic Ministry Training
 A Christian Response to Human Need
 Biblical Wholism
 Servanthood
 The Kingdom of God
 Kingdom Math
 The Church as a Window
 Seed Projects

Skills for Community Development
 Participatory Learning
 Leadership
 Project Management

The Kingdom Lifestyle Series (with Darrow Miller and Scott Allen)
 God's Remarkable Plan for the Nations
 The Worldview of the Kingdom of God
 God's Unshakable Kingdom

The Church as a Window (video)

A Vision for Carapita (video)

On Earth as It Is in Heaven (video series with Darrow Miller)

IF
JESUS
WERE
MAYOR

HOW YOUR LOCAL CHURCH
CAN TRANSFORM YOUR COMMUNITY

BOB MOFFITT
with KARLA TESCH

MONARCH
BOOKS

Oxford, UK & Grand Rapids, Michigan, USA

An earlier edition of this book was published by Bob Moffitt
and Harvest in 2004

First published in the UK in 2006 by Monarch Books
(a publishing imprint of Lion Hudson plc), Mayfield House,
256 Banbury Road, Oxford OX2 7DH.
Tel: +44 (0)1865 302750 Fax: +44 (0)1865 302757
Email: monarch@lionhudson.com
www.lionhudson.com

ISBN-13: 978-1-85424-763-6 (UK)
ISBN-10: 1-85424-763-8 (UK)
ISBN-13: 978-0-8254-6129-3 USA)
ISBN-10: 0-8254-6129-4 (USA)

Distributed by:
UK: Marston Book Services Ltd, PO Box 269,
Abingdon, Oxon OX14 4YN;
USA: Kregel Publications, PO Box 2607,
Grand Rapids, Michigan 49501

Unless otherwise stated, Scripture quotations are taken from the Holy Bible,
New International Version, © 1973, 1978, 1984 by the International Bible
Society. Used by permission of Hodder & Stoughton Ltd. All rights reserved.

The text paper used in this book has been made from wood independently
certified as having come from sustainable forests.

British Library Cataloguing Data
A catalogue record for this book is available from the British Library.

Book layout designed by Brian Gammill, Harvest, 2004.

Printed and bound in Malta by Gutenberg Press

This effort is dedicated to God's glory and to the advance of His reign—on earth as it is experienced in heaven.

Men are saying that Jesus Christ came as a social reformer.
Nonsense!

We are social reformers; Jesus Christ came to alter us,
and we try to shirk our responsibility by putting our work on
Him.

Jesus alters us and puts us right;
then these principles of His instantly make us social reformers.
They begin to work straightway where we live . . .

—Oswald Chambers

Contents

Foreword

Our church is on a journey. We believe God wants us to be relevant, practical, and effective in reaching our community for Christ. We have been learning how we can do this through the dynamic principles of biblical wholism contained in this book.

Bob Moffitt and the seed project principles have changed our corporate life. As a cell-based church, deeply committed to community and evangelism, we have been thrilled and excited to see the tremendous impact of these small demonstrations of God's love—both on the members of our church body and the members of the community at large.

The practical demonstration of the love of Christ in meeting the needs of our community is becoming a way of life for us. Over the past several years since learning these principles, we have been able to conduct hundreds of practical community development and service projects that have brought favor to our local congregation, souls into the Kingdom, and glory to the Lord.

I believe that Jesus is teaching His church some very important things that we have forgotten. Our social acts of kindness and righteousness do matter very much to Him. He is not only the Lord of the church. He is the Lord of all and cares for every facet of society, all of the community, and its structure. To neglect community involvement and development tarnishes the image of Christ and stands in opposition to the call of Christ to compassionately reach out in love to a world that is needy in every way—spiritually, socially, and economically.

We have been learning that we can do nothing for God, as though He needed anything. The only thing that we can do for God is what we do for others. This is what Jesus meant when He said in Matthew 25:40, "I tell you the truth, whatever you did for the least of these brothers of mine, you did for me."

I invite you to join us in this journey of faith by digesting the contents of this book and applying them wholeheartedly in your life and your church. Then stand back and watch while God begins to do something fresh, new, and living in you and in your community.

Gary M. Skinner
Pastoral Team Leader
Kampala Pentecostal Church
Kampala, Uganda

Preface

Have you ever thought about this: *What if Jesus were Mayor of your community?* I never had. I had worked for many years among people who were poor or disenfranchised. I knew that their conditions broke God's heart. But one day, twenty years ago, I was talking with discouraged pastors in a small slum community in Honduras. As I did, God broke through with a stirring vision and a question: *"What would Jesus do if He were Mayor of your community?"* We mentally walked with Him through the streets. We saw Him weep to see people's suffering. We caught a glimpse of His vision for the community. You will read the story yourself in this book.

The church—the Body of Christ here on earth—has exciting potential and responsibility. It has been commissioned and equipped by Jesus Christ. That day in Honduras, I thought, "The Body of Christ should serve the community just as Jesus would!" I understood that Jesus *is* Mayor of our communities as He works through His transforming agent, the church . . . us! That's His plan—His grand agenda—for His representative on earth.

I realize that some may respond to the title of this book by thinking, "Jesus didn't come to be a social reformer!" In a sense, they are right. I appreciate Oswald Chambers' comment:

> Men are saying that Jesus Christ came as a social reformer. Nonsense! We are the social reformers; Jesus Christ came to alter us, and we try to shirk our responsibility by putting our work on Him. Jesus alters us and puts us right; then these principles of His instantly make us social reformers. They begin to work straightway where we live . . . [1]

---

[1] Oswald Chambers, *My Utmost Devotional Bible,* Reading 92. This citation is also for the epigraph at the front of this book.

If Jesus Were Mayor is about the kind of evangelism that brings men and women to a sustained, "altered" relationship with Christ and then leads to the discipleship of their nations—through the church.

I originally intended to write this book for church leaders in the Two-Thirds World.[2] I had worked in that arena for a quarter of a century, and I knew of the need for such a book. But an interesting thing happened. Church leaders from the Two-Thirds World challenged me: *"Why write it just to us? Don't pastors and church leaders everywhere need this message?"*

They were right! The ministry principles in these pages are true everywhere! I am grateful to Monarch Books for helping deliver them to many areas of the world. Wherever you live, I invite you to read *If Jesus Were Mayor*, and I pray you find its message challenging and applicable to your church, your community, and your culture.

Let me broaden this invitation. In this work, I frequently speak of conservative (evangelical, charismatic, or Pentecostal) churches. These are the churches we most frequently encounter in our work. However, I invite people from *all* church traditions to read and explore the application of the messages in their own settings. One of my convictions is that the church is God's principal entity to heal the brokenness of the world. Another is that God wants to build unity among us as we serve together. Yes, please read, *whatever your tradition!*

Another reason I wrote for my brothers and sisters in conservative churches is their churches' frequently unbalanced, narrow focus on spiritual ministry. Many have never learned that God commands His children to intentionally and actively demonstrate His compassion for physical and social brokenness. They have often lacked the strategy, biblical "permission," and resources. Everywhere I teach—in more than thirty countries in the past twenty years—I

---

[2] *Two-Thirds World*: Geographical areas in Asia, Africa, Latin America, and limited regions of Europe and North America, characterized by contexts of need and by unique worldviews and cultures. Sometimes called the Third World (a term based on economic and quality-of-life indicators). Two-Thirds World, however, better indicates the percentage of the world's population in those geographical areas.

see church leaders who have an urgent sense that God has called them to do more, much more. This book was originally written for them, but will challenge all who are ready to bring themselves and their congregations into broader and deeper service.

God's agenda begins with the spiritual salvation of each individual, primarily through the ministry of the local church—but His full agenda is nothing less than the discipleship of the nations! Churches that are committed to this broad agenda continue to bring individuals to Christ—and God's *shalom* to communities. We will look at Scripture from the perspective of God's broad agenda for the church. One of our staff members who previously served with an evangelical ministry has been heard to remark: "I can't imagine how many times I taught students from the Scriptures, but I never even saw the Bible's broad implications. Yet, it's right there!" That's the kind of revelation I trust you will have as you read these pages. *If Jesus Were Mayor* also includes real-life stories of transforming service. These stories are interspersed throughout the book, so you can meet some of the many individuals and churches from around the world who have answered for themselves: *"What would happen if Jesus were Mayor of our community?"* I encourage you to "translate" the stories into your own context. Capture the spirit, dedication, and creativity of our brothers and sisters!

I am humbled to be one more voice in the movement God is developing, and I share my vision from the perspective God has given me at this stage in my journey. I urge you to measure what you read here by the written Word and the inner promptings of His Spirit. One of our staff members in Brazil said that reading the manuscript was like having a long chat with me. I invite you, too, for a nice, long chat. I am glad God has given us this opportunity to look together at something that means—quite literally—the world to Him!

BOB MOFFITT

Acknowledgements

I want to thank the following for their help in making this book a reality.

- Our worldwide Harvest staff who have done the hard field work in which the lessons have been learned—and who have helped develop and revise them.

- Our U.S. staff who have granted me the time and space to write.

- Food for the Hungry, International whose partnership in ministry has greatly expanded our vision and reach.

- Darrow Miller, my brother and colleague with whom my life and ministry has intertwined since seminary days.

- Karla Tesch, our Harvest "editor-in-chief" who reworked the manuscript, composed the topics outside our normal training curriculum, and clarified the obtuse.

- Many colleagues and readers who have reviewed the manuscript and made suggestions.

- Judy, my beloved partner in life, whose patience and first reading of this project have been truly encouraging.

- Most of all, our Elder Brother, Jesus, whose astounding mercy and grace allow us the high privilege of serving Him.

In Memoriam

Special acknowledgements in honor of Ruth Concha, a friend, colleague, trainer, and practitioner from Peru. "Ruthie" not only read the first draft with zeal but responded with timely examples, concrete applications, thoughts, and research. Many were so pertinent they made their way into the manuscript. She received a copy one month before losing her earthly life in a traffic accident in Peru. I am thankful that her voice of experience and zeal for transformation through the church have been captured for you on these pages.

How to Read This Book . . .

This book is both a definitive work about a "wholistic" ministry—and a handbook for practitioners. I recommend you read it from cover to cover. Here are some specifics:

1. Read Part One to catch a vision for Jesus' agenda for your community and church.

2. Read Part Two to examine God's agenda to restore all things. View the church's servant role in cultural transformation through the lenses of Scripture, history, and present-day examples.

3. Read Part Three to see how local churches can be equipped and mobilized for service. See how God multiplies the effects of faithful and sacrificial service.

4. Read Part Four for tools that help local churches and individuals plan, execute, and evaluate community ministry. The tools may also be used by trainers.

PART ONE

The Mayor's Agenda

*. . . Your will be done
on earth as it is in heaven.*

—Matthew 6:10

The Journey Begins | 1

My Journey

God has given me a passion. My passion is that Christ's Body—especially the local church—will see and fulfill the great purpose for which He created it. This is the story of how I came to this passion. It is the story of my journey—literally and figuratively! I trust it will help you understand the perspective from which I write and the reason I urge people to ask what Jesus would do if He were Mayor.

I have to be careful not to put my passion for the church above knowing Christ, its head. I desire to know Christ above all else, as the Apostle Paul told the church at Philippi.[1] Those of us who have a passion are in danger of placing greater focus on the task than on the Task-Giver. When our focus is on anything but Christ, we diminish the impact of our work. Strength for the harvest does not come from our work, but from the One who gives us our assignment. Lord, help us to desire You first!

I am a preacher's kid. From my infancy until I was fifteen, my father pastored a loving Baptist church in a working-class neighborhood in central Los Angeles. My parents had attended the Bible Institute of Los Angeles, now Biola University. It was there that God birthed in them a passion for world evangelism. They prepared to go as missionaries to Africa, but instead accepted the challenge to recruit and send others.

The words written above the baptistery in that church are still etched in my mind: "Does anyone have the right to hear the Gospel twice until everyone has heard it once?" Our family and our church supported missionaries, and visiting missionaries stayed in our home. I listened to their stories. They were my heroes. I wanted to be like them.

---

[1] Philippians 3:7-10

When I was fifteen, Dad became General Secretary of the Arizona Baptist Convention. He had a vision to plant churches. More than one hundred churches were planted under his twenty-five year ministry. World evangelism and church planting were a wonderful heritage, but my early adult experiences caused me to search hard for answers to troubling questions.

I spent two years in the Peace Corps teaching secondary school in Malawi, Africa. My placement was at a rural mission station school, much like the ones I heard about as a boy. The missionaries had done a good job. The school was academically one of the best in the country. It was well run and efficiently administered. The missionaries clearly loved the students and wanted to reach them with the Gospel. I, too, wanted to see our students come into a personal relationship with Jesus and joined one of the missionaries in private, early-morning intercession for our students.

However, some of the students were turning away from the Gospel. They sensed a message—right or wrong—that the missionaries' Christianity must serve as a pattern for Africans who became Christians. The students suspected cultural imperialism, and this suspision caused many to reject the culture and the faith of missionaries who truly loved them. At this point, I began to question cross-cultural evangelism—yet I believed I had been called to missions.

After my Peace Corps service, I began what was an almost two-year quest to understand missions and my possible role in it. I traveled through most of sub-equatorial Africa by motorcycle, where I met and spent time with many missionaries. On this trip, I met two young African men who have become my life-long brothers. They are now Christian leaders in their own countries.

I hitchhiked through the Middle East and completed a semester of graduate school in Israel. Next, I purchased a used two-cylinder Citroen in Belgium (nicknamed "The Ugly Duckling" by the French) and drove it to India, where it collapsed of well-earned fatigue. On the final part of my odyssey, I flew to nine countries in South and East Asia. Throughout this journey, I interviewed missionaries and national Christians. I wanted to know what did and did not work in the spread of the Gospel. I concluded that cross-cultural evangelism *is* valid, but its greatest potential is when cross-cultural missionaries come not as masters or "bwanas," but as brothers and servants to national churches. I confirmed my call to missions, returned home, and immediately entered seminary in Denver, majoring in missions. Unknowingly, I was headed for a difficult dose of reality that would radically change my feelings toward the church.

The seminary encouraged students to engage in community ministry. My response was to coordinate a new program to provide mentors for young law-breakers, many of whom were African-Americans and Hispanics. Even though our program was openly Christian, the court was willing to refer its young people to us. Adult Christians could provide needy youth with loving friendships and also tell them about faith in Christ—a perfect opportunity to combine the Great Commandment[2] and the Great Commission![3] The seminary president wrote letters to local churches, and I spoke to hundreds of church people. There was little response. Perhaps the racial tension of the times made people fearful. Fortunately, my fellow seminary students were willing. Ten seminary students began one-to-one mentoring relationships with youth. Results were good, and the court referred still more youth to us. We desperately tried to get Christians from local churches involved, but with little success. The need was so great that we reluctantly accepted non-Christian university students who literally begged to participate. Our program grew and became a national model. But the growth was primarily because non-Christians were willing to befriend needy young people. I became profoundly disappointed with the church of my

---

[2] *Great Commandment:* Jesus said that the first and greatest commandment is *"Love the Lord your God with all your heart and with all your soul and with all your mind."* The second is *"Love your neighbor as yourself."* Together, they summarize the laws and teachings of the Old Testament (Matthew 22:37-40).

[3] *Great Commission:* Jesus told His followers to go and make disciples of all nations, baptize them, and teach them to obey all His commands (Matthew 28:19-20).

heritage. I increasingly wanted little to do with people who talked about love but were reluctant to help troubled young people who might otherwise never encounter the love of God. I loved the Lord, but I was angry—very angry—with the church.

In the midst of my frustration, God spoke to me. Through the Word and prayer, He told me, "Bob, this is My church, My bride. As broken as she is, I love her. I gave My life for her. Until you love her with My love, I cannot use you to help her become what I intend her to be."

I felt like a dagger had plunged into my soul. "Lord," I confessed, "Forgive me. I can't love the church unless You fill my heart with Your love for her, but I am willing." The Lord answered that prayer. Today, I love the church in spite of her brokenness, and my passion is to contribute to her healing. Was I called to missions? Yes! I saw my mission was to serve the church, to help her claim her inheritance. I soon joined Food for the Hungry to initiate and direct volunteer programs. Before long, God had opened the next door—to churches in the Two-Thirds World.

Our Journey

In 1981, I founded Harvest. Originally, Harvest partnered Christians in the Two-Thirds World with believers in North America. We had many church-to-church partnerships. We also partnered Christian organizations—for example, a Dominican daycare center with an American preschool; a Dominican burn-treatment center with a U.S. nursing school; a Haitian farming cooperative with American families. The partnerships were intended to help the materially poorer churches or groups tangibly demonstrate Christ's love in their communities. A number of good projects were initiated. But in some church partnerships, we observed church leaders competing for control of the resources from their North American partners. One church in the Two-Thirds World even split over issues of money control, and a pastor succumbed to corruption. We also saw that local Christian organizations which we partnered could not sustain large projects without ongoing outside resources—and that was not our goal!

In 1986, our Harvest board and staff went to our knees, asking God for direction. God answered. Our focus became the local church—not other Christian organizations—and we began to move away from projects funded by resources outside the community. Instead, we focused on training local church leaders and congregations about the biblical imperative to live out their faith in word and deed—starting with *local* resources.

Our first efforts were in five Latin American and Caribbean countries. The results were exciting! Churches watched God multiply their efforts. Previously disinterested people in their communities came to faith in Christ through the demonstration of God's love. Churches grew, and these churches began to impact their communities spiritually and physically. Word spread in the missions community. Youth With A Mission (YWAM) invited us to train their community development students. In 1997 Harvest began to collaborate informally with Food for the Hungry. The collaboration opened the door for our organizations to train churches and church-related missions in more than forty countries, imparting a vision and strategy for biblical wholistic ministry.[4] Our training curriculum has been translated by local groups into more than twenty languages. In fifteen countries, local groups have formed to promote and encourage this approach. This simple understanding is transforming churches and communities. God has done it, and it is awesome to behold!

Our Growing Journey

God's intention for His church does not change, but my understanding changes as I continue on the path where God has placed me. Our collaboration with Food for the Hungry not only enlarged our training opportunities, but our thinking! We came to see that the church must not only impact its local community—*but disciple its nation.*[5] And we came to see that a biblical worldview

---

[4] *Biblical wholistic ministry:*   Ministry that reflects God's concerns for whole persons and the whole of creation, as revealed in Scripture.
[5] God has since led both organizations to become founding partners of Disciple Nations Alliance (DNA).

is essential if we are going to disciple our nations or serve our communities *as if Jesus were Mayor.* A worldview is, simply, a collection of premises by which people view their world and how it works. A biblical worldview tells us that we are a broken race. Without God's intervention, we are without hope—but, with God's Good News, there is hope for the healing of our brokenness! This is the worldview we embrace.

. . . Now, let's meet the Mayor!

If Jesus Were Mayor | 2
Catching a Vision of God's Agenda

❖ Two history-making prayer breakfasts were recently held in Nairobi, the capital city of Kenya. One prayer breakfast was for the National Assembly, where the President was the guest of honor. The Mayor of Nairobi hosted another one. This was the first time that the city leaders of Nairobi had met to pray. Several political figures declared their faith publicly. The government minister who spoke at the breakfast issued this challenge: "If you loved your neighbor as yourself, would things be different in Nairobi? How?" Does this sound familiar? *("What would Nairobi, Kenya, be like if Jesus were Mayor?")* After the breakfast, there was a newfound spirit of unity. Civic leaders decided to begin a weekly fellowship and make the prayer breakfast an annual event.[1]

❖ A colleague in India went to a village where his ministry team had been working for a year. They asked the village women what a "developed" village looked like. *("What would your village look like if Jesus were Mayor?")* Umrai, one of the more outspoken, described a village where there was unity and solidarity. She knew Jesus was not honored by how her village was divided. Each family lived only for itself. Because of her reply, the group formed a health committee and a self-help group. The self-help group, comprised of fourteen village women, began to meet regularly and with great enthusiasm. Group members collected small amounts of individual savings into a group account—and they began to solve community problems together. Umrai became president and used her leadership gifts to plan and mobilize the village to do the kinds of things Jesus would do if He were Mayor.

---

[1] Sources for stories marked by ❖ are listed in the Bibliography at the end of the book.

*"If Jesus were Mayor, how would your community change?"*² I often ask this of pastors and church leaders in our conferences around the world. Their answers help them catch a vision to engage their churches in their communities.

The Bible clearly says: *"Where there is no vision the people perish."*³ If young people lack a vision for their future, they don't know how to spend their time. They are unsure about their direction, and they accomplish little. Young people with a vision for their future, however, do not have a problem using time well or making decisions. Their lives are organized around specific visions for their future. In the same way, a church without a vision does little more than maintain the status quo. It has little chance of making an impact for the Kingdom of God in its community. But a church with a vision has an opportunity for earthly and eternal significance.

If Jesus were Mayor, how would your community change?

We do not want just any vision—but God's vision for the people and world He created and loves. Jesus always carried out the will of His Father.⁴

Knowing that, let's imagine: *What would Jesus do if He were Mayor?*

- What would He do about street children and the homeless?
- What would He do about alcoholism, drug abuse, and other addictions?
- How would He strengthen families?

---

² *Mayor:* The primary leader in a local community. (As you read, please substitute the term used for the primary leader in your community. What would your community be like if Jesus were in that role?)
³ Proverbs 29:18 (KJV)
⁴ John 15:10; John 5:19

- How would He promote safe drinking water, adequate housing and food, health services, garbage and sewer systems, and decent roads?
- What would He do about fair wages and adequate employment?
- What would He do about unwanted children and care for the sick and elderly?
- What would He do to bring beauty—clean streets, trees, flowers, and public parks?
- What changes would He make in the education of children and adults?
- What new public policy decisions would He institute?
- How would He help people evaluate problems and make just decisions?
- What would He do to change the way local government works?
- Would His teachings be televised? Would He hold "town meetings" where His agenda and Kingdom principles would be set forth?
- What would He do about crime and civil unrest? What guidelines would He use for police and community relations?
- What changes would He make in the courts? In the prison systems?
- What would He do about the gap between the rich and the poor?
- How would the "little people" be treated in the community? How would the powerful people feel about Him?
- What would He do about corruption and bribery?
- What regulations would He establish for business?
- What would He do about depression, loneliness, and mental illness?
- How would He deal with pornography, sexual immorality, and prostitution?
- What would He do about child and spousal abuse?
- How would He improve social relationships among the citizens?
- What would He do about recreation and entertainment?
- What role would the church play in the community?
- How would He encourage unity among the churches?

- What would He do about other religions?

- Would His teachings and actions put His life in jeopardy?

- How would the community be changed to reflect the administration's priorities?

We are working in the realm of our imaginations, and there is a caution. Before our speculations go off course, I should say what I do and do not mean. Let's use these as ground rules to imagine His governance in ways that are compatible with the realities of Jesus and the present world:

- Jesus' mayoral actions would match the character of God, revealed in Scripture. He would carry out God's will.

- Jesus would not be literally returning in the flesh as a community leader.[5] Instead, we are imagining what would happen if Jesus' character, values, laws, and teachings were the governing basis for our communities.

- Jesus would not establish a theocracy or a government ruled by the church.

- Individuals would have free choice.

- Jesus would not create a welfare state. For example, His government would not instantly provide free housing for everyone. He would not instantly and miraculously make everything perfect for all of the citizens. As He did in Scripture, He would involve the citizens in healing the brokenness around them.

We cannot know exactly what Jesus would do as Mayor, but we can study Scriptures and ask the Holy Spirit to reveal what they mean for our communities. We need to know God's Word and character—and hear His voice. The things Jesus would do as Mayor would reflect the Father's will for the community. Jesus taught us to

---

[5] The idea of Jesus as Mayor is only to help us think how it would be if His will were carried out in our communities and societies. We recognize that He did not establish a political kingdom on earth.

pray to our Father: *"Your kingdom come, your will be done on earth as it is in heaven."*[6] God wants His will done on earth—now—as it is in heaven. He desires this because He loves us and the world He created. He wants the very best for us. As we will learn, He wants to reconcile everything back to Himself.

We can also learn from others, as we will in this chapter and throughout this book, to see how they have already answered the question in their locales: *"What would Jesus do here if He were Mayor?"*

Imagine what would happen if God's will were done on earth as in heaven. Another way to think of this is to ask ourselves: *"What would happen if, next Monday morning starting at 9 a.m., everyone in our community started to live as God intends?"*

- What would happen to us, personally, if we fully obeyed God's intentions for our relationships, the care of our bodies, and our walk with God?

- What would happen in our families if all members fully obeyed God's intentions in their relationships to one another?

- What would happen in our church and the other churches of our community if all the leaders and members truly loved each other, served one another, advocated for the powerless, and lived in unity?

- What would happen in our community if our leaders worked together for the common good, with honesty and integrity?

- What would happen if cheating, dishonesty, or corruption were never used in our business community?

- What would happen if children respected their parents and learned from them?

- What would happen if there were no corruption in our nation—but real justice?

One time many years ago, I was praying and talking with pastors in a slum community of Honduras. Suddenly, God gave me a story

---

[6] Matthew 6:10

to share with them. After I finished, we explored God's vision for a wholly transformed culture. It was a journey I will never forget. Come with me again and listen to "The Parable of Juan."

The Parable of Juan

Juan sensed a call of God to move to an unchurched area in his rapidly growing city and start a church. Actually, every time he rode the bus to and from work, the bus passed by the squatter community of Las Palas. Juan felt a strange attraction for the people who lived there. He didn't have much training—just a few Bible school extension classes. What he did have was a passion to see people come to know Jesus.

Juan discussed it with his wife, and they decided to move to Las Palas with their two young daughters. They rented a small, one-room wooden shack. Las Palas had no water, no electricity, no school, and no clinic. The roads were dirt. The people were poor. They lived in shacks made of tarpaper, tin, old tires, cardboard, used boards, and anything else they could find for shelter. It was tough living, but Juan and his wife believed God had called them to live and minister there.

Juan worked during the day, but he used his evenings to visit neighbors and invite them to his home for Bible study. He devoted his weekends to being a pastor. Within a few months, a small group of women and children gathered each Sunday in Juan's one-room house. In a few more months, they were able to rent a room that served as a meeting place. Juan had about twenty women and numerous children in his congregation, but there were no men. The men in the community liked Juan, but thought religion was something for women and children.

Juan was a faithful and loving pastor. He rose early every morning to pray for his people and to study the Bible. After the first year, there was good fellowship but not much growth. Juan and his wife found that the living conditions were weakening them physically. His little daughters were often sick. He did not earn enough money to get them proper medical care. Juan was discouraged.

Early one morning, about 4:00 a.m., Juan got up quietly. As

usual, he was careful not to awaken his wife and daughters. He had hung a plastic curtain to divide the room. At night, it separated the sleeping area from the living area, which was furnished with a table and four chairs. Juan sat at the table and lit the wick of an old milk can. It was full of paraffin and served as a lamp. He opened his Bible and began to read. This particular morning, he was reading Isaiah 58. He read about God's concern for the hungry, for the naked, for the homeless, for the oppressed. Juan's heart cried out silently to God: "God, I see your concern for the poor in the Bible. Why don't I see it here in Las Palas?" Juan was deeply touched by the needs of the people, and a tear ran down his cheek as he prayed. As he was meditating on the difference between his experience and what he was reading, there was a soft knock at the door.

Immediately, Juan walked to the door, but he didn't open it. It was dangerous to open the door to a stranger in the dark. "Who is it?" Juan whispered.

A soft voice came from the other side and said, "I'm Jesus, Juan."

"Who are you really?" asked Juan.

The voice again said, "I'm Jesus, Juan."

The voice sounded so gentle that Juan almost believed it was Jesus. He quietly slid the locking bolt off the door and carefully opened it just a crack. He could see the silhouette of a man in the dark, and he did not look threatening. Juan opened the door a little wider and said, "Come in."

But Jesus said, "No, Juan, I heard your cry this morning. I came so you could show me the things that trouble you here in Las Palas."

Juan quickly and quietly stepped outside, a little surprised by his obedience to this invitation. He shut the door behind them. Juan said, "Okay, Jesus, but stay close by me. This is the rainy season, and I know where to walk to miss the puddles."

"Okay, Juan," Jesus said, "I'll follow you."

They began their walk down the winding path. As they did, Juan talked to Jesus. "Jesus, over in that shack, there is a single mother. She sells her body—in her house and in front of her little children—to make money for food." They walked a little further. "And in that tarpaper shack, there's a family. The man is an alcoholic. He often comes home drunk and beats his wife and kids. The whole area can hear him yelling. Jesus, I can't stand it when I hear the screams, but there's nothing I can do." They walked further and Juan said, "Hold your nose as we go by here. This is where the people throw their garbage and use the toilet." They could hear the rats scurrying among the trash. Then Juan pointed to another shelter. This one was larger than the rest. Juan said, "This, Jesus, is where the 'presidente' of Las Palas lives. He likes to feel powerful. He collects money and tells the people it is to bring water and electricity here. But everyone knows he uses it for liquor and women." Then Juan turned a corner, walked downhill, and began to circle back to where they had started. Juan pointed to a little shack at the bottom of the hill. "Jesus," he said, "This is one of the saddest things to me in all of Las Palas. The woman who lives there was abandoned by the father of her three little children. Whenever it rains, black water floods her little shack. They all sleep on the floor, and she has to hold the children so they don't drown!"

Juan heard someone softly weeping. He looked around. He could tell from Jesus' shaking shoulders that it was the Lord who was crying. Juan saw that the same things that broke his heart also broke the heart of Jesus! In a broken voice, Jesus turned and said, "Juan, I want to show you My intentions for Las Palas."

Juan didn't know how it happened, but all of a sudden he and Jesus were looking down on Las Palas. Juan could see the whole community. Jesus started talking about adequate housing. All of a sudden, the shacks turned into small, neat shelters. They weren't fancy, but they were nice. Jesus talked about jobs, and Juan could see the people of Las Palas going to work. Juan could tell that the jobs weren't high-paying, but he could tell that they paid enough to support the families of Las Palas. Jesus talked about water. All of a sudden, there were water pumps appropriately spaced in the community, and everyone had clean water. Jesus talked about education and health. Right before Juan's eyes, there was a school and a clinic. Jesus talked about beauty. Juan saw the garbage disappear. In its place, children played in a field with trees and flowers! Jesus talked about healthy families, where men and women and children respected and loved one another. Then Jesus talked about spiritual healing. Juan saw his little church full of families—including men. He was excited! He thought, "This is the kind of community I'd like!"

Of course, Jesus read his thoughts and said, "Juan, these are My intentions for Las Palas. I want you to tell the people about My plans and begin to lead them there."

"But, Jesus," Juan protested, "I can't do that! How could my little congregation of women and children do anything? We are just struggling to survive!"

"Juan, listen to Me. I want you to share my plans with the people here, and then I want you to instruct your congregation to begin to serve the neighbors. Visit the sick. Visit the single mothers. Share with their neighbors. They can bring a cup of rice, a little soap, some sugar or salt, a few vegetables, and extra clothes to church on Sunday. Collect them in baskets and take them to those who are in greater need. They should do this every week. Then, you go and develop relationships with the city officials. Explore what is needed to bring water and power to Las Palas. . . ."

"Jesus," Juan said, "We need to be realistic. These little things will never make a difference. I . . ."

"Juan, who created the world?"

"You did, Lord, but . . ."

"Juan, who divided the Red Sea so that the children of Israel could cross?"

"You did, Lord, but . . ."

"Juan, who fed the five thousand with five loaves and two fish?"

"You did, Lord, but . . ."

"Juan, I am the same yesterday, today and forever. You do your part, and I'll do the rest. Some things will not come to fulfillment until I return, but I want you to begin the process. You and your little flock are my ambassadors, my representatives. As you obey, I will begin to heal Las Palas."

Juan was thinking about what Jesus said. Suddenly, he heard a rooster crow. He heard his wife beginning to stir behind the dividing curtain. He looked around. He was sitting at the table. The oil wick had gone out. It was becoming light outside.

Juan looked around for Jesus, but saw no one. "What happened?" Juan thought. "Did I have a vision? Was it a dream?" Juan did not know. But he did know that Jesus had met him—and that he had a new vision for the church and community of Las Palas.

———————

I believe this is what Jesus wants for Juan's community and others. In fact, I have shared this parable with local church leaders of many nations to encourage vision and hope.

Until this point, I have asked questions, raised issues, and told a parable. Hopefully, those who are reading this will have already begun to consider the question: *"If Jesus were Mayor, how would our community change?"* I would now like to tell you my thoughts. If Jesus were Mayor, I imagine he would do several things:

- He would live a *life* that modeled what it means for His Father's will to be done.

- He would help the people of the *church* recognize their role, follow His example, live according to His Father's instructions, and intentionally promote His Father's will wherever they go and whatever they do in the community.

- He would be sure that the *community* knew His Father's will for all aspects of community life—business, education, health, police, housing, and every other area.

- He would compassionately present the benefits of following—and the danger of disregarding—His Father's plan. He would give each citizen the choice to accept or reject the plan.

Finding and carrying out the Father's will is a large task! Jesus is not physically our Mayor. He has not tapped on our doors, as He did on Juan's, and supernaturally given us His vision and shown us His compassion. Knowing this, one of my colleagues who has a difficult time imagining Jesus Christ as a community official rephrased the original question. She asked: *"If I were mayor and could carry out the intentions of Jesus by the power of the Holy Spirit, what would my community look like?"*

This is a great question—and one worth thought. However, the task is too large for one person! If only there were an organization—a group of people—that could be equipped for this . . . a group that exists in all sectors of our communities . . . a group that has a sound moral code . . . an organization that represents all ages and facets of God's creation—individuals, families, neighborhoods, local businesses, local government, education, health care, and the physical environment.

As a matter of fact, there is such a group—it's called the church! Through its varied members, the church is uniquely positioned to advocate and advance God's will in each sector.

Let me tell you now what some of the people who have heard our teachings have decided Jesus would do in their communities. They not only decided what He *would* do—they did it! I have used examples here that deal with community services because that is often what people expect of a mayor. It is a good place to begin. However, the list of things Jesus would do if He were Mayor would have enormous variety. After all, God cares about every single aspect of life!

❖   There is a small church located in a rural village among the rice fields of an Asian nation. The area is predominantly Buddhist. The pastor attended our training conference, returned to his church, and taught his people. The thirty members then decided to demonstrate God's love in their neighborhood. During the rainy season, the water collects in this village. Roads are impassable. The water rises and floods people's living quarters. Great swarms of mosquitoes bring Dengue fever and other ills. Even fish ponds—the community source of income—are flooded and lost. The church property stands between the flooded neighborhood and a rice field. Church members hand-dug a trench from the often-flooded neighborhood, across the church property, into the rice fields. They lined it with concrete pipe. The rain waters drained sooner, and no families were displaced by flooding! It was hard work, but it had a profound effect on the community. The church has developed relationships with previously antagonistic Buddhist neighbors. Many neighbors helped as the church members cleaned weeds and rubbish and added more drainage pipe. The church is not large (thirty members), not old (seven years), and not rich (many members are illiterate farmers). But they demonstrated the concerns of Christ in their community. They did something that Jesus would have wanted done as Mayor.

❖   Wanderlei and Dalva wanted to serve a community in Brazil. They did several small exercises, but knew more could be done. They organized an association and called it "Emmanuel," or "God with us." They planned fifteen different social projects for a single community. They raised funds for a daycare center for forty children; and they mobilized a large church, pastors, and government departments. Their zeal reflected the intentions, love, and Spirit of God. Their trainers comment: "Their enthusiasm was contagious." Jesus was at work.

❖   Ladies from a Bible study in rural Uganda decided to serve their village. They carefully planned their first project—cleaning garbage around a local bar. Two of the women courageously entered the bar. (Usually, the only women in that area who go into a bar are the prostitutes.) They asked permission to clean up the garbage. The surprised owners laughed, but agreed. The women then mobilized the community—even the headmaster of a local, prestigious school volunteered. The group dug two pits—one for biodegradable garbage and the other for non-biodegradable materials. When bar patrons saw others cleaning up their trash, they helped. To the delight of the community, the bar owners continued to keep the area clean. Encouraged, the women decided to build nine fuel-efficient stoves for local families and to provide water storage bins for needy people. Next, the Bible study group undertook a larger project—a community market. (The village women typically walk many hours, carrying their vegetables and goods to far-away markets; a nearby market would allow them to generate income while keeping them close to their families, community, and gardens.) Land was donated, but it was too steep to begin to build the market. The women from the Bible study prayed—and highway workers who were repairing a road nearby willingly came and bulldozed the market property at no cost. With God's help, the small group of rural Christian women discovered and collected resources, saved money, solved dilemmas, built a community market, and confidently and expertly shared their story at a conference attended by high government officials. Their spiritual lives grew as they served others on behalf of Jesus.

❖ A new church had been planted in Asia in a poor, small village of one-hundred homes. Church members wanted to respond to community needs. As there was no electricity in the community, they decided to buy a generator and provide the line and power for one light bulb per home. The children could read and study at night, and the adults could work later into the night. The pastor and denominational leaders discussed this idea in a teahouse. They agreed to initiate it, but first needed to find a generator. A man overheard their conversation. He said, "I am a new believer, and I have just heard your plans. I have a new generator that I will give you!" Electricity has now been provided for the homes. Each home pays a small fee, which covers gasoline and maintenance. Many community people have thanked the church for its interest in them. The denominational leader is also grateful to have discovered the power of "loving your neighbor." Jesus' agenda was served.

❖ To get water in Fonfrede, Haiti, people walked up to three kilometers to a polluted river, which was sometimes dry. One day, a group of foreigners arrived with machinery and announced they were going to dig a well. There was great excitement! But the area was filled with stones too large for their equipment, and they couldn't drill. Great disappointment was evident. The church leaders decided to explore what they could do to meet the community's need for water. They visited a development organization that owned equipment to help dig wells by hand. At first, the idea was not well received. If hand-dug wells were possible, the people reasoned, why hadn't they been dug before? However, the church rented the equipment, moved it to Fonfrede, and began to dig for water on church property. Water was struck at forty-five feet. The celebration was great! Non-church members, though, were not pleased. They thought church members would hoard the water. On the contrary, the church invited the community to share in God's blessings. Soon, representatives of other parts of the rural community asked the church for help in digging wells. In less than a year, fifteen wells had been dug by hand. If the machinery had worked, there would perhaps be only one well in Fonfrede today! The church did what Jesus would have done as Mayor, demonstrating God's practical love to their neighbors.

We opened this chapter by asking what Jesus would do if He were Mayor. Perhaps we need to ask the question another way. *"What would Jesus do if He served here through His people, the church?"* God has already commissioned and equipped the church to administrate His will in the sectors of the community where His people live and work. We, the church, serve the will of God, on earth as it is in heaven.

A friend recently heard the title of this book and wondered, "Why Mayor? Why not President? Prime Minister? Governor?" He thought awhile and then answered his own question: "This is about the ministry God wants to work through the *local* church. We have to think first what Jesus would want if He were the *local* ruler—the leader of the territory that the local church occupies on His behalf!"

We need to ask ourselves what Jesus would do if He were the leader of our village, hometown, or metropolis. As we do, I believe our findings will resemble the activities of the Christian church of history. From the time of the early church, the people of God cared for others and influenced the society around them, *as if Jesus were Mayor.*

Following are two thought-provoking examples from Nepal and Peru, written by people who took the time to ponder, "What would Jesus do if He were President of our village? What if He were Mayor of my hometown?"

What Would Jesus Do If He Were President of a Village? (Nepal)*

I work in Nepal in a training program. I teach church planters and community health workers. When I attended the conference in India, it changed my view of the Gospel and my teaching style. Now, I put the students in small groups. I give each group a large piece of paper to draw a picture of a village where there is no church or Christian people. I ask them two questions:

- "If you were going to stay in the village five years, how would you present the Gospel?"
- "What do you want to see happen after five years?"

As they draw their pictures, I see their understanding of the Gospel. Some want to build relationships and then have personal evangelism, mass evangelism, and plant churches. They have a spiritual focus. When all of the groups show their pictures, they all say that in five years they want to see many Christians in the village and a church established.

As soon as they finish sharing, I ask this question: "What would Jesus do if He were president of that village?" This question shakes them up. They discuss with each other, and I keep letting them talk. "What would He do?" "Would He build a toilet for the village? A school? Drinking water? A health clinic?"

This way, our students get a bigger picture of the Gospel. Now, they go to their villages with this question: "What would Jesus do if He were president of the village?"

Thank you,
Nar B. L.

* Report to Bob Moffitt, April 2004

If Jesus Were Mayor of My Hometown (Peru)*

In Peru, mayors are the highest authorities in town. When our people think of a mayor, they usually have a picture in their minds. Perhaps they see a progressive mayor—or a corrupt mayor—or someone hungry for power. It would be incorrect to see Jesus like this—yet we often err because we do not picture Him as being among the people!

The title of this book helps us interact with our own realities. If Jesus were mayor of Lima or Arequipa, my hometown, I think He would:

- Lead by His example of service
- Prioritize the solution of community problems
- Focus on improving the community—not fix a road only because it is election time
- Set an action plan based on the root of the problem, not the symptoms
- Confront sin and corruption
- Be a visionary
- Address more than physical needs (electricity, water, sewage)
- Establish a school for parents and a leadership training school for children, both based on biblical principles—to build the next generation
- Treat children and youth as future leaders—see their potential as agents of change
- Educate the people about values, using many different community activities—medical campaigns, drawing contests, art exhibits
- Value the local culture by opposing its lies, affirming its truths, and celebrating its valid elements

* Ruth Concha, manuscript review (Peru: October 2003).

PART TWO

Cultural Transformation through the Church

Biblical and Historical Roots

*His intent was that now, **through the church** the manifold wisdom of God should be made known to the rulers and authorities in the heavenly realms.*

—Ephesians 3:10
(emphasis added)

Cultural Transformation through the Church
Biblical and Historical Roots

"What would Jesus do if He were Mayor?" This is the central question we ask in this book, whether we are looking at one small act of kindness in a neighborhood—or the abolition of slavery in the British Empire.

We examine other questions, as well. What is God's role for the church? What contribution is the church to make to the society in which God places it? Is it primarily to bring the lost to Christ? Is it to instruct and encourage believers in spiritual discipleship? Is it to advocate for the vulnerable of society, minister to suffering humanity, or address the social injustices that God abhors? Or does the church have a broad purpose that begins with spiritual salvation but continues on to transform its culture?

In the next several chapters, we examine our biblical and historical roots as change agents in the world. We discover principles through Scripture and observe them through history. As foundations, they support the rest of the book, equipping the local church for its task.

Neglected

My pastor was a theological student at Cambridge. One day he was asked to meet John Stott, a well-known British theologian, at the train station and bring him to class where he was to lecture. Thrilled with this privilege, my pastor prepared a list of questions to ask Dr. Stott on the drive to class. His first question was, "Dr. Stott, what do you think is the most neglected area of theology in the church today?"

Dr. Stott's response was immediate: "Ecclesiology—the study of the church!"

The church of Jesus Christ is God's principal agent to represent His intentions in the world! Believing this, we would expect to see highly visible transformation in the societies and cultures where the church exists. Certainly, the church of history shaped its culture! Today, though, it is a different story. The Christian church has experienced rapid growth around the globe, but too often this multiplication does not make an observable impact on society. Even in cultures where nearly half of the population claims to be Christian, governments and businesses are corrupt, people live without respect for their Creator or each other, and nations and tribes battle one another. Tragically, there have even been genocides in countries where the majority of the population claims to be Christian.

Why has the church not transformed the world around it? On a global level, perhaps the principal lack is a biblical understanding of God's intentions for His church. Please note—without a biblical understanding of its role, the church of Jesus Christ *cannot* fulfill, or have a passion for, God's intentions.

Many churches in this generation would say that their principal task is to fulfill Christ's commission—to *"go and make disciples of all nations, baptizing them in the name of the Father and of the Son and of the Holy Spirit, and teaching them to obey everything I have commanded you."* [1] Often, though, these churches—whether liberal or conservative in theology—have not caught the fullness of the Great Commission.

The conservative branch of the Protestant church knows that the Great Commission relates to evangelism and church planting— but seldom recognizes that it also commands us to disciple nations to live under the Lordship of Christ the King. (The "conservative" church refers to evangelical, charismatic, Pentecostal, and other faith traditions that, among other tenets, believe that the Bible is the revealed Word of God and individual spiritual salvation is essential.)

---

[1] Matthew 28:19-20a

The liberal branch of the church knows that the church is to have a strong social impact, but downplays the importance of individual spiritual regeneration. (The "liberal" church includes many mainline denominations and other churches and organizations that refer to Scripture but interpret it less authoritatively than conservative churches. A key tenet is that the church has great social responsibility to speak for and minister to the vulnerable members of society.)

Neither branch of the church has fully caught the breadth of the Great Commission! Scripture is clear that God's purpose for the church is broader than evangelism. It is wider than church planting. It is deeper than spiritual discipleship. It is larger than addressing social injustices. It is greater than feeding the hungry.

"Preach the Gospel at all times and when necessary use words."

God's strategy is both for *proclamation*—and *demonstration*—of the Good News. In this book, I write primarily about *demonstration,* but both have a key role in communicating the Gospel. St. Francis said it well: "Preach the Gospel at all times and when necessary use words."[2] More and more churches and church leaders are coming to understand this. When people of all traditions who regard Scripture as authoritative hear ideas they believe are clearly reflected in God's Word, they accept and implement them. They are poised and waiting to learn how to be the people and the church that God intends. I have great hope. Christ continues to head His church!

In Part Two

- We will examine illustrations from history, from the early church through 1850. Why did the church influence social transformation in the Roman Empire, when only an estimated 10.5 percent of the population followed Christ?
- We will see that God's agenda is larger than spiritual

---

[2] St. Francis of Assisi. QuotationReference.com. St. Francis lived from 1182 to 1226.

salvation. How is God's big agenda reflected in creation? In His covenants? In His concern for nations? In Jesus' shed blood? In God's plan to redeem *"all things"*?

- God's big agenda was obscured through sin. So was His image in man, especially the characteristic of servanthood. We will examine how God again revealed His servant image to mankind through Jesus and through the church. What does this mean for us, the people of the church?

- From Paul's writings to the Ephesians, we will learn that the extensive brokenness created by sin is to be healed through Christ. What is the church's role? How will it serve as the agency through which God accomplishes this mystery? Is the church really more important in accomplishing God's purpose than any other entity—even kings and presidents?

- We will explore reasons that the church of today has not brought transformation to its societies, even where over half of the citizens claim to be Christians. We will look at a "divided" understanding within the church. We will see why the evangelical church of the mid-nineteenth century entered a time of "Great Reversal" from the spiritual, physical, and social ministry of the past. How are churches around the world today beginning to "reverse the Reversal" and once more carry God's healing message to broken people *and* broken societies?

- Finally, before examining how the local church can serve its society, we will look at four characteristics that the church needs in order to be useful—humility, love, works of service, and unity. How do these characteristics lead the church to maturity, to displaying the fullness of Christ?

- Throughout the book, we emphasize the practical outworking of the "big picture" themes we explore. We relate stories from our archives and correspondence—from staff, colleagues, and practitioners who have studied wholistic ministry and have implemented what they learned. Stories are powerful tools!

Premises for Part Two

A premise is a foundational principle, a basis for our reasoning and action. Premises shape how we *think* and *act*. In this case, they shape what we *think* about the world, God, Scripture, and the church. Because of our premises, we *act* as we do. Here, they compel us to help the church accomplish its task.

Premise 1: *The world is seriously broken. Human wisdom and material resources cannot heal it.*

The nation of Haiti is a poignant illustration of brokenness that has not been healed by human wisdom and material resources. Haiti is the most impoverished nation in the Western hemisphere. I first visited Haiti in 1980 and have been there many times since. Since 1980, thousands of international, governmental, and nongovernmental programs have been carried out. Billions of dollars have been directed toward healing the economic, social, political, and spiritual wounds of Haiti's eight million inhabitants.[3] Political crises caused the distribution of international aid to drop drastically in recent years, but international donors in 2004 again pledged more than one billion dollars to "rebuild Haiti."[4]

Despite the work and resources that have been invested by human experts, Haiti today seems as broken as in 1980. Its citizens are suffering. Hope is elusive. Eighty percent of Haiti's people live in poverty. Factories and businesses have shut down. Unemployment is at least 70 percent. Inflation is rampant. Over 10 percent of the children do not live past age four. Urban slums are overpopulated, filled with makeshift shacks and streets strewn with garbage. Crime is rampant. Political turmoil, poor governance, and civil unrest continue. Haiti ranks as one of the most corrupt nations of the world.[5] Roads are in disrepair, and safe drinking water is in short supply. The rural countryside is beautiful but fragile. After years

---

[3] U.S. Department of State, *Background Notes: Haiti*, Internet.

[4] *Scottsdale Tribune*, A-20.

[5] Transparency International, *Corruption Perceptions Index 2002*, Internet.

of extensive deforestation and soil erosion, many villages have little defense against frequent natural disasters—tropical storms, hurricanes, and floods.[6]

Even with massive investments of funding, technology, and social engineering, there is little evidence of broad-scale healing in Haiti. Economic resources have not healed the land. Nor has some of the best secular development "know-how" that the world offers. My Haitian colleagues agree: The world's brokenness cannot be cured by human wisdom, technology, or material resources alone. Something more is needed.

Premise 2: Healing for a nation or society comes as God's people respond in obedience and live as He instructs. As a consequence, He supernaturally intervenes in their history.

People who hold a secular worldview would call it nonsense to think that healing—especially the healing of a nation or a society— would come from obedience to God. For them, the physical world is the only real world. Healing would come from the mind of man. They would apply human wisdom, knowledge, money, and technology to the world's brokenness. Sickness, famine, poverty, economic underdevelopment, and social inequity would eventually be healed by human efforts.

However, people who hold an animistic worldview would also find Premise 2 hard to believe. For them, the spiritual world is the only real world. The physical world is operated by spirits or gods, and the world's brokenness is the work of these capricious and unpredictable spirits. Societal healing, then, would come from trying to live in harmony with the gods, appeasing the spirits, and escaping suffering in a future life.[7]

A biblical worldview, though, says that a nation or society is *not* healed by human wisdom or creativity or by appeasing spirits—but by God's intervention and man's obedience. God revealed to Solomon:

---

[6] Lord, "Poverty prevalent in Haiti," *The Cincinnati Post*, Internet.
[7] Miller, *Discipling Nations*, 57.

If my people, who are called by my name, will humble themselves and pray and seek my face and turn from their wicked ways, then will I hear from heaven and will forgive their sin and will heal their land.[8]

God provides healing for the world's brokenness. He works through people, too. He has created us in His image and has placed His Spirit within us. Nonetheless, without God working in and through us, there is no real healing. As Scripture reminds us, the world's brokenness is healed when God supernaturally intervenes in lives, society, and history; and His action comes in response to His people's humble obedience.

Premise 3: The Bible is God's revelation for our healing.

Some products have owner's manuals—instructions written by the products' designers or manufacturers. Manufacturers know how their product was made and how it should be used to obtain maximum benefit. God is our maker—our manufacturer. His written revelation, the Bible, is like an "owner's manual" for us. Not only did He make us and all creation, He told us how He designed us to operate, or live, in every area of life. In the Bible we also find the instructions, principles, and wisdom to heal the world's brokenness. God revealed in this manual how our individual lives and communities can be healed when broken—and how we can flourish.

Premise 4: The church is God's principal entity to accomplish His purpose of healing all that was broken in the Fall.[9]

God uses individuals, rulers, secular states, and anything else of His choosing to accomplish His purpose in history. However, He has appointed the church as the principal administrator of His agenda to heal the broken world. His plan will not be fully

---

[8] 2 Chronicles 7:14
[9] *The Fall:* Man's rebellion against God and the consequences of this rebellion (Genesis 3).

accomplished until the return of Christ. Until that time, the church is to represent and pursue God's purpose in history: *"to reconcile to himself all things."* [10]

The church—whether universal or local—is the expression of the Body of Christ. It is the local church, though, that is the primary expression of God's purpose in its community. The church—especially the local church—is God's principal agent to carry out His grand agenda in the world.

———————

May these thoughts encourage and impel you as you and your church catch a vision to carry out God's broad agenda, *as if Jesus were Mayor.*

What is the Difference?

Culture: All of the ways of life that define who we are as individuals and as a society. Culture includes the behaviors, patterns, beliefs, thoughts, institutions, values, habits, traditions, practices, and characteristics that we pass along to the next generation.

Society: A distinct group of people distinguished by their common institutions, relationships, and culture.

Culture defines how a *society* thinks and operates. If we want to transform a *society*, we do so by transforming its *culture*.

Transformation: A substantial change in nature and character. Biblical transformation brings people into alignment with God's intentions.

---

[10] Colossians 1:20a

Cultural Transformation
and the Church of History

3

This is not only the "history" of the role of the church in society. It is HIS-story—the story of God at work in His world, redeeming it to Himself. In this chapter, we will see God's hand in HIS-story—from the simple service and generosity of the early church to the culture-impacting revivals and missions of the nineteenth century. We will see the people of the church carrying out acts of Christian love; enabling social change; and affecting how their societies thought, believed, and acted. We will see, century after century, the people of the church carrying out the kind of changes that would happen *if Jesus were Mayor.*

Church History???

When I attended seminary, I had little interest in church history.

Everywhere I looked, I saw pressing social needs. Somehow, church history seemed irrelevant. But I was wrong!

The church of today can learn and profit from the church of the past. Today's church leaders need to see how God has used His church for His purposes in history. We have much to learn . . .

Throughout history, the church has usually understood social and cultural transformation as an essential part of its task. Maybe the churches around you no longer believe this. Maybe you agree with them. If so, you will be challenged as you see how the church of many generations has impacted the world around it. Scripture reports that Jesus not only taught, but went about doing good. Jesus' intention was that evangelism and social concern be intimately related to one another, and many periods of church history have reflected His intention.

This understanding of HIS-story not only informs us, but helps us grasp the potential for the church of today. These are stories of the people who loved God and neighbor and were salt and light in their worlds. This is our legacy. These are our forebears in the faith. This is *our church!*[1]

The Early Church

The followers of Jesus in the early church were looking for the soon return of Christ. Filled with faith, zeal, and love, they eagerly shared their possessions with one another. Their generosity made a profound impact. Not only did nonbelievers watch and benefit, but the spread of the Gospel was founded on—and funded by—the sacrificial giving and service of these humble believers. In the second and third centuries, the church spread into North Africa, Arabia, and India—reaching the entire Greco-Roman world by the end of the fifth century.

The early church was characterized by generosity and sacrifice. Listen to the advice of a second-century church leader, Commodianus:

> God Himself cries out: Break your bread with the needy. There is no need to visit with words, but with benefits. . . . Do not try to satisfy him with words. He needs food and drink.[2]

The early church was also characterized by the persecutions and executions suffered by thousands of believers. Yet, the church grew. In fact, the church and its view of humanity changed ancient Rome!

How the Church Changed Ancient Rome

Three centuries earlier, when Jesus had finished His earthly ministry, He had charged a handful of followers to deliver His message to the world. They did—and God eventually used the message carried by this tiny, persecuted, oppressed, rejected, reviled group of one-hundred twenty people to change the Roman Empire

---

[1] I am sensitive that what I am presenting is from a Western historical perspective. Yet, that perspective is necessary to understand the background of the Protestant church in the world today. I am aware, too, that my focus on the Protestant church does not tell the full story of God at work in His world.

[2] Oden, "Two Thousand Years of Caring for the Poor," *Stewardship Journal,* 50.

and put into effect the greatest social transformation within Western culture in the last two millennia![3]

Jesus had also commanded the little band of disciples to wait in Jerusalem for the Holy Spirit to fill, empower, equip, encourage, and embolden them. They did—and the church was launched. God Himself was working through His people. This is the most important reason the church affects the world, then and now. Yet, it is also helpful to look at the human element—to learn what the Christians believed, thought, and did that so influenced the society around them.

Social scientist Rodney Stark[4] examined the link between social transformation and the early church. He found that this small group of early Christians had introduced a new vision of humanity to the Roman world. Seven beliefs and practices of the early church especially impacted Roman society and, eventually, the world. Stark discovered these seven beliefs and practices—this new view of humanity—by looking at historical data and documents. Yet, all are biblical principles:

1. *Christians have a God who loves those who love Him.* For the first time in the pagan world, people heard of a God who loves those who love Him. This God was radically different from the Roman gods. Pagan gods had their own agendas. They spent much of their time fighting each other, competing for dominance. They had little interest in the people who worshipped them, and they needed to be bribed for favors with sacrifices and ceremonies. By contrast, the God of the Christians actually loved those who loved Him.

2. *The Christians' God instructs those who love Him to love others—all others.* The Christians' God loved all of humanity. He demonstrated that love through His own sacrifice. Further,

---

[3] Stark, *The Rise of Christianity*, 161-162. See also Acts 1:15.
[4] Rodney Stark is an internationally recognized social scientist who studies the social implications of religious movements, applying methods of social science to historical data.

He directed those who love Him to also love and serve others. This was revolutionary! Pagan Romans loved only those in their families and social class—or those it was politically or economically advantageous to befriend. By contrast, this "new" God was essentially saying to His followers, "Because I love you, I want you to love as I love—regardless of blood relationships, class, political alliances, or economic attachments. I want you to love those who are poor and hurting. I want you to especially love those who are in socially humble positions."

3. *Christianity has a culture stripped of ethnicity and rank.* Christians were not separated by social rank or ethnicity. This was quite different from Roman culture! Romans wondered why a nobleman would allow a slave to address him as "brother." The church created a pattern of human relationships that had not existed in pre-Christian Rome.

4. *The God of the Christians is a merciful God who requires mercy.* The Christians believed in a merciful God. This merciful God required that those who follow Him also practice mercy to others. Mercy was not part of life in pagan Rome. Rome was well known for casual cruelty. One emperor celebrated his son's fourteenth birthday by bringing gladiators into the coliseum to kill each other. He wanted his son's transition to manhood to include the "manly" experience of shedding blood to death. Roman writers ridiculed Christians because they were merciful, especially to the poor. They could not understand why mercy and care for the poor would be a central belief and practice of Christianity.

5. *In Christianity, men are to love their wives as themselves.* Romans laughed at the Christian view that men must love their wives and children. Roman men *owned* their wives and children. Children were property, and they could do anything they wished with their own property. They could even kill their children without legal consequences. In the new Christian religion, however, men were to love their wives as they loved themselves—a radical concept and practice.

6. *Christians rejected the Roman practice of abortion and infanticide.* Christianity rejected abortion and infanticide, standard practices in Rome. A Roman soldier wrote his pregnant wife from the battlefield: "If you are delivered of a child [before I come home], if it is a boy keep it, if a girl discard it."[5] Dozens of baby skeletons were found in the excavation of a Roman sewer—probably unwanted baby girls. In this new Christian religion, all of life—handicapped, unborn, male or female, slave or nobleman—was sacred.

7. *Christians love others—even at personal risk.* Christians were to love others, even those outside their faith. It was not easy. Daily life in Rome was arduous. The poor lived in outlying areas in squalid, cramped quarters. Their ramshackle houses were so crowded that people went home only when it was their turn to sleep. Sanitation was poor. There was no running water or toilets. Human waste was discarded through windows onto the streets. When severe illness came to those filthy, cramped quarters, it quickly spread. Epidemics claimed many lives. Christians, with love and charity as central duties of their faith, showed mercy and charity in times of raging epidemics.[6]

Christians were not afraid to die. They knew that death was not the end. Roman pagans, though, had no reason to serve the sick. Even the doctors fled infected areas whenever they could. Those who stayed were afraid of contamination. They often took their sick outside and left them on the street to die. Sick people's chances of survival greatly improved, though, if they received even minimal nursing care, food, and water—which Christians provided. Using historical information, social scientist Rodney Stark designed a hypothetical case study (see box on next page), showing how Christianity might have grown during epidemics—through the loving care of Christians.[7]

---

[5] Stark, 97-98.
[6] Stark, 82-87, 97-99, 151-156, 212.
[7] Stark, 88-93.

In summary, the Christian religion provided a compelling new vision of humanity that drew many to the faith.[8] This new view of humanity was observable—not in organized programs of the church, but in the lives of its followers.

Christianity's influence was larger than its numbers indicate:

• By AD 40, there were perhaps 1000 Christians—only .0017 percent of the Empire's 60 million people.

• By AD 300, they had likely grown to 6.3 million Christians—still only 10.5 percent of the population.[9]

Christians constituted a small percentage of the population, but there was such a significant influence that, by AD 313, the Emperor Constantine declared Christianity legal and gave the church freedom from persecution

---

Hypothetical Case Study

How Christianity might have grown during epidemics
(Note how ratios changed, in italics.)

SCENE: AN EPIDEMIC IN ROME

- 5 Roman acquaintances
  (4 pagans, 1 Christian)
- 1 pagan fled the city
  (3 pagans, 1 Christian)
- 4 became ill
  (3 pagans, 1 Christian)
- 3 sick pagans were left to die— Christians cared for the sick pagans and Christian
  (3 pagans, 1 Christian)

RESULTS

- 2 pagans died (despite care)*
- 1 pagan survived
- 1 Christian survived
  (1 living pagan, 1 Christian)
- 1 surviving pagan would be likely to convert after receiving the Christians' care
  (0 pagans, 2 Christians)

ANALYSIS OF CHANGE

- From   *4 pagans, 1 Christian*
- To   *0 pagans, 2 Christians*

---

* The 2 pagans who died may have converted, too.

---

[8] Stark, 214.

[9] Stark, 7.

and social contempt. He and his successors continued to broaden policies that favored the church. By 381, Christianity was declared the state religion. Pagan Rome was now officially "Christian" Rome.

The Roman Empire gave state support to Christianity in 392. The growing cooperation between church and state—with the desire to transform the world under the banner of the Roman Empire—introduced radical changes from the humble and simple service of the early church.[10] The changes were not always godly. Yet, God continued to use the church during the coming period in HIS-story. He always does.

A Changing Church, Changing Society—the Middle Ages

In the early church, charity was the result of spiritual conversion. Good works were the normal and intentional fruit of a believer's life in Christ. In the period known as the Middle Ages, though, the motivation for Christian charity was changing. Evangelism and social responsibility in this period can be understood only in the context of the institutional church of the time, which taught that the only way to grace was through the church, headed by the Pope. Earning merit for salvation through asceticism and good works was a key doctrine. Both church and state were viewed as God's instruments to achieve God's purpose for man. Church-related charity helped the unemployed, orphans, widows, injured, sick, travelers, disaster victims, and the poor of the community. Caring for the poor was a consistent subject of concern among such well-known church figures of the Middle Ages as St. Thomas, Ignatius Loyola, St. Patrick, and St. Francis of Assisi.[11]

Practical service and faith expanded into other concerns and nations through the monks of the fourth to eighth centuries. The Nestorians moved from Asia Minor into Arabia, India, Central Asia, and China. The Orthodox went north into the Balkan states and Russia. The

---

[10] Ro, "The Perspectives of Church History," *In Word and Deed,* 17.
[11] Ro, 17-20

Celts left Ireland for Scotland, England, and central Europe. The Benedictines were in the Western church. As they traveled, they founded monasteries, which were organized for daily prayer and work. Incidentally, the monks' discipline of manual labor was radical. Labor had normally been considered as fit only for slaves.[12]

The Roman Empire fell to barbarians in the fifth century. Libraries throughout Europe were vandalized and burned, and Europe was in danger of losing thousands of classical masterpieces. The fifth-century Irish, new to Christianity *and* literacy, rescued manuscript after manuscript from Europe and preserved them, copying them by hand. The monks continued to build abbeys and go on missions to find more books in Latin, Greek, Hebrew, and Coptic. While Europe descended into near-barbarism and its libraries were completely closed or destroyed, the books copied in the abbeys of Ireland became treasures. Later, when the monks returned the classical texts safely to the continent, the new rulers asked them to educate their children,

The church was used to transform Europe.

and the monks founded monasteries and schools throughout Europe. They eventually brought both their faith and the literature of antiquity back to the continent of Europe. In fact, one author commented, the reintroduction of intellectual thought may have kept Europe from turning to Islam in the Middle Ages.[13]

Another observer described monasteries as "Christian leaven in a rude society, to implant and preserve a Christian culture like a cultivated garden amid a wilderness of disorder."[14]

---

[12] Pierson, "Missions and Community Development," in *Christian Relief and Development*, 9.

[13] Cahill, *How the Irish Saved Civilization*, 4,181-184,193-196,207.

[14] Hannah, *Monasticism*, 86, cited in Pierson, "Missions and Community Development," in *Christian Relief and Development*, 13.

Later in the Middle Ages, St. Francis of Assisi offered dignity to the poor—and reformed a social system. Poor serfs began to enter the order he began by the hundreds of thousands, crippling the feudal system.[15] One commentator wrote:

> The poor little man of Assisi conquered by that strange power called Love, and overthrew a political theory on which the whole fabric of European statecraft rested. Feudalism fell, democracy began, and society, instead of falling to pieces, became purer, stronger, and freer than before.[16]

As the Middle Ages came to a close, the church and society were ready for change. Despite low points in the Middle Ages, God was moving in HIS-story.

Church Impact and Practices during the Reformation

God used the church and the Protestant Reformation to transform societies in Switzerland, Germany, and Holland. The Reformation began in 1517, when Martin Luther nailed ninety-five theses to the door of the Wittenberg castle. He was particularly opposed to the sale of indulgences[17] to fund the coffers of the church. The church was, apparently, in a time of profound corruption, and Luther urged it to return to the purity of the early church. Luther's theological differences with the Roman church came from his study of Romans and Galatians. The doctrines of *sola gratia, sola fide, sola scriptura,* and *soli Deo Gloria*[18] challenged the tenets and practices of the Roman church of the day.

Though Luther believed that good works could not atone for sin, this did not lighten the Christian's responsibility to care for

---

[15] *Serf:* A person in condition of servitude, required to render service to the landowner. *Feudal system:* The system of political organization and landholding in Europe during the Middle Ages, in which tenants became servants to landowners.

[16] Newton, "Social Saviors," in *Union Life,* 21.

[17] *Indulgences:* Remission of sins, normally through penance.

[18] Paraphrased in English: Salvation is through grace alone and faith alone. Only Scripture is authoritative. Only God is to be glorified.

the poor or influence the world. Luther taught that there are two Kingdoms—the Kingdom of God and the kingdom of this world. The Christian is to be involved in both. He also established the practice of a common chest in each church. Pastors were to preach about serving the poor; church members were to give; and deacons administered the funds, using common-sense guidelines for effective help for the needy. [19]

Meanwhile, Swiss reformer John Calvin envisioned the church as a small society inside a larger society—an embryo of a new world order.[20] Calvin often preached about Christians' responsibility to the needy—and acted. When 60,000 refugees flooded into Geneva from France beginning in 1550, Calvin founded a private, church-based ministry that became a model throughout Europe. The ministry cared for a broad range of needs, serving the sick, orphans, elderly, incapacitated, travelers, disabled, and terminally ill. Aid to the needy was tied to a work ethic. Deacons were trained to find long-range solutions to poverty—job-retraining, temporary housing, tools to set up a trade—and to distinguish between the deserving and undeserving poor.[21]

Actually, God used many Christian leaders in a movement that spanned Europe. As they sought to reform the church and societies throughout Europe, they also developed well-managed outreaches to the needy.

Church Impact on Societies through Revivals

Evangelical revivals stirred the seventeenth and eighteenth centuries. The revival movements not only converted sinners, but included an emphasis on good works that profoundly affected societies on both sides of the Atlantic. The movements renewed the church, brought spiritual conversion to thousands, enacted social reforms, and launched the Protestant missionary movement.

---

[19] Ro, 22 and Hall (ed), "Earlier Paradigms for Welfare Reform," in *Welfare Reformed*, 156.
[20] Ro, 24.
[21] Hall, 158.

The Wesleyan Revival, led by John Wesley, was one of the most important of these movements. It brought about major transformation in England. Prior to this, England had been one of the most corrupt and immoral societies of the Western world. Women and children were abused in the labor force. Immorality was rampant. Greed ruled the Empire and fueled the British slave trade, the largest commercial trading of human life the world had known. When a biblical worldview was brought to England through the Wesleyan Revival, the culture experienced a remarkable transformation.[22]

John Wesley was an evangelist and preacher, but the Gospel he preached also inspired people to take up social causes in the name of Christ. In fact, some historians believe that the revival movement did more to transform the moral character of the populace than any other movement in British history—and may have saved England from facing a sweeping revolution like France suffered from 1789-95.[23]

A small group of friends, including Wesley, formed a Holy Club while at Oxford in 1729. As Christian politicians, they continued to meet over the years, specifically to confront injustices in their society. They delegated assignments according to what each member could do best. They implemented a wide variety of spiritual and social projects, including William Wilberforce's efforts to end slavery in the British Empire.[24] Others from the group addressed a wide range of other concerns—prison and parliamentary reform, education, England's obligation to its colonies (especially India), literacy, child labor, factory legislation, dueling, gambling, drunkenness, immorality, cruel animal sport, the plight of lunatics, chimney sweeps, trade unions, education for the poor, women and children in mines, children in slums, factory conditions, and schools in slums. Outgrowths included the founding of Sunday schools, the YMCA, the YWCA, the Salvation Army, a Bible society, and Church Missionary Society.[25] Faith was practical and strong!

---

[22] Stott, *Involvement*, 21.

[23] Ro, 27.

[24] Stott, 21.

[25] Stott, 22.

John Wesley's motto served him and his colleagues well: "Do all the good you can, by all the means you can, in all the ways you can, in all the places you can, at all the times you can, to all the people you can, as long as you ever can."[26]

God used British statesman William Wilberforce to advance the abolition of slavery in England. Wilberforce took his stance because of his beliefs and regarded John Wesley as his spiritual father. The first year that Wilberforce introduced an abolition law in Parliament, he was virtually alone. He continued to introduce his anti-slavery legislation for more than thirty years. Each year, more parliamentarians voted for the law. During that same period, the Wesleyan Revival was spreading through England—and the law eventually passed. Although Wilberforce played a specific parliamentary role, it was the growing body of Christ and its members' way of life and thinking that influenced the change in British worldview and culture. That change allowed Wilberforce's anti-slavery passion to become reality.

Finally, the evangelical missionary movement crossed the Atlantic Ocean and erupted as the first and second Great Awakenings in the United States. After the second Great Awakening, nearly all Protestant denominations were engaged in social services and were addressing such issues as women's rights, slavery, temperance, prison reform, public education, and world peace. The close association between evangelism and social concern yielded a new wave of missionaries and men and women of the church who preached and pioneered evangelism and biblically-based social reform, not only on their own continents but also in Africa, Asia, and Latin America.[27]

Cultural Impact and the Protestant Missionary Movement

Nineteenth-century traveling missionaries carried bags of medicine and seed with their Bibles. They brought coffee and cocoa to Ghana.

---

[26] Warren, *The Purpose Driven Life*, 259.
[27] Ro, 28-29.

They eliminated smallpox, malaria, and leprosy in Thailand. They addressed forced labor issues in Congo. In China, they dealt with the opium trade and fought the practices of foot-binding and exposing baby girls to die. In India, they fought against widow-burning, infanticide, temple prostitution, and the caste system. They built wells and schools. Virtually all missionary movements were involved in what we now call "community development." As part of communicating the Gospel, they cared about education, health, agriculture, and social improvement for the neglected and oppressed.[28]

A British man named William Carey knew that God had transformed England, Germany, Switzerland, and Holland through the efforts of Christian reformers. Carey reasoned that what God could do for them, He would accomplish anywhere. India became Carey's new home, where he began an amazingly broad-based approach to the restoration of India. He was a missionary, botanist, industrialist, economist, medical humanitarian, printing and newspaper pioneer, agriculturist, translator and publisher of the Bible in forty different Indian languages, educator, astronomer, library pioneer, forest conservationist, crusader for women's rights, public servant, moral reformer, and cultural transformer. He was "an evangelist who used every available medium to illumine every dark facet of Indian life with the light of truth."[29]

For 2000 years the Hindu and Buddhist leadership had instilled a fatalistic view of life. Life was about suffering, and souls were sent to earth because of previous misdeeds. William Carey, though, taught India that the Creator intended life to be good! Transformation was both possible and desirable![30]

Other nineteenth-century missionaries, while focusing on spiritual conversion, also demonstrated concern for physical, social, and cultural problems where they served:

---

[28] Stott, 24.

[29] Mangalwadi, *The Legacy of William Carey*, 17-25.

[30] Mangalwadi, "William Carey and the Modernization of India," in *William Carey: A Tribute*, 43-49.

- Missionaries to Hawaii evangelized—and protected the islanders from economic and sexual exploitation by traders, sailors, and business people.

- David Livingstone wished to evangelize Africa—and demonstrated a strong concern for economic and community development in isolated villages.

- Nationals served as "Bible women" in Korea and China, making a powerful impact on the growth of the church and status of women in their societies.

- An anthropologist compared two remote Brazilian villages. One village benefited from a missionary's evangelism and leadership in community development; the other village lived according to traditional folk religion. The first village was thriving in nearly every way; the second was decaying in nearly every way.[31]

- The most prominent feature of nineteenth-century Kerala (India) was "the revival of education that transformed the society from medievalism to modernism." The London Missionary Society pioneered the work of schooling girls, intending not only to educate them but also to raise women from their low status in society.[32]

How appropriate that a rational God—a Creator who did not design a world of endless suffering—would use His people to carry His love and concern as a demonstration of the Gospel they spread.

In Conclusion

The church cannot be proud of everything that has been done in the name of Christianity—the Crusades, the Inquisition, the wars between Protestant and Catholics. The church has had cause to repent many times. Even so, it has had an important role to carry out in HIS-story. The church has long assumed that the Gospel would transform individual and community life. Dr Michael Green wrote:

---

[31] Pierson, 17.

[32] Hepzi Joy, *History and Development of Education of Women in Kerala*, 20,58,61,63.

Is it not true that the great forward movements of the church have been through the proclamation of the good news? Peter, Paul, Origen, Savonarola, Luther, Wesley, Whitfield, J. Edwards, William Temple, Martin Luther King moved the hearts of people through telling them of Jesus. *But in each case there was an inescapable social implication in their proclamation. . . .* The only gospel worth having is rooted in an encounter with the living God which has as its necessary fruit and stamp of authenticity a passionate concern for people's needs (emphasis added).[33]

Perhaps you wonder why this chapter stops in the middle of the nineteenth century—or why you don't always hear about the church's role in cultural transformation today. Something happened, as we will see later. The church became divided. The conservative branch lost some of its historical connection with the church that transformed society, and the newly formed liberal branch lost some of its zeal for spiritual conversion.

God has a broad agenda, and He ordained the church to carry it out—to heal brokenness, to transform individuals and societies, and to enable the kinds of changes that would happen *if Jesus were Mayor.* The Christian church of HIS-story played a large role in the transformation of entire societies and their cultures. Today, there is a growing movement in the Christian church around the world. The church of this generation is returning to an understanding of its role in spiritual and cultural transformation. In the coming chapters, you will be reading HIS-stories from many of these twenty-first century "reformers."

---

[33] Green, *Evangelism in the Early Church*, cited in Ro, 39.

God's BIG Agenda | 4

If Jesus were Mayor, I believe He would have an overall agenda and a long-range plan. God does have a grand plan. This grand plan affects and includes His church everywhere, in every generation.

What is God's agenda in the world? What is His mission? It depends who we ask—or observe. In this chapter, we will be examining Scripture, looking at the biblical roots of God's big agenda.

"Agenda"

Dear Brother Bob:

Just one question: I understand very well the idea of "God's Agenda," but if you choose another word for "Agenda," which word in English could it be?

In His service,
Pastor T.P. (Brazil)

Dear Brother:

I could equally use "Purpose." "Plan" would be another word to use.

Under the same wings,
Bob Moffitt

The church of history seemed to believe that God had a broad mission in the world. Today, though, we see many churches working hard for the spiritual redemption of man—evangelizing and planting churches around the globe. At the same time, we see other churches investing their energies in vigorously addressing human suffering, poverty, hunger, and injustice. We cannot easily see God's full agenda by observing His church today.

"What took you so long?"

❖   A few years ago a colleague and I were teaching church leaders on the Muslim-dominated island of Mindanao in the Philippines. The last day of the conference, ten people dressed in Muslim clothing came into the large church where we met. They took their places. A hush fell over the audience. There had been skirmishes between Muslim rebels and the government. Tension between Muslim and non-Muslim was high. We discovered that these were new Christian converts. They had been delayed four days at military checkpoints on their way to the conference. They asked if they could give their testimonies.

For many years, Christians had come to their village, preaching and handing out tracts. The village people rejected the message. Recently, a group of people had come to the village simply to minister lovingly to the needs of the people. Only later did the village people discover that these caring people were Christians. The impact of this ministry was so powerful that a number of villagers came to Christ. The final testimony still burdens me. A teenage girl told her story. Christians had come to her village doing traditional evangelism for years—perhaps even before she was born. Yet, only when the Gospel came wrapped in love and good works did it reap a harvest. She concluded with an unforgettable question: *"What took you so long?"*[1]

As the church of today, let's learn from her question! Let's understand the breadth and depth of God's agenda. Scripture tells us that God's agenda is much bigger than we imagine. Let's start at the *very* beginning—at creation.

---

[1] Sources for stories marked by ❖ are listed in the Bibliography at the end of the book.

God's Agenda Revealed in Creation

The Bible opens with a detailed account of creation. Each day except Day 2, God evaluated His work. It was "good," He declared. (If God evaluates something as "good," it must be truly good!)

God is magnificent beyond human description. He is glorious! He is good! He is wonderful! Everything He does reflects His goodness—and His intention is that *everything* He created would reflect His goodness and His glory. The Psalmist proclaimed: *"The heavens declare the glory of God and the firmament shows forth his handiwork."*[2]

When creation reflects God's goodness, it reflects God. When creation does not reflect God's goodness, it dishonors Him and promotes the lie that He is not good. People are attracted to a God who lovingly created them, but they are driven away by the lie that His intentions are not good. This is an essential insight! It explains God's intense concern for His goodness, His glory, and His agenda.

The creation shows us an amazing picture of God's glory. The perfect, holy, and loving God made a creation filled with an enormous variety of sizes, colors, and textures. His creation is complex. It is interconnected—and it works! Humans cannot fully understand or describe it. The cosmos—the earth, sky, vegetation, animals, and mankind—function together so well that God evaluated this totality of His creation as "very good." God clearly appreciated the work of His hands. It reflected not only His glory, but His agenda.

Here is a summary of creation and God's evaluation of it:

	What was created?	Genesis 1	Evaluation
Day 1	Light – Day and Night	verses 3-5	Good
Day 2 & 3	Sky, Land, Sea, Vegetation	verses 9-8	Good
Day 4	Sun, Moon, Stars	verses 14-19	Good
Day 5	Animals	verses 20-25	Good
Day 6	Mankind, All He Had Made	verses 26-31	Very Good

---

[2] Psalm 19:1

Mankind was the final step—the crown, the high point—of God's great work. After man was created, God evaluated all creation as "very good." God not only formed man, but "created man in his own image . . . male and female he created them."[3] Then, He appointed us to be His vice-regents—to act on His behalf to fill, subdue, and rule the earth.[4]

The biblical understanding of "ruling" is very different than the selfish ruling we observe in fallen mankind. When we look at Jesus, we see how God intends mankind to rule the earth. We see the One who came from heaven's glory to serve—even sacrificing His life for those He created. Biblical rule is not motivated by self-interest, but by service and sacrifice. This kind of rule reflects the servant character and glory of God.

The Bible tells us that, unfortunately, our ancestors did not rule as God intended. Instead, Adam chose to serve his own interests. With Adam's disobedience, known as the Fall, his relationship with God was severed—as was the relationship between God and all future humanity. Rebellion, tension, conflict, destruction, disintegration, and death were introduced into the creation that God had so carefully and lovingly made to reflect His glory.

The sin in the garden affected not only Adam and Eve, but all of creation. Many human beings are still in rebellion against God's purpose. Our individual lives, families, societies, and even the environment groan under the consequence of that rebellion. The Apostle Paul explained that *"the creation was subjected to frustration."* [5] Scripture tells us: *"The Lord was grieved that he had made man on the earth, and his heart was filled with pain."* [6] No wonder God's response to Adam's disobedience was so great—God was protecting His agenda from the consequences of Adam's selfishness!

---

[3] To be consistent with Genesis 1:27, I use "man" and "mankind" in the generic sense—male and female—throughout this work.
[4] Genesis 1:26-28
[5] Romans 8:20
[6] Genesis 6:6

God's Agenda Revealed in a Covenant

God continued to protect His agenda from the selfish misrule of Adam's descendents when He sent the Flood. After the Flood, God made an amazing covenant. Though speaking with Noah, God clearly made His covenant not only with Noah's descendents, but with *all* other surviving life, and with the earth. Noah, his sons, and their descendents, are listed nine times in the covenant. Other forms of the living creation—birds, livestock, wild animals, every living creature, and all life—are listed ten times, and the earth itself is mentioned twice.[7] Through this covenant, God reflected His concern for all creation.

> ## God's Covenant with All Life
>
> Genesis 9:8-17
>
> Verse 9—Noah and his sons
>   10—Every living creature
>   11—All life
>   11—The earth
>   12—Every living creature
>   12—The earth
>   15—All living creatures
>   15—All life
>   16—All living creatures
>   17—All life living on the earth

God's concern covers all of creation, and He made this clear through Noah. His broad agenda was again reflected in His covenant with Abraham—when God revealed His concern for all nations.

God's Agenda and Nations

God told Abraham that *"all peoples on earth will be blessed through you."*[8] He later confirmed the covenant, promising that *"all nations on earth will be blessed through him."* [9] God's agenda for the nations is a principal theme of the Bible—from Genesis to Revelation. In

---

[7] Genesis 9:8-17 Total word counts as seen in English NIV Bible. Other translations will be similar.
[8] Genesis 12:3
[9] Genesis 18:18b

the very last chapter of the Bible, the angel tells the Apostle John that the leaves on the tree of life are *"for the healing of the nations."*[10] The word "nations" is listed more than 2,000 times in Scripture.[11] God's concern for nations is not abstract! He expressed specific concerns for the social and economic well-being of the societies that make up nations.

In 2 Chronicles 6 and 7, we see a fascinating dialogue between King Solomon and God. As Solomon prayed at the public dedication of the temple, he acknowledged that the people had sinned. He was conscious that the consequences of sin brought a broad range of social and economic tragedy to the nation, which he described:

- Individual judgment against wrongdoers
- Defeat by an enemy
- Drought
- Famine, plant disease, insect infestation
- Attack by enemy, exile
- Natural disaster, disease

Solomon pleaded for God's mercy for the people if they would turn from their disobedience to walk in obedience to God.[12] God assured Solomon that He heard his prayer, including his request to forgive people's sin because of their repentance and obedience. Then He did something consistent with the agenda He had already expressed to Noah and Abraham. He promised Solomon He would heal the land!

---

[10] Revelation 22:2

[11] In the Old Testament, "nation" (*mishpachah*, in Hebrew) means a family group, tribe, or clan. The New Testament uses the Greek word *ethnos*, indicating a race, people, or ethnic group. Here, the biblical references to "nations" are to people groups (not countries). In later chapters, we look at impacting "nations," and both meanings will apply—we can influence our cultures, and we can influence our governments.

[12] 2 Chronicles 6:22-38

If my people, who are called by my name, will humble themselves and pray and seek my face and turn from their wicked ways, then will I hear from heaven and will forgive their sin and will heal their land.[13]

This healing of the land, Israel, would encompass the social and economic issues Solomon articulated in his prayer—issues that would sustain a healthy society. The healing of the land would depend on the people honoring God's will.

God *wanted* the land and the people of the land to be healed! God made all people to flourish. He made us in His image. When we flourish, we reflect who He is and His glory.

With fallen natures, we do not naturally flourish. We do not intuitively choose to live right.

God needed to reveal to us how He made us to live and relate to Him, to each other, and to creation.

Flourishing nations reflect God's glory.

God invited Israel to be His model nation—to live as He called it to live and to disciple nations by example.[14] God intended that Israel would show other nations that life is superior when they follow God's instructions:

Observe them [decrees and laws] carefully, for this will show your wisdom and understanding to the nations who will hear about all these decrees and say, "surely this great nation is a wise and understanding people."[15]

As a consequence of Israel's obedience to God, other nations

---

[13] 2 Chronicles 7:14

[14] Israel was to be an example to the nations by following the moral and social laws, as reflected in the Ten Commandments. I am not saying that other nations are called to obey Levitical laws, such as Old Testament dietary laws.

[15] Deuteronomy 4:6

would be drawn to God's splendor and glory. God spoke to Israel through the prophet Isaiah:

> *Surely you will summon nations you know not, and nations that do not know you will hasten to you, because of the Lord your God, the Holy One of Israel, for he has endowed you with splendor.*[16]

Throughout the Old Testament, it is as if Israel were on a public stage, demonstrating God's intentions and the consequences of obedience and disobedience.[17] Israel was to be a model nation, a messenger, a priest—pointing other nations to God.

In some ways, Israel did impact the culture. Or, more correctly, the way God dealt with Israel has influenced *many* cultures, to this day. Before Abraham, people understood life as endless cycles— birth, life, death, birth, life, death, plant, cultivate, harvest, plant, cultivate, harvest. Then God called Abraham out of this meaningless cycle.

> God intended that Israel point the nations to Himself.

He called him to leave a former way of life and start a new one. He gave him hope and a future promise. Could even one person be used to change the course of history? What a concept! Through Abraham, God showed the world that life has meaning and purpose. Life is going somewhere! The Ten Commandments are another blessing to the nations through the Jews. They were given to Israel, but today they provide a foundation for just and moral societies around the world.[18]

Israel, however, did not point other nations to God by obeying God. The nation that was to be an example to other nations became a disgrace, and God protected His glory. The prophet Ezekiel recorded God's disappointment:

[16] Isaiah 55:5
[17] Wright, *Deuteronomy*, 47.
[18] Miller, *God's Remarkable Plan for the Nations*, 30, and Cahill, *The Gifts of the Jews,* 240-241.

But the people of Israel rebelled against me, and they refused to obey my laws there in the wilderness. They wouldn't obey my instructions even though obedience would have given them life. And they also violated my Sabbath days. So I threatened to pour out my fury on them, and I made plans to utterly consume them in the desert. But again I held back in order to protect the honor of my name. That way the nations who saw me lead my people out of Egypt wouldn't be able to claim I destroyed them because I couldn't take care of them.[19]

God continued, not pleased:

Therefore, give the people of Israel this message from the Sovereign Lord: "I am bringing you back again but not because you deserve it. I am doing it to protect my holy name, which you dishonored while you were scattered among the nations."[20]

Israel had misrepresented God's glory, and He sent them into captivity. Here, and throughout the Old Testament, we see God protecting His agenda.

The New Testament also tells the story of God's concern for nations. Jesus' final commission to His disciples was to take the Gospel to the nations, so that *"repentance and forgiveness of sins will be preached in his name to all nations."*[21] Those nations, said Jesus, were to be discipled to understand and observe God's pattern for life: *"Therefore go and make disciples of all nations . . . teaching them to obey everything I have commanded you."*[22]

> # Jesus' last command: Take the Gospel to all nations and disciple them.

Sharing the Gospel—the Good News—includes proclaiming

---

[19] Ezekiel 20:13-14 (NLT)
[20] Ezekiel 36:22 (NLT)
[21] Luke 24:47
[22] Matthew 28:19,20a

Jesus not only as Savior, but as Lord. When the Lordship of Christ is acknowledged, we submit to *"obey everything"* Jesus has commanded us. Without the Lordship of Christ, we may be saved, but we will not be healed of our brokenness. The Lordship of Christ over every aspect of life is essential. Without it, the Gospel is incomplete and the church is immature. An immature church, not fully discipled itself, is incapable of fulfilling the commission to disciple all nations.

Finally, following the pattern of God's concern for the nations in the Old and New Testaments, we even see the nations represented at the return of Christ. This is an amazing truth! In the future Kingdom, the nations will see, abide by, and enjoy the blessings of God's glory. The Apostle John wrote that *"the nations will walk by its light, and the kings of the earth will bring their splendor into it."*[23]

God's agenda clearly encompasses the healing of people and nations—in the past, present, and future.

God's Agenda and Jesus

I often ask seminary and Bible school students: "Why did Jesus shed His blood?" One after another, students say, "He shed his blood to save our souls."

"Yes," I answer, "that's right. But why else did He shed his blood?"

"He shed His blood so we could be redeemed, and when we die we can go to heaven and have eternal life."

"Yes," I answer again, "that's right, but why else did Jesus shed His blood?"

They are focused on the spiritual aspect of God's redemptive purpose. They often have no other answer. We then look at a passage in Colossians 1. Time after time, the students express great surprise at the answer. Like the students, let's look at Colossians 1:15-20, counting how many times the word *"all"* appears in this amazing narrative:

---

[23] Revelation 21:24

He is the image of the invisible God, the firstborn over <u>all</u> <u>creation</u>. For by him <u>all things</u> were created: things in heaven and on earth, visible and invisible, whether thrones or powers or rulers or authorities; <u>all things</u> were created by him and for him. He is before <u>all things</u>, and in him <u>all things</u> hold together. And he is the head of the body, the church; he is the beginning and the firstborn from among the dead so that <u>in everything</u> he might have the supremacy. For God was pleased to have his fullness dwell in him, and through him to reconcile to himself <u>all things</u>, whether things on earth or things in heaven, by making peace through his blood, shed on the cross" (emphasis added).[24]

In the New International Version, *"all"* appears six times and *"everything"* appears once.

Seven times, this passage reminds us that God's agenda is as big as *"all creation."* Paul was making a point! Jesus' blood was shed for the restoration of *"all things."* Why? *"All things"* were broken in the Fall. God loves His creation, and He wants *"all things"* reconciled to Himself!

Jesus has the same agenda as His Father. This should not surprise us. The Bible says that Jesus is *"the image of the invisible God"*[25] and *"the exact representation of his being."*[26] As we look at Christ, we see God in human form.[27] There's more! Scripture tells us that *"God was pleased to have all his fullness dwell in him."*[28] Since He is the exact image of God and God's fullness dwells in Him, Jesus' agenda is the same as His Father's. It includes the spiritual regeneration of mankind—*and* the reconciliation of *"all things."*

> # The blood of Jesus was shed to restore all things!

[24] Colossians 1:15-20
[25] Colossians 1:15
[26] Hebrews 1:3a
[27] This truth is also affirmed in John 1:1 and Colossians 2:9.
[28] Colossians 1:19

Wonderful things happen when churches respond to God's larger agenda! However, far too few churches equip their people to restore *"all things."* Some concentrate on spiritual salvation, where restoration *begins*. Others concentrate on social and physical reform, to the neglect of spiritual regeneration. But the church must equip its people to represent God's whole agenda, to bring *"all creation"* under the Lordship of Christ.

This may seem like a huge task, but God has placed all believers in spheres they can influence—in their marriages, families, homes, neighborhoods, schools, work sites, offices, farms, marketplaces, friendships, common interest groups, societies, governments, and environments. The church must equip and encourage its people to impact their own spheres of influence and cooperate with God's big purpose in the world—the restoration of all things. When a church disciples with an *"all things"* understanding, it equips its people to bring their spheres of influence under the Lordship of Christ. A story from Haiti shows what happens when one person catches a bigger understanding of God's agenda and carries it out in his sphere of influence:

❖ Dougé is a remote village, populated by families of poor, subsistence farmers. Existence is meager, and people's well-being is dependent on the land and weather. Life is hard in Dougé. But there is a church in Dougé that cares deeply about these hardships. The church leaders invited our Harvest staff in Haiti to train leaders and members of eleven area churches. Though reaching Dougé requires arduous travel, our staff was glad to help. The training began much like we began this chapter—God's view of creation and man's responsibility in creation. The very first training session was attended by a church member who, by training, was an agricultural technician. His vocation had already trained him to care for the land, but something much deeper happened when he realized that *God* commanded him to manage *and rule* the earth and care for creation.[29] He realized he was not only trained—but commissioned and called by God!

---

[29] Genesis 1:28; 2:15-17

It was the rainy season, and the technician helped church members plant a vegetable garden for the community. The rainy season stopped, though, before the first harvest was ready. A river was the water source for the community, but it was not plausible to run a culvert that far, through rocky soil. "How would the plants grow?" the leaders pondered. The Dougé church houses a one-room school for one-hundred area children. The technician and other leaders enlisted the students to each carry a full gallon of water every morning when they came to school, to water the garden until the rain started again. They were successful. After the first harvest, the little church distributed more than 20,000 tomato seedlings around the community. Seed is a treasured commodity. Seedlings—ready to plant—must have been a great gift.

The people in the area, the church, and the school cooperated to carry out this means of community provision—because one agricultural technician saw the depth of what it means to "rule" the earth. We cannot know the long-lasting effects on people's lives as the church ministered to the physical needs of its community. Imagine what happens when thousands of local churches and millions of individual Christians cooperate with God to restore *"all things,"* to carry out God's BIG agenda!

There is another important lesson here. The agricultural technician lives in a small, impoverished nation, but that does not diminish his importance or ability in the sight of God. He was created in the image of God. He reflects the creativity, intelligence, serving spirit, and abilities of the Creator. He represents the One whose image he carries. He can do something Jesus would do if He were Mayor!

God's BIG Agenda

God's BIG agenda reveals His goodness and glory in all He has created. It includes the healing and restoration of all that has been broken.

- It includes the physical—the creation.
- It includes the social—the societal ills of our lands.
- It includes the spiritual—the personal redemption of our spirits.

In short, it includes the restoration of all!

Is There a Priority?

As followers of Christ, is it our priority to work for the spiritual salvation of mankind? There are at least three compatible answers to this question:

1. *Spiritual salvation is more important than any other kind of restoration.* There is nothing in the whole world that compares with it. Without salvation through Christ, we would have total separation from God. Jesus said:

   > *What good is it for a man to gain the whole world, yet forfeit his soul? Or what can a man give in exchange for his soul? If anyone is ashamed of me and my words in this adulterous and sinful generation, the Son of Man will be ashamed of him when he comes in his Father's glory with the holy angels.*[30]

   At risk is how people spend eternity—and their present lives. With Christ, *"the gift of God is eternal life in Christ Jesus our Lord."*[31] Without Him, *"the wages of sin is death."*[32] With Christ, comes full and abundant life.[33] Believing in Him, we *"shall not perish but have eternal life."*[34] Without Him, we are *"condemned already."*[35] The contrasts are as strong as they can be.

   Life comes through Jesus. He told His disciples: *"I am the way and the truth and the life. No one comes to the Father except through me."*[36] He later defined eternal life as He prayed to His Father, *"Now this is eternal life: that they may know you, the only true God, and Jesus Christ, whom you have sent."*[37] Eternal life is *knowing* Jesus and His Father. What an amazing privilege!

---

[30] Mark 8:36-38
[31] Romans 6:23b
[32] Romans 6:23a
[33] John 10:10
[34] John 3:16b
[35] John 3:18
[36] John 14:6
[37] John 17:3

Spiritual salvation is much more than a ticket to Heaven. Even the priority of spiritual salvation points us to God's larger purposes:

> *For it is by grace you have been saved, through faith—and this is not from yourselves, it is the gift of God—not by works, so that no one can boast. For we are God's workmanship, created in Christ Jesus to do good works, which God prepared in advance for us to do.*[38]

2. *Jesus ministered according to each context—sensitive to His Father's will.* Sometimes, Jesus ministered to spiritual need first, as in the healing of the paralytic man.[39] He was always concerned about people's spiritual needs, yet did not routinely minister to them first. Sometimes, He ministered to people without ever addressing spiritual needs. For example, when He healed ten lepers, we never saw Him deal with the spiritual needs of the nine who did not return to thank Him—but only the one who returned and fell at His feet.[40] Jesus knows men's hearts. We might expect He would heal only the one He knew would return—or would speak to all ten about their spiritual need before He healed them. He did neither. I believe Jesus reflected God's compassion for the physical *and* spiritual leprosy of all ten—even when He knew that nine would not respond spiritually. This is not a ministry strategy. Rather, it is the very character of God the Father, who *"causes his sun to rise on the evil and the good, and sends rain on the righteous and the unrighteous."*[41]

There are a number of other contexts in which Jesus ministered to physical or social need before He addressed spiritual need. Here are a few examples:

- He raised a widow's son (Luke 7:11-17).
- He calmed a storm (Luke 8:22-25).
- He healed an invalid at the pool of Bethesda (John 5:1-15).

---

[38] Ephesians 2:8-10
[39] Matthew 9:1-8
[40] Luke 17:11-19
[41] Matthew 5:45

- He changed water into wine (John 2:1-11).
- He fed 5,000 (as recorded in Matthew 14:13-21).

3. *Service is often the most effective means of ministering to spiritual needs.* People who are resistant to the spoken word are often open to seeing the living expression of God's love. Jesus, of course, knew this principle and ministered first to the need His Father knew would open people's hearts.

Allow me to share some insights from a colleague who works with impoverished children—and trains pastors in a South American seminary: "Most Christians agree that spiritual restoration is first. But when I see children being taught how to wash their hands before eating or how to brush their teeth well, I also see God's supernatural concern for His creation and human well-being."

As her pastoral students heard this kind of remark in class, one objected:

"No, this is wrong. We may fall into the extreme of just addressing the social area of development."

She replied: "But we may also fall into the extreme of just addressing the spiritual area and neglecting others. Falling into extremes is not good—be it focusing only on the spiritual area or addressing just the social area. There needs to be balance. Otherwise, we will be like a pendulum going from one side to the other, but going nowhere."[42]

Is there a priority for ministry? In eternal terms, yes—spiritual ministry takes priority. However (and this "however" is of critical importance), how we minister depends on the context into which God sends us and our sensitivity to the Holy Spirit. Always, it is important to keep in mind that our God has a big agenda. We don't want to be a pendulum, swinging from one extreme to the other, going nowhere!

---

[42] Ruth Concha, manuscript review (Peru: 2003).

God's All-Encompassing Love

Scripture helps us catch a glimpse of God's BIG agenda. This agenda includes the healing and restoration of all things that have been broken. It includes the physical—the redemption of the creation. It includes the social—the healing of the societal ills of our lands. It includes the spiritual—the personal redemption of our spirits. In short, it includes the redemption of all! The brokenness from the Fall was comprehensive—and so is God's plan to redeem all that was broken.

The Bible is clear that God not only loves the *people* He created, but His agenda includes the healing of *all creation*. God's now-broken creation will one day

> God so loved the *kosmos* . . .

be liberated from its bondage, and this liberation will be tied to the "glorious freedom" of the children of God.[43]

We can see God's broad intentions throughout Scripture as we read familiar passages in light of God's broad agenda. Let me give an example. Even one of the dearest passages to Christians offers potentially new insights:

> *For God so loved the world that he gave his only begotten son that whosoever believes in him shall not perish but have eternal life.*[44]

In this passage, *kosmos* is the Greek word used for "world." Sometimes in Scripture, *kosmos* means "earth" or "the created world." Other times, it can be interpreted as "people."[45] Our usual interpretation of John 3:16 is that "God so loves the people of the world" that He sent Jesus, so the people of the world could believe

---

[43] Romans 8:19-20

[44] John 3:16

[45] Earth/created world: Matthew 13:35; John 21:25; Acts 17:24; Romans 1:20; Hebrews 4:3; Hebrews 9:26. *Kosmos* also appears in Matthew 5:14; John 1:9,10,29; John 4:42; and passages in Romans, 1 Corinthians, and 1 John. It is interesting to note that John could have written that God so loved the *anthropos* (people), but did not.

in Him and have eternal life. Clearly, only people can choose to believe and have eternal life. Thus, God so loves the *kosmos*—the people of the world—that He provided a Savior, and the people who come to Him become children of God.

I believe this passage may also be telling us that God loved the *kosmos*—all creation—so much that He sent His Son, Jesus, to reconcile all things by His sacrifice on the cross.[46]

People are a significant part of His creation. Because of His love, He has now assigned the *kosmos* (His beloved children) a role in the restoration of the *kosmos* (His beloved creation). Because we have been loved and restored, we have a role in liberating creation from its brokenness. The Apostle Paul concurred. He wrote that the entire *"creation waits in eager expectation for the sons of God to be revealed."*[47] The creation is eagerly waiting for us to mature in Christ, so we will increasingly manage His creation according to His intentions.

God knows how we ought to live our lives. He wants His intentions, His will, and His laws obeyed at all levels on earth—now—as they are in heaven. Why? He loves us and all creation. He knows that we and the rest of creation will flourish to the degree that His will, His intentions, and His purposes are fulfilled. We, His beloved people, can again exercise our roles as vice-regents of all of His creation. We can once again steward it to reflect God's goodness and glory.

Wholistic Ministry

God's agenda to restore *all things* is addressed by what is known as "wholistic ministry." Let me define and illustrate this:

- Wholistic ministry is based on the whole Gospel for our whole lives. It ministers to the whole person and the whole of God's creation, based on the whole commission and God's whole agenda.[48] It reflects God's desire for wholeness, the opposite of brokenness. For these reasons, I choose to spell the word with a "w"—"wholistic"—rather than "holistic."

---

[46] Colossians 1:20
[47] Romans 8:19
[48] Disciple Nations Alliance, "Regaining Biblical Wholism," in *Wholistic Ministry* course, Internet, www.disciplenations.org.

- Wholistic ministry looks to God and the application of biblical truth to transform lives, churches, communities, and nations.

- Wholistic ministry reflects God's care for whole persons—for their spiritual, physical, social, and wisdom needs.

- Wholistic ministry is a lifestyle of obedience and love, based on Jesus' Great Commandment to love God and neighbor.

- It is the responsibility of all local churches and all individual believers.

- It does not depend on large financial outside resources, but on God.

As I was working on this section, a wonderful story—"A Treasure Wrapped in Rags"—arrived from a colleague in Peru. It is a story of wholistic ministry:

"Wholistic" or "Holistic"?

- Both are accepted English words.
- Both are found in the Oxford English Dictionary.
- Some development agencies use "holistic."
- "Wholistic" is more appropriate for Christian ministry.
- "Wholistic" is consistent with the "whole" Gospel, for the "whole" person, for the "whole" world.
- "Wholistic" distinguishes us from movements that use "holistic" in ways that are not consistent with Scripture.

❖ God had given Frances a heart for the street children of Peru. The children are often known as "piranhas," after the dangerous man-eating fish. They survive by assaulting and robbing people. Violence and drugs are part of their everyday lives. Burdened by God, Frances began a center to work with them. She knew that, no matter how hopeless they seem, they have been created in God's image and have God-given potential. Instead of calling them "piranhas," the center calls them "treasures wrapped in rags." Before Frances started the center, she shared her vision with her pastor. He was a well-intentioned Christian man with a narrow view of the church's mission. He told her, "You are concerned about social things. This is not what the church is called to do. If we are not evangelizing the lost, we are not doing anything!" Saddened, she left the church to begin what she was convinced God had called her to do. (The pastor has since apologized and now supports her efforts and vision.) Frances started the center in 1999 with few resources. One day, she spoke in a church about proclaiming the Gospel from a wholistic perspective, and someone offered her materials from one of our conferences. She says: "The materials confirmed God's plan. We need to impact all areas of life." The center does exactly that. There is a school that trains adults to work with the street children. The adults meet with the children regularly to provide spiritual counsel and encouragement to leave street life. When feasible, the children return to their families—but many cannot. A home is being built for these children, on land donated by the Peruvian government. It will house the children and provide them with education, spiritual and emotional counsel, and biblical values. The center has already built a medical center that provides health care for the children and for the public—as a community service and source of income. The children also help run a poultry farm and bakery on the ministry property, teaching a work ethic and providing funds for the ministry. God has blessed the center's wholistic ministry to these "treasures wrapped in rags."

The Kingdom of God

There is another important way to describe God's agenda:

God's primary agenda is to advance the Kingdom of God.

Jesus taught His disciples to pray: *"Your kingdom come, your will be done on earth as it is in heaven."* [49] In heaven, God's will, laws, and ordinances are completely obeyed by those who inhabit it. On earth, God's will is not fully obeyed, but His Kingdom advances on earth as His will is done. The Kingdom of God is one of Jesus' primary teachings. It is much larger than our comprehension, but here are some things we do know about the Kingdom of God:

---

[49] Matthew 6:10

- It reflects God's original intentions for the earth and all that inhabit it.

- It is the primary biblical metaphor[50] for God's redemptive work in history.

- Sin interrupted those intentions, but God's plan is to fully reestablish it.

- It is a present reality. It offers present hope for substantial healing and restoration, though its fullness is yet to come.

- God calls His people to be a present expression of the future reign of Christ. We are adopted into His family and have, therefore, entered the Kingdom of God.

- The Kingdom of God is advanced as God's will is carried out—as individuals live as He intends and as we disciple others, including nations, to do the same.

- The local church is the principal visible agent for this agenda on earth.

- When the King rules in us, we are privileged to take His healing to others.

❖   The Kingdom advances as God's will is done on earth, as it did among the Pokomchi Indians. The Pokomchi were among the poorest people in Guatemala. Missionaries of earlier generations had planted churches and many Pokomchi had accepted Christ, but their communities remained desperately poor. Next, development organizations arrived. They completed projects with large amounts of outside funding. The result? The Pokomchi had latrines and schools they didn't use! Clearly, transformation had not taken place. Arturo, a young Peruvian pastor, began to work among the Pokomchi. He knew that the Pokomchi needed to know God's view of the world and that it would take wholistic ministry to heal the broad-scale brokenness he saw. He began to teach the illiterate pastors and their

---

[50] *Metaphor:* An implied resemblance of two very different things.

people the very things we have covered in this chapter. For example, if the people harvested a good crop but rats ate it because it was poorly stored, Arturo would ask: "Who is smarter, you or the rats?" They would laugh and say: "The rats." Arturo would then ask: "Do you have dominion over the rats, or do the rats have dominion over your lives?" They had to acknowledge that the rats currently had dominion over their lives. Arturo then showed them that God had already blessed them to have dominion and rule over creation. God had already given them creativity, since they were made in His image. Arturo encouraged them with these truths. Gradually, they began to think differently—biblically. As their minds were transformed, so were their churches. Through the churches, the communities began to be transformed. Children went to school, women learned to read, men used new farming techniques, and women created storage to keep rats out of the food supply. They knew that God designed them to live better. A seminary professor from the U.S. visited. He saw lives and communities healed and transformed as people lived according to a greater awareness of God's broad agenda. Greatly touched, he said, "This is the coming of the Kingdom of God to the Pokomchi!"[51]

In Conclusion

Certainly, God's agenda is broad! The Psalmist wrote: *"The Lord is good to all; he has compassion on all he has made."*[52] Yes, God's concern covers all creation. It clearly includes the spiritual salvation of those who are dead in sin. Yet, when individual Christians and local churches *expand* their concern and ministry beyond the spiritual, they reflect the Good News of God's intentions to reconcile *all* that was broken in the Fall. God's agenda will not be fully completed

---

[51] The Pokomchi society is not yet fully transformed, but redemption *began* in the parts of Pokomich society where people started to live as God intends in all areas of life. As this happens, the purpose and Kingdom of God are advanced.

[52] Psalm 145:9

until the Second Coming of Christ. He *"must remain in heaven until the time comes for God to restore everything."* [53] In the meantime, the church must understand, embrace, and represent God's full agenda.

There is nothing outside the scope of God's agenda. The restoration of all things represents a total, global transformation. The entire world is to be purified of evil. It is to be full of the glory of God. The scope of God's redemptive work encompasses all of creation, including all mankind, all relationships, and the stewardship of all creation. If Jesus were Mayor, He would have a very BIG agenda!

---

[53] Acts 3:21a

God's Image Revealed | 5
The Servant Nature of the Church

God's Image Distorted . . . His Agenda Obscured

God's big agenda is to reconcile *"all things"* to Himself, even us. On the sixth day, says the Bible, God created man, male and female, in His image.[1] In His image—no wonder He wants to reconcile us to Himself!

The Bible then simply says that God saw all He made, and it was very good. In my imagination, I see God smiling and nodding with satisfaction as He carefully looks at each part of His creation. Here is daylight. It is good. Here are trees. They are good. Here is the moon. It is good. Here is a butterfly. It is good. He is pleased with His creation.

> ## "Image"
> - An "image" is a copy, likeness, resemblance, or reflection.
> - The "image of God" in man is about our characteristics, not physical appearance.
> - Only God is all-powerful, all-knowing, and omnipresent. Mankind is not.
> - The "image of God" is not like man-made images of false gods.

His gaze finally rests on His final masterpiece, which He fashioned after Himself. "Very good!" he exclaims! "These are my image-bearers. They reflect *Me!*"

Man was distinct. God Himself was the pattern, the model. Though other parts of creation reflected His glory, it was only in mankind that God placed such a rich reflection of Himself!

I often say that God's image-bearers were the "crown" of His creation. A crown is the pinnacle, the highest point of something

---

[1] Genesis 1:27

tall and grand. Genesis reveals that human beings were the high point of God's creation. A crown is also a symbol of supremacy and authority. If a nation crowns a king or queen, this person has been singled out as supreme leader of the land. Indeed, God has given mankind leadership over creation—to *"subdue"* the earth, *"rule over living creatures,"* and steward a broad range of creation.[2]

Created in the image of God, people were given attributes of God's image at a much higher level than He gave the rest of creation, including these:

- Creativity—ability to make something new[3]
- Language—ability to communicate ideas and abstractions through words
- Relationships—ability to form intentional, purposeful interaction with people, nature, and work
- Moral choice—ability to discriminate between constructive and destructive alternatives; ability to discern beauty
- Servanthood—ability to act in loving, compassionate selflessness toward others

These reflections of God's image are often found in other parts of the creation—but there is a profound difference between how they are reflected in man and in the animal kingdom. Monkeys can be creative, but they cannot make a bicycle, automobile, or space station. Wolves can communicate with each other, but they do not leave their written histories for future generations.

I did not list love as a separate attribute of God's image. The Bible tells us that *"God is love."*[4] The love of God permeates each of these characteristics. In fact, *everything* about God is love. Especially,

---

[2] Genesis 1:28-30. Not only does man steward the physical creation, but God has given mankind leadership in the spheres of society—science, arts, sports, philosophy, government, law, etc.

[3] Only God created something out of nothing. We discover and create something "new" out of substance already created by God.

[4] 1 John 4:16

love describes the *kind* of service that reflects God's image. The Apostle John asked how the love of God can be in someone who says he loves, but does not serve a brother in need.[5] Compassionate and sacrificial servanthood is the most important mark of God's image in man. Without this kind of servanthood, all other attributes can be corrupted and distorted:

- Creativity can produce an atom bomb.
- Linguistic ability can produce pornography.
- Relationships can lead to tyranny.
- Moral choice can be used to justify ethnic cleansing or abortion.

Compassion and sacrifice are distinguishing qualifiers for the kind of servanthood that reflects God's image in man. Other parts of the animal kingdom sacrifice for one another. A mother hen, for instance, instinctively sacrifices her life in a fire to protect her chicks. God, however, consciously chooses to sacrifice. He chooses to identify with our distress and to heal our brokenness. His conscious identification and decision to enter into our need at His own cost defines compassionate service. With animals, sacrificial service is instinctive. With God, sacrificial service is a compassionate choice— and He has placed this distinguishing mark of servanthood in us.

The distortion of God's image in man began almost immediately after creation. Ironically, man's sinful effort to become *more* like God actually distorted the image of God in man! Throughout the Old Testament, man was not able to see what it meant to bear the image of God, especially the attribute of loving and sacrificial service. God had intended that man would use the attributes of His image to serve others and creation. Instead, man acted selfishly. He did what he wanted, rather than what his Maker had purposed. He used the attributes of God's image for selfish advantage. Man distorted the image of God, and this distortion has continued through human history. The Apostle Paul confirmed this many years later. Man

---

[5] 1 John 3:17

worshiped himself and creation rather than the Creator, wrote Paul, and caused enormous havoc:

- Sexual impurity
- Depraved minds, filled with evil and greed
- Envy, murder, strife, deceit, malice, gossip, and slander
- God-hating, insolence, arrogance, boasting, evil intent, and disobedience
- Living in ways that are senseless, faithless, heartless, ruthless
- Approving others who do the same[6]

The image of God had become distorted. God's agenda had been obscured. Yet, God loved His creation so much that He would not allow the distortion of His image to destroy His agenda! In the Old Testament accounts of the Flood, Babel, the Law, and the Captivities, God can be seen protecting His agenda from mankind's selfish choices.

> ## In Jesus we see what God intended for Adam.

In the New Testament, too, we can again see God's broad agenda—in the coming of Jesus and the founding of the church.

God's Image Revealed in the Servanthood of Jesus

After Jesus came to earth, people could look at someone and *see* what God is like. Jesus was the perfect and complete image of God, but in human form. He is the exact representation of God.[7]

We see not only Jesus' divinity, but *humanity as God intended it.* Jesus perfectly modeled what it means to be made in the image of God. When we look at Jesus, we see the image of God—the crown of creation.

---

[6] Romans 1:24-32
[7] Hebrews 1:1-3b

When we look at Jesus, we also see the most important attribute of God's image, the brightest jewel in the crown. The shining feature that we see in Jesus is not the physical stamina and strength of the carpenter. It is not Jesus' wisdom—the wisdom that exceeded that of the Pharisees. Neither is it His perfect spirituality, nor is it the relational skills that endeared Him to the humble and silenced the proud. It is not even a combination of these. The jewel in the crown is Jesus' compassionate servanthood.

Jesus affirmed His servanthood when He replied to James' and John's mother. She had asked that her sons sit on thrones next to Jesus in the Kingdom. Jesus told her that *"the Son of Man did not come to be served, but to serve, and to give his life as a ransom for many."*[8] Paul affirmed Christ's servanthood in his letter to the Romans: *"For I tell you that Christ has become a servant of the Jews on behalf of God's truth . . ."*[9]

Finally, let's consider Paul's strongest description of Jesus' servanthood.

[Jesus], being in very nature God, did not consider equality with God something to be grasped, but made himself nothing, taking the very nature of a servant, being made in human likeness. And being found in appearance as a man, he humbled himself and became obedient to death, even the death on a cross.[10]

As the passage continues, we see God's response to Jesus' servanthood:

God is a servant!

Therefore God exalted him to the highest place and gave him the name that is above every name . . . and every tongue confess that Jesus Christ is Lord, to the glory of God the Father.[11]

---

[8] Matthew 20:28
[9] Romans 15:8-9
[10] Philippians 2:6-8
[11] Philippians 2:9-11

Because Jesus voluntarily and sacrificially became a servant, God exalted Him. He gave Jesus the highest position that could be given, a name that supersedes every name. Every tongue will confess that this Servant is Lord. He is exalted more than any other being. God honored Jesus in this manner *because* Jesus fully reflected what God intended when He created man. Jesus fully expressed the highest example of God's image—voluntary, compassionate, and sacrificial servanthood. God is

God is glorified when we serve.

a servant, and Jesus modeled that servanthood!

Paul introduced this description of Jesus' servanthood by telling his readers: *"Your attitude should be the same as that of Christ Jesus."*[12] Man, created in God's image, was also created to serve voluntarily, compassionately, and sacrificially. When we serve as Jesus did, we most fully bear the image of God.

Mankind is the crown of creation, and servanthood is the "jewel" in the crown. When Jesus was honored for being a servant, God was glorified. In the same way, God is glorified when His children reflect His image as they serve. Jesus told His disciples: *"Let your light shine before men, that they may see your good deeds and praise your Father in heaven."*[13]

The Bible describes the high calling of servanthood:

- God said He is pleased by service to the poor and oppressed.[14]
- Jesus told His disciples that service is the distinguishing mark of those in the Kingdom—they feed the hungry, clothe the naked, and visit those who are sick and in prison.[15]

---

[12] Philippians 2:5
[13] Matthew 5:16
[14] Isaiah 58:6-7
[15] Matthew 25:35

- Pure and faultless religion includes serving widows and orphans—those who need protection.[16]
- Jesus emphasized God's high priority on loving and serving our neighbors.[17]

God intends that His people be conformed to the image of His Son.[18] This is a process, as we *are being transformed into his likeness with ever-increasing glory, which comes from the Lord, who is the Spirit.*[19] We conform to the image of Christ as His Spirit lives within and conforms us—and as we model our lives after the highest point of our likeness to Christ, servanthood.

God's Image Revealed in the Servanthood of the Church

After revealing His image through Christ, God revealed His image in His church. One of the tasks of the church is to birth and disciple others to bear the image of God, especially His servant-image. As we will see, it is God's intent to use this community of believers to demonstrate and administer His agenda. The local church does so by facilitating new birth, equipping, and sending its people out as servant-ambassadors.

God does not command compassionate and sacrificial service for its own sake. He commands it because it results in the demonstration of His greatest attribute, love. Jesus told us to love God and love our neighbors as ourselves. We demonstrate our love for God by loving our neighbor as we would want to be loved. Similarly, God's love was demonstrated to the world through Christ's compassionate service. Sacrificial service is the way that the full character of God is still expressed in the world today. When God's love is expressed through human agents, it expresses itself not only in words, but in sacrificial service.

---

[16] James 1:27
[17] Mark 12:31
[18] Romans 8:29
[19] 2 Corinthians 3:18b

Godly love results in compassionate and sacrificial service. Loving service heals brokenness. It restores. It redeems. This is God's agenda. When it is fulfilled, He is glorified.

GODLY LOVE | **YIELDS** | **COMPASSIONATE, SACRIFICIAL SERVICE**

❖ This was certainly the case one November day in 1999 in Addis Ababa, the capital of Ethiopia.[20] Three months earlier, we had presented a conference there, where I was introduced to Gizachew, a young man in his twenties. Gizachew was one of ten children in a poor Christian family. He and other volunteers—also from poor families—identified with the hundreds of teenage boys living on the streets. They occasionally went to a nearby mountain to seek God's vision to help the boys. They also began to work with twenty-two street boys, giving them Bible studies, food, baths, and used clothing.

After the conference, Gizachew and his friend excitedly shared with the other volunteers what they learned. They systematically studied the teachings and put them into practice.[21] The group then planned a garbage cleanup near a busy bridge in the center of the capital city, on the road to the biggest market place. They invited the street boys to join them. At 6 a.m., the group met. They divided into two groups. One group picked up garbage from the street, despite the foul smell of mixed garbage and waste. The other group prayed, offered first-aid, and witnessed to people who asked what was happening. At 9 a.m., the first people carried trash to the dumpsite. As they started to throw the trash into a large metal box—a dumpster—they looked inside. They saw something like a

---

[20] The source for the story marked by ❖ is listed in the Bibliography at the end of the book.

[21] Two teachings that particularly impacted them were Kingdom Mathematics and Seed Projects. Both are covered later in this book—Kingdom Mathematics in Chapter 11 and Seed Projects in Chapter 13. In fact, the second part of Gizachew's story is used to introduce Kingdom Mathematics.

human foot! They uncovered the trash and found a young man. The dumpster had been his home. They checked the movement of his chest to see if he was still alive. He could barely move his lips. He was not in his right mind. They carefully led him out of the garbage dump and began to remove his filthy rags. His clothes were attached to his body from sweat and dirt. He had not removed them or bathed in years, and his body smelled rotten. Some of his clothes were stuck to wounds from burns he had gotten when hot coals were thrown on top of him as he slept. The believers cut off his clothes, bathed him in a nearby open-air shower, and trimmed his hair. They later shaved his head to relieve him of lice. Meanwhile, they tried to communicate, but received no response.

In awhile, he began to talk, but his speech was like a baby's. Listening carefully, the believers could understand. His name is Jemal. He was born 200 kilometers from the city. His parents are Muslim. Years ago, he went to the capital in search of better living conditions. He thought the city would provide him whatever he needed. He found no food, shelter, or clothes—only five dogs that had been abandoned by their owners. After years of wandering, he finally chose to live inside the dumpster. He explained that it gave him hope because it was like a home. He ate garbage. No one ever asked him who he was. He preferred to spend his days with the dogs and never wanted to associate with people. He had no one to speak to until the volunteers served him with love and compassion. They soon told him about the love of Jesus.

He asked them, "Is there a God who cares and loves me?"

"Yes!" they assured him. He didn't hesitate—he accepted Christ.

A woman who had been watching the volunteers asked them: "Why are you doing humble service?"

The Christians replied, "We do this to show people that Jesus loves them."

Jemal was taken to the hospital for health checkups and medical treatments. After several months, his physical health had improved, and the psychiatrist who examined him expected him to recover. He bathed and washed his clothes by himself, ate and socialized with people, and went to church regularly. Two years after the first conference, I was teaching in Addis Ababa again. I had the privilege of meeting the young man who was found at the dumpster. He was *"dressed and in his right mind,"* [22] like another man who had encountered Jesus many years ago!

Clearly, the Christians embodied the image of God in their servanthood. I believe they also saw Jemal through God's eyes and understood that he was created in the image of God, with the capacity for creativity, language, relationships, moral choice, and servanthood. When they first met him, his life lacked all creativity, language, and human relationships. Moral choice and servanthood were unknowns. Love had no meaning. Since then, God's image has become visible in Jemal, little by little.

When Jesus raised Lazarus from the dead, He told Lazarus' friends to take off the grave clothes. [23] God preserved Jemal's physical and spiritual life, but Gizachew and his friends, literally, took off his grave clothes.

A Call to a Biblical View of Servanthood

Many Christians—especially those who have seen a long history of economic and political abuse—are offended by the concept of servanthood. To them, servanthood means involuntary service or slavery. As a consequence, servanthood is considered degrading.

Involuntary servitude assumes many forms. It can be outright slavery. It can be degrading servitude, required by economic realities. It can be servitude forced on the

Some Christians may be offended by servanthood.

unwilling by those who are mentally, socially, or politically more

---

[22] Luke 8:35
[23] John 11:44

powerful. None of these are the servanthood of which the Bible speaks. God's church needs to help its people reclaim the biblical meaning of servanthood.

If we have not been servants in the biblical sense, we are called to change. Picture the Christian life as a journey on a long road. When we sin, we travel down the road in the wrong direction. We hear Jesus say, "Go and sin no more." We turn around and face the other direction.   Having turned, do we stay at the same place on the road? No, we *walk* in the new direction, toward the righteousness that God intends.

The Apostle Paul encouraged believers to put on the new self—and become like God. Liars become truth-tellers, thieves become givers, unwholesome-talkers become edifiers, and bitter people become forgivers.[24] Where we have served our self-interests, we turn and walk in the other direction—toward

> ## The Image of God is Motivating!
> ## Listen to These Words*
>
> [God's] righteousness is an essential expression of his love. He loves justice and hates oppression. He champions the cause of the poor, the alien, the widow, and the orphan. He feeds the hungry, clothes the naked, heals the sick, finds the lost. He wants all mankind to be saved and to come to know the truth in his Son Jesus Christ. Now this biblical vision of God profoundly affects our attitude to society, since God's concerns inevitably become his people's too. We also will respect men and women made in God's image, seek justice, hate injustice, care for the needy, guard the dignity of work, recognize the necessity of rest, maintain the sanctity of marriage, be zealous for the honor of Jesus Christ, and long that every knee will do homage to him and every tongue confess him. Why? Because all these are God's concerns.
>
> * Stott, Involvement, 80.

---

[24] Ephesians 4:30-32

God's agenda, serving the interests of others.

Biblical servanthood is not possible without the indwelling Christ, but it *is* possible through the power of God's Spirit. Paul reminded his readers that God and people work together to achieve the purposes of God: *"Continue to work out your salvation with fear and trembling, for it is God who works in you to will and to act according to his good purpose."*[25]

In the ninth chapter of Acts, Aeneas the paralytic was healed, and Dorcas was raised from the dead. Dramatic! Just as dramatic is the fact that the instrument of healing was not Jesus, but Peter. God wants to show Himself through His image in His children! As we express His love, we are the instruments through which God's life-transforming power is expressed. We reflect and communicate the great miracle of lives once vandalized by sin, now restored to God's image. Who would have dreamed that the Lord of the universe—our "Mayor"—would want to use His "citizens" to reveal Himself, His love, His servanthood, His image, His power, and His agenda? It is His plan that His image be reflected in the church and its people. What a legacy! What a challenge!

---

[25] Philippians 2:12b-13

The Purpose of the Church
The Mystery Revealed

6

Adam was created in God's image. He was then appointed as God's vice-regent to rule the earth.[1] Instead of reflecting the image of God and ruling in a way that demonstrated God's character, Adam rebelled and initiated a process of selfish choice. The Bible reveals that, at that point, everything God created became corrupted.

Since then, throughout history, God has been redeeming His creation, reversing the carnage that began with Adam. He made covenants. He chose a model nation. He sent His Son. Step by step, He made known His divine secret—His mystery—revealing how God will resolve the brokenness and restore *all things* to Himself.

Introducing the Mystery

In his letter to the Ephesian church, the Apostle Paul introduced the mystery of God's intentions, His plan to restore a world

> ## "Mystery"
>
> Tomorrow I'll fly to Jamaica to teach. I'll board the airplane, buckle my seatbelt . . . and *fall asleep!*
>
> For centuries, others have not been so fortunate. They tried to fly. They strapped on home-built wings, jumped off cliffs, flapped their "wings," and failed (*ouch!*). They didn't know the mystery of flying. Year after year after year, they failed. The secret was understood only by God.
>
> Finally, the mystery was revealed. It was revealed through people who were knowledgeable—and now we can fly.
>
> In the Bible, a "mystery" is a divine secret that is undiscoverable by human reason, revealed only by God.
>
> There is an amazing mystery that was hidden through the ages. At the right time, Paul was chosen to reveal it to the Ephesians—and to us . . .

---

[1] *Vice-regent:* A person who acts in the place of a ruler, governor, or sovereign.

vandalized by sin. God revealed the mystery to Paul. Paul was to tell others. It was no longer a divine secret! Paul wrote: *"And he made known to us the mystery of his will according to his good pleasure, which he purposed in Christ."* [2]

The "mystery," in summary, is this: All that was broken in Adam's rebellion will be brought back into unity and peace. God intended before creation that Christ would come and restore all things to Himself. This will happen as creation submits to the intentions, will, and rule of the One who created it—through Christ.

But let's hear it in Paul's words. The purpose of the mystery, said Paul, is *"to bring all things in heaven and on earth together under one head, even Christ."* [3]

All things together under Christ? Imagine the enormous revelation this was in the first century! One commentator wrote:

> How far then was He from being merely the national Messiah of Jewish expectation! Even "the Savior of the world" is not a great enough designation for Him: He is the Savior of the universe. [4]

Before Paul introduced the mystery, he gave his readers a clear indication that this mystery was going to include them—and us:

> *In him we were also chosen, having been predestined according to the plan of him who works out everything in conformity with the purpose of his will.* [5]

We have a part in this mystery! As Paul prepared to reveal the mystery, he prayed that his readers' eyes would be opened, able to deeply know the grand inheritance and resurrection power available to those who carry out His grand purpose. [6]

---

[2] Ephesians 1:9
[3] Ephesians 1:10b
[4] Davidson et al (eds), *The New Bible Commentary*, 1018.
[5] Ephesians 1:11
[6] Ephesians 1:18-20

Revealing the Mystery

The mystery, wrote Paul, is to *"bring all things in heaven and on earth together under one head, even Christ."*[7] He then began to reveal the details to the church at Ephesus. Let's review each phrase of the following passage to discover several facets of the mystery. They are important! They are as true for us today as they were when Paul's scribe first recorded them:

> ## We have a glorious part in the mystery.

And God placed all things under his feet and appointed him to be head over everything for the church, which is his body, the fullness of him who fills everything in every way.[8]

1. *"And God placed all things under his feet."* Paul confirmed God's agenda to reconcile *"all things"* through Christ. *"All things"* are placed by God under Christ's feet.

2. God *"appointed him to be head over everything for the church."* Christ is head of all—*"for the church."* We can understand why God would put everything under Christ and why He would appoint Him as head over everything. But why did He do this *"for the church"*? What wondrous purpose could He have for His church? Paul clarified this later, in Ephesians 3.

3. Paul wrote of *"the church, which is his body."* The church is Christ's body. A body carries out the intentions of its head. Clearly, the agenda of Christ (the head) is also the agenda of His body (the church). This is important. The church has the same agenda as Christ, who has the same agenda as His Father!

4. Paul then explained that the church, Christ's body, is *"the fullness of him who fills everything in every way."* The Bible says that

---

[7] Ephesians 1:10b
[8] Ephesians 1:22-23

the church *is* the fullness of Christ. Yet, many churches today are good illustrations of the world's brokenness—not Christ's fullness! The church *is* the fullness of Christ, but it has not yet reached its potential. It has not lived up to its identity as the fullness of Christ. As it does, the church (like Christ) will *"fill everything in every way."*

5. Paul described this mystery later in Ephesians: *"This mystery is that through the gospel the Gentiles are heirs together with Israel, members together of one body, and sharers together in the promise of Christ Jesus."* [9] In the body of Christ, explained Paul, Gentiles are now members of Christ's body. People who were formerly hostile to one another are united into one family. Christ brings peace to divided, warring humanity through His body, the church. (Even today, former enemies

---

Kigali, Rwanda
April, 1997

Dear Brother Bob:

This is a month of mourning for the victims of the 1994 genocide. Yesterday, 10,000 Christians marched through the streets of Kigali—singing, praising God, and praying for peace, security, repentance, and 2 Chronicles 7:14.

We ended at the National Stadium, where an amazing thing happened. Helen M., who used to be a member of our church, stood in front of the multitude next to a man, E____.

The man, E____, had killed Helen's husband. She had suffered loss, grief, hardship.

As they stood in front together, E____ told the crowd: "I no longer want to say I am a Hutu, because a Hutu or Tutsi who is not saved makes no difference. I was among the people who murdered your husband, and I made sure he was dead simply because he was a Tutsi. When I came to know the Lord Jesus Christ, I did not have peace in my life until I confessed to Helen that I murdered her husband. I wrote her in Burundi and then went there to ask for forgiveness."

Helen forgave E____. She said: "If God has forgiven you, who am I not to forgive?" They hugged while everyone else was shedding tears!!!

Your co-laborer and brother,
Simon

---

[9] Ephesians 3:6

are united through Christ's body. See the letter in the box on the previous page.)

6. Paul related next that he had been given grace *"to make plain to everyone the administration of the mystery."* [10] He revealed how this mystery would be administered. "Administration" comes from *koinonia,* Greek for "participation." The mystery is Christ, whose shed blood reconciles the broken world to God. Thus, the reconciliation of *"all things"* to God is administered through the *participation of the church!* Paul told the church of its great role in administering the mystery.

7. Paul continued: *"His intent was that now through the church the manifold wisdom of God should be made known."* [11] God's plan is to restore *all things*—and His wisdom is manifold. It is not one-dimensional. It is multi-dimensional. It is expansive. His agenda is not only spiritual, but includes the restoration of *all* that was broken in the Fall. As the church obeys Christ's purpose, it administrates

> ## The Eternal Cup
>
> A stadium is full of people. A match is in process on the field.
>
> On the field are two teams—the Kingdom of Darkness and the Kingdom of Light, the Church. For the sake of discussion, let's assume that the stands are crowded with spectators from both sides, as is the case in most sporting events.
>
> Each team has a coach. Jesus Christ is Coach of the Church. Satan is the coach for the Kingdom of Darkness. Jesus, God's son, has a strategic game plan. His plays are brilliant and multi-faceted.
>
> As the Church follows its Coach's game plan, it wins a cup greater than the World Cup—the Eternal Cup! The church wins the contest on earth and for all eternity!
>
> ———
>
> All analogies break down at some point. Yet, they are instructive, so we use them. The same is true of this analogy. Jesus and Satan are not parallel! Jesus is the almighty Son of God, a member of the Godhead. Satan is a fallen angel, and his power is limited.

[10] Ephesians 3:9a
[11] Ephesians 3:10a

the mystery and makes known the manifold agenda of God. I thoroughly concur with a comment I read about this very passage: "The ecclesiastical implications of such a verse as this are staggering, indeed."[12] Yes, the implications for the church are staggering! And, there's more . . .

8. The passage resumes: *"Through the church the manifold wisdom of God should be made known to the rulers and authorities in heavenly realms."*[13] God's great and multifaceted plan—which Paul said was hidden in God in ages past—would now be made known, not only to the people of the earth but to the rulers and authorities of the spiritual world. These are the powers of the dark world, the spiritual forces of evil. They may also be the holy angels, the spiritual forces of the Kingdom of God. Through the church, God will demonstrate to Satan and his army—and to the entire spiritual realm—that He, God, will restore *all things* through Christ. The rulers and authorities in heavenly realms will look on the theater of earth. They will see God's manifold wisdom—His amazing plan for bringing peace, breaking divisions, healing brokenness, and restoring all things. All of this will be administered through the church!

The *administration* of
God's redemptive purpose—
His manifold wisdom

THROUGH
THE CHURCH

---

[12] Graelein, *The Expositor's Bible Commentary, Volume 11*, 47. "Ecclesiology" is the study of the church.
[13] Ephesians 3:10-11

Resolving the Mystery

Ephesians 1 raised perplexing questions about the mystery. We now have some answers:

Question: Why would God place all things under Christ's feet and appoint Him head over everything *"for the church"*?[14]

Answer: God did this *"for the church"* because He has chosen the church to be the instrument through which He will accomplish His purpose. I cannot imagine a greater purpose or privilege than to have a central assignment in our Creator's eternal purpose for the restoration of all things! This is *our* privilege.

Question: What are the implications for the church as Christ fills *"everything in every way"*?[15]

Answer: His body—the church—must do the same. Christ fills every aspect of societal life. The church, then, should creatively infiltrate every aspect of its society with God's agenda to heal brokenness. The people of the church should penetrate individual, family, and community life. The body of Christ must demonstrate God's intent and ability to restore all things to Himself. The church is not proclaiming a hope based on human initiative, but on *"the glorious riches of this mystery, which is Christ in you, the hope of glory."*[16]

Therefore . . .

God wants to accomplish His redemptive purpose, His big agenda, through the church—not through individual believers alone, but through the local and global church. His purpose will be fulfilled in communities and nations when the church carries out its mission.

---

[14] Ephesians 1:22
[15] Ephesians 1:23
[16] Colossians 1:27b

Therefore, the church is far more important for the transformation of a society than the president of the nation, its legislators, or its business leaders. The principal and most strategic institution God appointed to carry out His big agenda is not found in the political or economic spheres. Instead, it is the church. We serve the head of the church. We work for the Mayor, and His agenda is total restoration!

> ## The church is more important than the nation's president!

Locally Expressing the Mystery

Each generation of each local church has a choice—to be an administrator of God's agenda for its community, or not. The combined churches of a country have a similar choice to make. The generation of Israel that Moses led out of Egypt had a choice. God told them that His agenda was for them to move into the Promised Land. They were afraid, and they stayed in camp! Because of their lack of faith, they did not see His faithfulness and purpose. That generation did not arrive in the Promised Land. God removed His blessing from one generation and gave it to the next.

God chose the local church for a grand purpose and equipped it with unique strengths:

- The local church is a microcosm of the community. When it submits to God's intentions, it becomes a model of God's agenda in its society.

- As it submits to God's intentions, it increasingly reflects His image and character. It is in a position to serve as God's vice-regent in the part of creation where God has placed it.

- God has prepared and given leaders to the church. These leaders then equip the people of the church for God's grand purpose. This is the overarching job description of all church leaders—to equip God's people to carry out His work and to extend His rule through service.[17]

- The local church ministers corporately. It also equips and sends its individual members to serve in their own spheres of influence.

- The local church has the mandate to represent God's whole agenda. Other Christian institutions have narrower mandates.

At Harvest, we have hundreds of ministry stories that demonstrate how service to God's agenda transforms individuals, churches, communities, and nations. I have been sharing some of these stories with you, and this would seem like the ideal time to feature more of them.

In this chapter, though, I'm going to ask you to do something different. I'm going to ask you to step back and think. Think of the specific areas of brokenness in your community. Then, picture *your* church as the agent of reconciliation and healing. Picture the individuals in your church, filling their society with the fullness of Christ. What do you see? What is your vision? What changes would there be in your community *if Jesus were Mayor?*

Summarizing the Mystery

When Paul wrote the believers in Ephesus, He brought them a mystery revealed. His letter covers God's revelations about the church, its purpose, and its strategy. He communicated the mystery to them—and to us:

God's grand purpose will be carried out through the church!

- *All things* are placed under Christ.
- Christ is head of all—for the church.
- The church is Christ's body.
- The church is the fullness of Christ.

---

[17] Ephesians 4:11-12

- Former enemies are united.
- The church is to administer the mystery.
- The church is to reveal God's manifold wisdom.
- The church is to make God's plan known to rulers and authorities.
- The overall job description of all local church leaders is to equip and disciple the local church members for service.

The church is dynamically related to God's big agenda!

- God's overarching purpose is to restore all things under Christ.
- The task of the church is to carry out God's great agenda.
- The church is the body of Christ and the fullness of Christ.
- God's plan to place all things under Christ is done "for the church."
- We—the followers of Christ—are the church.
- We play a role in this purpose—a role so grand it is called an "inheritance."
- Christ shed His blood in order that all things would be restored, first by reconciling the breach between God and mankind.
- The work of restoration begins by bringing people who were "far away" back into relationship with God through Christ.[18]
- As restored people take on the image of Christ, they reflect His concern in every dimension of the creation—especially in the spheres they influence. As they do, God's big agenda—the transformation and restoration of creation—is advanced.
- Full restoration will follow Christ's return. Now, God's people are charged with the responsibility to extend His rule and "occupy" the territory until He returns.[19]
- God's people are once again being given the privilege of being His vice-regents.

---

[18] Ephesians 2:13
[19] Luke 19:13 (KJV). The Greek word for "occupy" means "do business."

Proclaiming the Mystery

For a different declaration of the grandeur of the mystery, let's look at the Ephesians 1 passage in a contemporary paraphrase, *The Message*. It is powerful!

> *He is in charge of it all, has the final word on everything. At the center of all this, Christ rules the church. The church, you see, is not peripheral to the world; the world is peripheral to the church. The church is Christ's body, in which he speaks and acts, by which he fills everything with his presence.*[20]

How privileged we are that God has revealed His mystery to us! Christ's fullness dwells in the church, and He has equipped us to reflect it. As the church of today, we are still commissioned to proclaim the mystery to the world we serve.

---

[20] Ephesians 1:22-23 (The Message)

Ephesians

Ephesians presents Scripture's most complete vision of the church and its purpose. It was in Ephesians that Paul revealed the mystery hidden through the ages—the relationship between God's big agenda and His plan to carry out that agenda through the church.

The church at Ephesus was best prepared to receive this revelation. It was possibly founded by Apollos. Priscilla and Aquila—long-time colleagues of Paul—served as leaders. Paul sent Timothy to pastor there. Tradition even says that the Apostle John and Jesus' mother were part of that body.

Paul's time at the Ephesus church was longer than at any of the other churches. During his first three months in Ephesus, he taught about the Kingdom of God in the local synagogue. He met opposition and moved to the lecture hall of Tyrannus, where he taught two years. After he left, as was his custom, he wrote a letter to the church, which has become the book of Ephesians. It, like other letters, was likely circulated to other churches, but it was directed to the believers in Ephesus.

The church at Ephesus was prepared to move beyond the basics of the faith and understand deeper theology revealed to Paul about the church. Paul—and the Holy Spirit—wanted these mature disciples to move beyond individual redemption. He revealed the mystery to them—God's grand purpose for the church.*

* Scott Hahn, *The Splendor of the Church*, St. Joseph Communications, Inc., videocassette.

The Church and Today's World

7

Reversing the Reversal

We have seen that the church of history introduced great social transformation. Here, from Kosovo, is an example from the present, as told to me by a missionary friend:

❖ The Secretary General of [a major city in Kosovo] had invited our team leaders into his office to thank them for what they were doing. He said:

> You have my unqualified support. There's no one else like you here. Even our Muslim brothers from abroad come and spend millions of dollars, but they aren't helping the people. They're building mosques from one end of the country to the other; but they're not feeding us; they're not clothing us; they're not building our homes like you are. You're the only ones who really care about us.

Before our meeting was over, this Secretary General and a number of his people asked for Bibles and other Christian literature. The Secretary General told our team leaders: "You go out and help my people. You can do whatever you want. You have my unqualified support. You don't even have to ask my support ahead of time—that's how much confidence I have in you."[1]

Certainly, all communities would be different if Jesus were Mayor—and there would be many stories like those from Kosovo. Is this the kind of positive transforming effect the church is having

---

[1] Sources for stories marked by ❖ are listed in the Bibliography at the end of the book.

around the globe? The past one-hundred fifty years have seen explosive growth of new churches and new believers around the world. When there is a large and growing percentage of Christians in a nation, it would seem that the reign of Christ should be dramatically reflected in the fabric of its society. After all, only 10.5 percent of the population radically influenced the Roman Empire!

Unfortunately, we often hear the opposite today. In many societies, while the church is growing numerically, the society is simultaneously decaying. The church is not making a strong, visible impact on its culture.

I was recently with a Christian brother in Africa who shares my passion for the church. During the 1990s, he led a coalition of church-planting ministries in a southern African country with a population of over eleven million

> ## Babies Who Make Babies
>
> My friend, a Guatemalan who is a Quiche Indian, trains native pastors among his people. He has a passion to build a church with God's full agenda. He told me:
>
> Bob, we don't really need more churches like the ones among my tribe. There are churches on every street corner in some villages. One church preaches against the next church. Another church says, "If you go to that church, you'll become a heretic. We are the true church and the only one that has the power of the Holy Spirit." The problem is not evangelism, but immature believers and weak churches. We have babies making babies! New churches think their first responsibility is to plant a new church. But neither the believers nor the churches are spiritually mature. They can't nurture new believers or new churches.*
>
> How perplexing, I thought. In my culture we think it is tragic when young people have babies before they know how to raise them to maturity. Yet, we tend to celebrate when it happens spiritually—when spiritual babies produce babies!
>
> * Interview with Isaias C., circa 1995.

people. This coalition reported 10,000 new churches during the 1990s. He thought that the numerical growth in churches would bring visible transformation to the society. On the contrary, the country seriously deteriorated at almost every social level. Politically, it moved from democracy to dictatorship. Corruption was rampant. There were sharp declines in economics, health, and education. Yet, there were ten thousand new churches! Seventy percent of the citizens considered themselves Christians! (Thirty-three percent were evangelical, charismatic, or Pentecostal believers; only twenty percent were active church-goers.) There was such a disconnection between church growth and societal transformation that my friend decided he could not remain in his position with integrity.

This African nation is not unique. Forty percent of the people in Guatemala claim to be evangelical believers. Yet, the country still suffers from corruption, poverty, and ethnic division. A 2004 United Nations report concluded that the Guatemalan government failed to resolve 200,000 deaths and disappearances during the country's 36-year-civil war, which ended in 1996—and that people who were implicated in the deaths remain unpunished.[2]

In Rwanda, eighty percent of the people claimed to have been converted to Christianity; yet, Rwanda suffered a terrible genocide in 1994.

In the United States, 85 percent of the people identify themselves as Christians, and one-third claim to be "born again."[3] Yet, America is in steep moral decline.

What factors prevent us—the church—from having the kind of transforming impact on society that we could and should have? Here are a few factors I propose:

- *The people of the church are often hearers but not doers of the Word.* Leaders in the Reformation and revivals preached and taught the necessity of faith and works together. There was no such thing as faith without works or works without faith. But many churches today do not teach people to serve.

---

[2] "Thousands of deaths unsolved in Guatemala," *Arizona Republic*, Briefs.
[3] Barna Research Online, "Beliefs," Internet.

- *Confessing Jesus as Lord requires obedience, not merely words.* Belief itself is insufficient. Even demons believe that Jesus is the Son of God and Lord of the universe, but they do not obey Him. Real faith is a supernatural gift of the Spirit of God. Biblical faith results in loving obedience.

- *The Great Commission has been narrowly interpreted.* Although many churches today base their ministry on the Great Commission, they interpret it narrowly—as a call for evangelism and church planting. As we look at the passage, though, we find a vision of lasting transformation that is very broad and very deep. *Nations* are to be discipled, baptized, and taught to obey *everything* Jesus commanded:

  Therefore go and make disciples of all nations, baptizing them in the name of the Father and of the Son and of the Holy Spirit, and teaching them to obey <u>everything</u> I have commanded you.[4]

The "Greek" Commission

Many in the church today have been following what I call the "Greek"—rather than the "Great"—Commission. There is no Greek Commission, but if there were, it might say: "Go and make spiritual converts of all individuals, teaching them to evangelize and plant churches."

Why would this be "Greek"? The early church had to contend with a Greek heresy, Gnosticism. Gnosticism taught that everything in the spiritual world is good—and everything in the physical world is evil. This is not biblical. Scripture tells us that evil exists in both the physical and spiritual realms, but it also affirms that God's physical creation was "very good" and that He wants to redeem it.

The church of today did not set out to embrace a Greek heresy, of course. Yet, it happened. A missionary named Amy Carmichael

---

[4] Matthew 28:19-20a (emphasis added)

encountered "Greek" thinking on her arrival in India in the early twentieth century. She found that ritual abortion and female infanticide were still practiced and that young girls were being sold as slaves to pagan temples, to be raised as cult prostitutes. She was horrified! Despite persecution from Hindu sects and resistance from the British colonial government, she established an effective, compassionate ministry to protect and shelter the girls. Sadly, she also faced accusations from many of her fellow missionaries, who believed that her efforts to build an orphanage and school were "worldly activity" that distracted her from the "saving of souls." She did not give up, but reminded her accusers: "Souls are more or less firmly attached to bodies."[5]

Yes, souls are more or less firmly attached to bodies! Why did we ever act as if they were not?

The Divided Mind and the Divided Church

The "divided mind" of the modern church led to an unbiblical separation between spiritual and social ministry. It also divided the Protestant church in the nineteenth century into two branches, with sharply contrasting positions on evangelism and social responsibility:

- The "conservative" church focused on evangelism and church planting. It believed that the Bible is the Word of God and interpreted the world from a spiritual perspective. It eventually included most evangelical, Pentecostal, charismatic, fundamentalist, and other theologically conservative churches and organizations.

- The "liberal" branch focused on the church's responsibility within society. It interpreted the world through science and a physical understanding, rather than a literal interpretation of Scripture. It sought to impact issues of social justice, but downplayed spiritual evangelism. It eventually included many mainline denominations and other theologically liberal churches and organizations.

---

[5] Grant, *The Micah Mandate*, 241.

How did the church get to this point of division? The Western[6] world had changed. The United States had undergone a civil war, and the church was severely divided on issues of slavery, alcohol, and "end times" beliefs. In Europe, natural science had gained momentum and respect, and a philosophy known as naturalism[7] had developed. "Enlightened" man could now understand the workings of the physical universe through science and human reason. There seemed to be a scientific explanation for everything—except the origin of the universe. Soon, a botanist named Charles Darwin offered a solution. He proposed that life began accidentally and evolved slowly and without guidance into the forms we see today. This evolutionary theory—and the larger philosophy of naturalism— spread throughout the world. In the naturalist interpretation of reality, humans could discover the truths of the physical universe through reason and science alone, but the spiritual world was unreal and irrelevant.[8]

The Social Gospel and the Liberal Church

As naturalism became the dominant philosophy of the nineteenth-century West, the church found itself in a new and puzzling position—its views challenged by science and reason. German philosophers responded by integrating naturalism into their theologies, interpreting Christianity with a naturalistic

---

[6] *Western:* While *Western Hemisphere* is a geographical term relating to the Americas (North, Central, South), there is also a *Western mindset,* referring to cultures originally marked by Greek, Roman, and Judeo-Christian influence. In this sense, the *West* refers to the conditions of life that characterize the worldviews of North American and European cultures, including contexts of relative affluence. Definition submitted by Eleuza Alves de Oliveira (Brazil, 2005).

[7] *Naturalism:* A system that sees the world as ultimately physical and limited, controlled by the blind operations of impersonal natural laws, time, and chance. Also known as secularism, secular humanism, or humanism.

[8] Disciple Nations Alliance, "The Divided Mind and the Divided Life," in *Wholistic Ministry* course, Internet, www.disciplenations.org.

understanding. A theological movement called "higher criticism" came out of the seminaries of Europe in the 1850s. It was generally adopted by mainline Christian denominations and seminaries in the U.S. and gradually made its way into pulpits of liberal churches throughout the world. Higher criticism eventually produced something known as "social gospel."

The focus was shifting from an emphasis on the future, spiritual Kingdom of God to a present, earthly, physical kingdom—an improved society that would be achieved here and now through social action, enlightened government programs, and human effort and good works. Believing this, the liberal wing of the church began to focus heavily on social issues. In short, the social gospel said that the Kingdom of God would come to earth as a result of good works. It was no longer necessary for individuals to be personally converted to Christ.

The "Great Reversal" and the Evangelical Church

This was heresy to the conservative branch of the church, which firmly believed that each individual must be born again. In reaction, the evangelicals became preoccupied with the defense and proclamation of the Gospel. They began to focus on the spiritual side of God's concern and had little time for His social concerns.

In much of Christian history, there had been a "massive investment . . . in projects designed to bring about social transformation."[9] Thus, the rejection of social concerns by the conservative church became known as the "Great Reversal."[10] Although the greatest reason for the reversal was evangelicals' focus on traditional biblical doctrines, there were other factors, too. Widespread disillusion followed World War I. By all appearances, human evil had prevailed. Social programs had failed. Attempts at reform seemed useless. Man and society, it appeared, could not be reformed.

---

[9] Pierson, 22.
[10] Stott, 25. The term was used by church historian Timothy Smith.

The evangelical church's attention was soon riveted on evangelism and church planting, often to the neglect of other areas of God's concern. Evangelicals established seminaries and Bible colleges, where students were trained in evangelism and spiritual conversion. Many in the schools and churches were influenced by "dispensationalism," an interpretation of biblical history developed by John Nelson Darby and popularized by C. I. Scofield's version of the Bible, first published in 1909. The "Scofield Bible" was used in many evangelical schools and seminaries during the first half of the twentieth century. Its extensive notes and commentary—influenced by Darby—were treated as authoritative. As the men and women who had been trained in dispensationalism left school and planted churches throughout the world, they passed along two dispensational beliefs that eventually hurt the conservative church's influence on society:

- The world will inevitably get worse until Jesus returns.
- The Kingdom of God is only for the future, after Christ returns.

The World Will Inevitably Get Worse

There was little reason, said the evangelicals of this period, to involve the church in healing society. After all, society was destined to decline until Jesus returns. Evangelicals had a pessimistic view of the world's future, but they looked forward to the future reign of Christ. The world was destined for hell. The biggest need was to save souls for heaven.

The inevitable decline of the world contributed to a "lifeboat mentality," expressed by evangelist Dwight L. Moody. I paraphrase one of his well known statements: "The world is like a sinking ship. God has put me in a lifeboat and given me a life preserver and said, 'Moody, go out and save all you can. Don't worry about the ship. It's sinking anyway.'" Though Moody himself was involved in social implications of the Gospel, the imagery of the world as a sinking ship is one of his legacies. This belief was shared by a generation of missionaries, who exported it around the world.

Moody was certainly correct that there is evil in the world. Each generation of Christians has struggled to be *in*—but not *of*—the world. Each generation has devised ways to resist, flee, shun, avoid, self-protect, and separate itself from the evils of society. Yet, believers who insulate themselves and the people they love from the evils of the world ignore God's desire to use His people as lights in a dark world—bringing God's hopeful, transforming story to their lives and societies. In every generation since Jesus, Christians have believed that theirs was the generation in which He would return. Yes, we need to live as though Christ is coming back tomorrow, next week, or next year. No man knows the day or the hour—only the Father. Jesus may not come for another ten, one hundred, or one-thousand years. When He comes, He expects His church to be "occupying"[11]—doing His business—until He returns.

The Kingdom of God is Only for the Future

At the same time, the evangelical church, influenced by dispensationalism, taught that the Kingdom of God was a spiritual reality for the future, after Christ's return.

Jesus said, *"My kingdom is not of this world."*[12] But He also said, *"The Kingdom of God is within you."*[13] It is *both* present and future. Jesus taught His followers to pray, *"Your kingdom come, your will be done on earth as it is in heaven."*[14] The prayer was not for God's will to be done on earth *after* Jesus' returned, but to be done *here, now,* just as His will is carried out in heaven. *To the degree that God's will is done on earth now, His Kingdom comes to earth—now.*

The belief in a future-only Kingdom prevented churches from carrying a great concern for the restoration of *all things* in the present. Christians who thought the Kingdom of God was only for the future certainly were not going to work to see it expressed in the present!

---

[11] Luke 19:13 (KJV)

[12] John 18:36. Jesus was telling Pilate that His authority as King was not of human origin—His *kingship* was not of this world.

[13] Luke 17:21

[14] Matthew 6:9-10

In summary, in the first part of the twentieth century, thousands of newly trained evangelical pastors and missionaries fanned out across the globe in pioneering mission endeavor. As they served outside the West, they evangelized, planted churches, trained national pastors, discipled others to do the same—and unintentionally helped transport the "Greek" Commission to Latin America, Asia, and Africa. Even today, all around the world, church-goers who have never heard about the nineteenth-century division in the church have had their beliefs and their ministry focus shaped by the division and the philosophies that surrounded it.

Spiritual Revival Fostered by Pentecostal and Charismatic Movements

The conservative branch of the church was soon enlarged by a new expression of the faith that was also highly committed to spiritual ministry—Pentecostalism. Decades later, the charismatic movement brought still more explosive growth within theologically conservative circles.

Pentecostalism entered as the twentieth century opened, fueled by revivals in the U.S. in 1901 and 1906. Like evangelicals, Pentecostals had a strong emphasis on spiritual ministry.[15] Pentecostalism focused on personal salvation, the baptism of the Holy Spirit, and spiritual gifts. Though evangelicals and Pentecostals had very conflicting doctrines on spiritual gifts, they both opposed nineteenth-century theological liberalism. Where evangelicals responded to liberalism with corrective theology and biblical apologetics, Pentecostals responded with personal experiences of the power of God.[16] Pentecostals did address physical problems, noted one observer, but with spiritual answers: "Why save souls and not pray for the sick? These acts cannot be divided from Jesus' ministry,

---

[15] This historical/theological view differentiates evangelicals from Pentecostals, but labels vary. In some Latin American contexts, Pentecostals *are* evangelicals; and the two primary religious classifications are known as Evangelicals and Catholics. Explanation by Eleuza Alves de Oliveira (Brazil, 2005).

[16] Spittler, "Children of the Twentieth Century," *The Quiet Revolution,* 79.

for he came preaching, healing, and casting out demons. Who gave us permission to do less?"[17]

Pentecostalism did not intentionally focus on the social implications of the Gospel. Yet, early Pentecostalism did address society:

> Although Pentecostals did not engage in politics directly, their actions reveal political and social protests, nonetheless. Early Pentecostals were often pacifists as well as prohibitionists. Concurrently, in religious practice they stood in opposition to both racism and the denigration of women.[18]

The movement began as a multi-ethnic, multi-racial movement. Its original adherents were economically lower and lower-middle class who believed that the imminent return of Christ would resolve the ills of society. Meanwhile, they coped with economic problems, social ostracism, and racism through their faith, supernatural help, and shouldering one another's struggles. They worked to restore some of the values of first-century Christianity by promoting personal holiness and abstaining from "worldly" activities.[19] Pentecostalism had only a handful of followers at the opening of the twentieth century, but the movement's concern about the end times led to heavy missionary activity around the world. Spurred on by urgency concerning the soon return of Christ, Pentecostal missionaries kept evangelism and church-planting as their primary focus—and they were fruitful. By the middle of the twentieth century, Pentecostalism was on the brink of a worldwide explosion, and the primacy of spiritual ministry continued during coming decades.

During the social turmoil of the 1960s, a representative of a major Pentecostal denomination summarized the troubled times: "War, racial tension, corruption—these are today's problems. Men are searching for answers to the cultural, social, and moral upheaval of the day."[20] The denomination then commissioned leaders to study

---

[17] Farah, "America's Pentecostal," *Christianity Today*, 25
[18] Stephens, "Assessing the Roots of Pentecostalism, Internet, 8.
[19] Stephens, 4.
[20] Carlson, *The Assemblies of God in Mission*, 10,16.

its response to the turbulent times. While liberal churches were choosing to champion social causes, this denomination concluded that it should respond to social ills with a renewed, reorganized effort for evangelism, worship, and building up the church. It—like many liberal, evangelical, and other Pentecostal churches—chose a "Greek" ministry approach to a complex era.

The charismatic movement came onto the scene in the U.S. in the 1960s, as well. Charismatic gifts were no longer the doctrine and practice only in Pentecostal churches. Interest surged in the 1970s and 1980s among mainline denominations, independent congregations, and Roman Catholics. With an emphasis on miracles, signs and wonders, and spiritual power, the charismatic movement had a zealous spiritual message to communicate to the nations. Throughout the remainder of the twentieth century, spiritual renewal was the primary mission of the charismatic movement—spiritual renewal on both the personal and church levels. New local churches and new parachurch organizations were established, and new endeavors were begun. Trained workers carried the message worldwide—primarily through evangelism, worship, revivals, healing and miracle services, teaching, literature, music, and media.

The Pentecostal and charismatic movements brought spiritual renewal to a spiritually hungry society. But there were also great physical and social hungers in the world! Many in the conservative church *did* minister to physical/social needs, but usually as a *secondary* focus. Despite the "Great Reversal," not all had stopped doing physical and social ministry. At home and abroad, they founded and ran hospitals, clinics, schools, orphanages, and relief work. Their work was compassionate. Yet, it was sometimes said—even by those in the ministries—that their outreach to physical need was an evangelistic *tool*, a means to the greater goal of evangelism, rather than an expression of God's concern to heal physical or social brokenness.

Physical and Social Ministry—Why? How?

For Christians who are still pondering this issue, I suggest great caution here, for two reasons:

- First, we do not need to justify acts of compassion. After all, we have been commanded to love our neighbor.

- Second, deeds of compassion do not require a positive spiritual response. Jesus healed all ten lepers, though only one responded to Him.

> ## What Did Jesus Do?
>
> Ten lepers came to Jesus for healing. He knew the hearts of men, and He knew that only one would return to thank Him.
>
> - If He were healing them solely as a means of evangelism, He would have healed only the one who would respond, but He healed all ten.
> - He reflected the heart of God for the brokenness of all ten, regardless of their response.
>
> We are created to know God and be like Him. We need to express His love and His compassion to all people, regardless of their response.

We must continually examine our acts of service, asking ourselves such questions as these:

- How can we act so as not to be perceived as manipulative by those we intended to help—and possibly evangelize?

- How can we show people that we love them as persons, not only as "souls"?

- What would be our feelings if, as Christians, we were receiving medical help from a hospital operated by Muslims or Hindus who, we suspected, were more interested in our conversion than our medical need?

Church Ministry in the Two-Thirds World

The two diverse Western models—social gospel and evangelical soul-saving—were copied in the Two-Thirds World in the nineteenth and early twentieth centuries as liberal and evangelical missionaries carried their differing theologies and practices into their countries of service. Evangelical missionaries' ministries may have *included* medicine, education, or orphanages--but their ultimate purpose was always spiritual conversion.

Some national church leaders also combined evangelism and social action. In Japan, for example, Rev. Toyohiko Kagawa, a well known evangelist and social reformer, became a spokesperson for Christian social action in Japan in the 1930s.[21]

As the church spread outside the West, it usually reflected strong feelings of nationalism and independence—yet it was also negatively impacted by paternalism and issues of dependency. Let me tell you what we have discovered in the past twenty-five years about paternalism and dependency as we have worked not only with local church leaders in the Two-Thirds World but also with missions and development agencies.

Unintentional paternalism from missionaries and help agents has frequently *discouraged* wholistic ministry by the local church in the Two-Thirds World. That may sound harsh, but it is my observation. Most missionaries come from the materialistically affluent West, as do most development agencies. Historically, their efforts assumed that local people were unable to help themselves without money, goods, or technology from the outside. Outside resources were used to develop—and maintain—projects. Local people were often not helped to discover or use the resources God gave them. Many well-intended efforts actually created dependency and reinforced a mentality of poverty.

> They can't do it without our help.

But people of *all* nations need to know that God has placed in them the same intelligence, abilities, creativity, and reflection of His image as He has given to people of materially developed nations. They need to catch His vision for them and be encouraged to discover

---

[21] Ro, 33.

their God-given potentials and resources. The people of Rwanda and Kosovo have the same potential as people whose countries enjoy peace and prosperity. They are created in the image of God. They have His potential. God works through all people, with all of their resources, to build all of their nations.[22]

As we encourage people to look for local resources, we are often reminded that Scripture says that those with material resources should help those who have less.[23] This is true. But if outside material goods or resources are provided *before* the people of the local church have looked to God and have used the resources He has already given them, outside help can abort or delay God's desire to heal the land. This is a cooperative venture, however. Look at this comment from a South American trainer of pastors:

> Often the West's tendency to fix things and fix them quickly has been reinforced by the nations in the developing world. It happens because the nations do not see their local potential. They hold lies as truth regarding their own sources of development. Poverty of mind can be worse than poverty of circumstances.[24]

Despite encounters with theological division, nationalism, and paternalism, the evangelical and charismatic/Pentecostal church was growing and thriving outside the West by the end of the twentieth century. While the "Christian" West lost 7,600 believers each day, the church in sub-Saharan Africa was gaining 16,400 per day. Six new churches were being planted daily in South Korea.[25] Yes, the church had been exploding outside the West! What kind of church would it be? What kind of influence would it make on the world around it?

---

[22] "Resources" are not only money, as is commonly thought—but all manner of provision, including manpower and creativity. Money, of course, is a resource, and it must be stewarded well, also.

[23] 2 Corinthians 8:14 says, "At the present time your plenty will supply what they need, so that in turn their plenty will supply what you need. Then there will be equality."

[24] Ruth Concha, manuscript review (Peru: 2003).

[25] Ro, 35.

The Great Loss to the Church

The church of the nineteenth and twentieth centuries experienced a tragic loss. Despite the growing number of churches and professing Christians in the world, the church had lost its ability to impact its culture.

It developed an unbiblical distinction between the physical and spiritual realms—and an unbiblical distance between "word" and "deed." The liberal church had lost its awareness of the supernatural, Scriptural authority, and personal redemption. The conservative church had lost its impetus to minister to the whole of God's concerns.

The church has been robbed! The church did not cause this division. Naturalism did not cause it. Historical events did not do it. Many factors contributed, but Satan caused the division. Satan hates the church. He would like to destroy it. Satan "tricked" both parts of the church. The church needs to take back the territory that has been snatched from it. We need to stay true to our beliefs—but repent of our judgments and seek ways to serve together. We need to find ways to be relevant to

> **Survey**
>
> One of our staff heard of an informal survey taken on a downtown American street. Many people were asked:
>
> *"If you were facing a major crisis in your life, where would you turn for help?"*
>
> The people who were being surveyed gave many answers. But—no one thought to mention the church! People do not know the church as the church that Jesus intended.
>
> The loss to the church has, indeed, been great.

those who are spiritually lost *and* to societies that are broken spiritually, physically, and socially. The whole church needs to reclaim its whole task. A friend reminded me that each part of the church has something to give: "The liberal church shows us the need; the evangelical church shows us the plan; and the charismatic/Pentecostal church reminds us that God is in it!"[26]

What road did your church or denomination follow in the past? More importantly, where is it going today? And tomorrow?

"Reversing the Reversal"—The Church's Return to Social Concern

The evangelical church's trend to reject social concern was once termed the "Great Reversal"—a reversal of the Christian church's historic social witness. Eventually, conservative churches began to return to social concern—while maintaining their focus on evangelism. Not surprisingly, this has been called "reversing the Reversal."[27]

The 1960s, a decade of protest in much of the world, awakened the conservative church to social realities it had denied. The initial turning point was the International Congress on World Evangelization, held in Lausanne, Switzerland in 1974. Participants from over one-hundred fifty nations met and endorsed the Lausanne Covenant, which lists both evangelism and Christian social responsibility as key tenets.[28] Further work was done at a 1982 gathering that produced *Evangelism and Social Responsibility: An Evangelical Commitment.* It defined social activity as both a consequence of, and bridge to, evangelism. They are partners, united by the Gospel: "For the gospel is the root, of which both evangelism and social responsibility are the fruits."[29]

The following year, there was a consultation known as Wheaton '83. Brothers and sisters from all over the world—evangelicals—met to discover biblical principles and create new ways to respond to human need. The consultation wanted to know how to integrate wholistic mission, evangelism, and church planting. I was privileged

---

[26] Meg Crossman, manuscript review (Arizona: 2003).

[27] Stott, 28. The term was used by David O. Moberg.

[28] Harvest, the organization I lead, uses this covenant as our Statement of Faith.

[29] Stott, 30, citing Keele, *The National Evangelical Anglican Congress* (Eastbourne U.K.: Falcon, 1967).

to participate and to write a chapter in the consultation's book, *The Church in Response to Human Need.*[30]

The story did not end in 1983! More voices continued to call the whole church to return to the whole Gospel. Decades later, there is still much to do—but many more are catching the vision and speaking out! Many have begun to reverse the reversal. I see the vision embraced and carried out in growing measure . . . in Pentecostal churches in East Africa . . . in cell churches in Asia . . . in an association of evangelical churches in Northern Africa . . . in a variety of individual churches in the United States . . . . in several large Latin American denominations . . . in Eastern European apartment churches . . . in a charismatic ministry in the Pacific . . . in mainline churches that integrate spiritual and social outreach . . . in the lifestyles of followers of Jesus, all over the world:

❖ As this chapter was being written, we received an e-mail from a staff member who was conducting training conferences in French-speaking Africa:

> The Swedish Pentecostal Church has not only preached the Good News to the pygmies, but they are helping them to become self-sufficient through farming. Without this kind of help, the pygmies would be pushed further into the forests and closer to extinction. The church is in the very center of the community development here. The Swedish missionaries who came in the 1930s had a good balanced approach to meeting the needs of the people.

❖ A few days later, at a meeting of our Board of Directors, another staff member related the local church's transforming effect on communities in Ethiopia. He and his wife spent three weeks interviewing local church and organization leaders who had previously received our training—to see if the training was being

---

[30] Sine (ed), *The Church in Response to Human Need* (California: Missions Advanced Research and Communication Center, 1983), v,vi.

applied and if the society was showing signs of transformation. He was not disappointed!

❖ In one Ethiopian village, they asked local leaders what they recalled and applied one year after training. The villagers said they were most impacted by a biblical worldview teaching [31] on the values of the Reformation: "Work as hard as you can, save as much as you can, and give as much as you can." The village leaders had incorporated these very words into their village charter—and the principles were being practiced throughout the society. The report came that the community was remarkably transformed in only one year—and that it was observably different from other Ethiopian villages that did not live by those words. Their final analysis: Yes, communities look and act differently after local churches are trained and are implementing what they learn! Yes, the local church can be a vital transforming agent in society!

The Lord often guides local church leaders to discover wholistic ministry principles through Scripture and prayer. This is the amazing story of the birth of a village church that Harvest worked with in the 1980s:

❖ A European missionary hiked alone into a mountainous territory of Mexico—into an area known for lawlessness, deadly feuds, and cash crops of marijuana. He spoke about Jesus to the people, and one man came to the Lord. The missionary returned the next week, intending to baptize the man. The new convert had been killed! He had decided to stop carrying a gun—and he was one who had been involved in vengeful feuds between village families. Instead of baptizing him, the missionary had his funeral. Before he was killed, though, he had led one other man to the Lord. This man eventually became the village pastor. The missionary hiked back regularly to disciple him—and soon a few other men. The men asked the missionary how to begin a

---

[31] Harvest and Food for the Hungry founded a partnership, Disciple Nations Alliance. Harvest teaches wholistic ministry through the local church, while Food for the Hungry teaches biblical worldview. The combined messages are presented in Vision Conferences. Many such conferences have been conducted by local staff in Ethiopia.

church. He advised them to go to the mountains for several days to fast, pray, and search the New Testament. They also wanted to know the implications of their faith for their community. The missionary assured them God would tell them. He did! They read that James said it was important to care for widows. God reminded them, "You have seven widows in your village. The first thing I want you to do is to build houses for each of the widows." These women were widows because of the endless cycle of feuds and revenge. (Building houses for them was counter-cultural. In the prevailing *macho* culture,[32] the men might have built homes for themselves—after all, they were the leaders—but they would not have built homes for *women!*) The community needed so many things. It had no running water, clinic, church building, latrines, good roads, or electricity. But God told them to first express His Kingdom by building homes for widows, and they did! It was a shock to the community. God used the activity to spearhead a revival and bring transformation to the village and surrounding district. The men frequently went to the mountains to fast and pray, the church grew, and all but one village family put their faith in Christ.

This story is dramatic and impactful—but it is also powerful when local churches express God's love through simple acts of love:

❖ Members of a small urban church in Brazil gather on Saturdays to do numerous small-scale projects to express God's love. Together, the projects are making a lasting impression on the community.

❖ Several small churches in Africa leased a plot of land. From one harvest, the churches supported more than thirty needy and displaced people. More than twenty of these people recently came to faith in Christ.

❖ To feed their families, field workers often labor in other people's fields, leaving no time to plant their own fields. To break this cycle of

---

[32] *Macho:* Spanish term for behavior that is seen as manly, strong, virile, dominant, powerful, aggressive, masculine. *Macho* behavior avoids showing sympathy or weaknesses.

poverty, a local church in Africa gathered food, seed, and money for the field workers, who then planted crops on their own land. When the harvest arrived, the workers had adequate food for their families.

❖   Boats are the only means of transportation for an isolated village in Asia—even for school. Transportation is costly, and children from poor families frequently missed school. A church in Asia bought a boat and provided service, taking community children to school daily. The community was overwhelmed by the love of the church, and the children are being educated.

Today's Prophets for God's Larger Agenda

Let me mention two other evidences of growing change:

- One of our staff randomly studied three denominations' doctrinal statements on the Internet. She noted in this instance that a major evangelical denomination had carefully included both traditional evangelical beliefs and God's bigger agenda.[33]

- A member of Harvest's Board of Directors observed that pastors' seminars in the U.S. are beginning to feature workshops on community service. "In this postmodern era," he remarked, "actions speak louder than words. Pastors know they have to show—not only tell—that Christianity is a relevant faith and that the church is a valid institution."[34]

There is a new breeze blowing among the churches today as they learn to be embassies of God's full intentions. This breeze has the mark of the Spirit. It creates a longing to demonstrate God's agenda in a broken world. There are individuals and churches whose sails are catching that breeze. It is my prayer that God will use them

---

[33] Southern Baptist Church, "The Baptist Faith and Message, Section XV;" Internet.
[34] Dr. Tom Davis, Harvest Foundation Board of Directors, March 2004. "Postmodernism" questions traditional teachings based on doctrine or logic until their reality can be tested by experience.

to turn the breeze into a mighty wind. In fact, the Spirit has been relaying the *same message* to the church around the world. Listen to some of today's prophets for God's agenda:

> The vision of the church's influence on society is best described in terms of "reform" rather than "redemption." As A.N. Triton has expressed it, *"Redemption . . . results in individuals restored to a right relationship to God. But that sets up horizontal shock waves in society."*
>
> —John Stott
> Church theologian, England, 1985[35]

> When a person becomes a Christian, even the situation around him needs to change because of him.
>
> —Patrick Byakika
> Local church leader, Uganda, 2001[36]

> When done in a fully biblical way, evangelism creates new persons who turn from sin, live new lives, experience new dignity and worth, and consequently challenge structures of oppression in the name of the biblical God who, they know now, lives in their hearts and reigns in the world. . . . *Christian mission works best when evangelism and social concern come together in the name and power of Jesus.*
>
> —Ronald J. Sider
> Professor of religion and history, U.S.A., 1993[37]

> Dr. Chao's entire life was devoted to a three-fold vision of the evangelization of the Chinese people; the Kingdomization of the Chinese Church; and the Christianization of Chinese Culture.
>
> —In memory of Dr. Jonathan Chao
> China Ministries International, 2004[38]

---

[35] Stott, 48, citing A.N. Triton, *Whose World?* (Leicester U.K.: IVP, 1970), 35-36 (emphasis added).

[36] Tom Polsin, Seed Project report, 2001

[37] Sider, *One-Sided Christianity?* 178,186.

[38] China Prayer Watch, Vol 11.

A woman in Uganda explained why her group ministered wholistically: "The spiritual and biblical integrate with all things." *Group members echoed:* "You cannot separate body and soul."

—Rebekah and grass-roots practitioners
Uganda, 2001[39]

No church should have a prayer group unless it also sponsors a social action cell, for prayer and worldly need must be conjoined.

— Donald Bloesch
Church historian, U.S.A., 1970[40]

The Gospel is to be proclaimed and demonstrated. We need to share the Gospel of the Kingdom of God so recipients see a relevant proposal for their lives, which goes beyond being saved from hell.

— Ruth Concha,
Wholistic ministry trainer, Peru, 2003[41]

Most of the twentieth century was a story of separation. Of an *either/or* Christianity. But isn't the cross a bridge? . . . For liberals, that will mean painfully re-embracing orthodoxy.[42] For evangelicals, that will mean humbly re-engaging the community and addressing real needs. . . . It is time to re-embrace the *both/and . . . [both]* truth *and* proof, *[both]* proclamation *and* incarnation . . . *[both]* common grace to the needy *[and]* amazing grace to the receptive.

— Robert Lewis
Pastor, United States, 2001[43]

Finally, let's listen to a prophet from an earlier time, speaking a timeless message from God!

---

[39] Ben Homan, Food for the Hungry informational letter.
[40] Bloesch, *The Reform of the Church*, 169.
[41] Ruth Concha, manuscript review (Peru: 2003).
[42] This orthodoxy refers to an adherence to the basic biblical tenets of the Christian church.
[43] Lewis, *The Church of Irresistible* Influence, 208,211.

A *Shout* to Turn from Incomplete Worship

Theological imbalance in ministry was evident even as far back as the Old Testament. In the opening verse of Isaiah 58, God told Isaiah: "Shout it aloud!" God wanted to strongly correct the people's misunderstanding of His big agenda. He didn't tell Isaiah to *tell* the people—but to *shout*. The message God wanted to give His people through Isaiah was no ordinary message. They were not going to hear it unless it was shouted. "Don't hold back!" He said. I imagine Him commanding Isaiah: "Raise your voice like a trumpet! My people will not hear this unless you make it exceedingly strong!"

"They are looking into My Word day after day," God continued. "They seem eager to know what I want them to do—as if they were doing the right thing but just needed to 'fix' it a little. No, they have turned their backs on My commands!" Isaiah was to hear more: "They ask Me for justice, for right decisions. They say they're eager for Me to come to them. They fast and then they complain: 'We're fasting, we're humbling ourselves, and You don't seem to notice!'"

God continued: "The reason I don't notice is because your humility—or what you think is your humility and openness to My voice—is sin. It's rebellion. It's rebellion because you are going through the religious activity that appears to be humble . . . that appears to be prayerful . . . that appears to be an investigation into My law and intentions. From outside appearances, it looks very good. But it is rebellion and sin. Why? It is rebellion and sin because you are hearers only. You are not doers of My Word!"

What the Israelites thought was worship was not—it was sin. What they considered as their appeal to God was not—it was rebellion. They thought they were worshiping God as He wanted. They thought they would obtain God's blessing by religious activities, like fasting and self-denial. They did have His attention—but not His approval. Their question revealed their motivation. When they saw

> ### Isaiah 58:1
>
> *Shout it aloud, do not hold back. Raise your voiced like a trumpet. Declare to my people their rebellion and to the house of Jacob their sins.*

> ## Isaiah 58:2-3a
>
> *For day after day they seek me out; they seem eager to know my ways, as if they were a nation that does what is right and has not forsaken the commands of its God.*
>
> *They ask me for just decisions and seem eager for God to come near them. "Why have we fasted," they say, "And you have not seen it? Why have we humbled ourselves, and you have not noticed?"*

no sign of God's blessing, they complained. God replied firmly: *"You cannot fast as you do today and expect your voice to be heard on high."* [44] God was not pleased by religious acts of "humility" on the part of people who did not treat others with compassion and justice. The ritual of fasting was being observed, but the expression of selflessness— loving service—was absent.

Several generations later, God would send His suffering servant into Israel's midst. Not all who called Him Lord, Jesus would explain, would enter the Kingdom. Instead, they would hear Him say: *"I never knew you. Away from me, you evildoers!"*[45] Why did He call them "evildoers?" They heard His instructions, but did not follow them!

After a very clear introduction to what God considers unacceptable worship in Isaiah 58, God continued to explain the kind of worship He wants. These appear in three pairs of verses, or couplets. In each couplet, God explained the *activities* of acceptable worship— followed by the *blessings* of appropriate worship:

> ## Isaiah 58:3b-5
>
> *Yet on the day of your fasting, you do as you please and exploit all your workers. Your fasting ends in quarreling and strife, and in striking each other with wicked fists. You cannot fast as you do today and expect your voice to be heard on high.*
>
> *Is this the kind of fast I have chosen, only a day for a man to humble himself? Is it only for bowing one's head like a reed and for lying on sackcloth and ashes? Is that what you call a fast, a day acceptable to the Lord?*

[44] Isaiah 58:4b
[45] Matthew 7:23b

- In the first couplet, God said that true worship includes ministering to the physical and social brokenness of the powerless. Then, He promised to heal Israel's own brokenness as the people obeyed.

- In the second couplet, God said that true worship includes reconciliation among people, and He reaffirmed the need to care for the powerless. Then, in one of the most beautiful word-pictures of Scripture, He promised healing.

- In the third couplet, God affirmed the practice of spiritual Sabbath activities. Spiritual activity, however, is not acceptable in the absence of love. Specifically, those who honor the Sabbath are not to go their own way and are not to speak "idle words" against others. Then, God again promised joy, restoration, and inheritance if they hear and obey.

True Worship and Our Healing—from Isaiah 58	
Verses:	
1-5	Unacceptable worship
6-7	Acceptable worship
8-9a	Promise of healing
9b-10a	Acceptable worship
10b-12	Promise of healing
13	Acceptable worship
14	Promise of healing

Isaiah 58 gives us a balanced view of true spiritual worship. It is not an outward expression of duty and laws, but an inner attitude of the heart that results in serving God *and* others. Isaiah 58 "shouts" to us that it is rebellion to display religious form without obeying God. The Apostle Paul cautioned Timothy to be on the alert for those who have *"a form of godliness"* and who are *"always learning but never able to acknowledge the truth."*[46] Satan loves to get us to focus on our religiosity. If he can do that, he is subverting the intentions

---

[46] 2 Timothy 3:5-7

of God. People think they are worshiping God, but religious activity without service is unacceptable. It is sin. If people attempt to worship through religious activity alone—unaware of God's requirement for service—they sin unintentionally.

Moses introduced three kinds of unintentional sin—community, leadership, and individual. Moses saw that sin, though unintentional, required repentance and change.[47] I believe the same is true for the church of today. I would suggest this kind of response:

- First, as the Holy Spirit draws church leaders and members to repentance, they acknowledge they have not been faithful to give God appropriate worship—whether from ignorance, apathy, or disobedience.

- Second, they ask the Holy Spirit for a fresh revelation of God's intentions for the church's role as His embassy in alien territory.

- Third, they obey what they understand as God's agenda. Individually and corporately, they faithfully respond to the physical, social, and moral brokenness of their communities.

In Summary

Jesus expects His church to *"occupy"* until He comes. "Occupying" means "doing business." It means actively representing what Jesus would do if He were Mayor:

- The church "occupies" by equipping *individuals* to move into society—to persuade by their lifestyle *and* dialogue that God's way is for the good of society.

- The church also organizes itself as a *corporate* entity—to move into society as a healer of brokenness.

Each local church, each pastor, and each member needs to serve God's larger agenda, pursuing and doing the kinds of things Jesus would do if He were Mayor. The church in each culture needs to

---

[47] Leviticus 4 and 5

consider how its context affects social and physical ministry. Latin America has strong Roman Catholic roots and exposure to liberation theology, which shape its evangelism and social concern. African Christians have to consider their culture's animistic roots as they serve the whole person. Asia has to deal with massive starvation, unevangelized peoples, and government opposition.[48] Americans so treasure individualism that the church must continually rekindle a concern for the good of all.

But Christ is Lord of all! Transformation in the biblical sense will not, cannot, be accomplished until the church is both proclaiming and demonstrating the Lordship of Christ in all areas of personal and community life. The world has a difficult time understanding God's compassion unless it hears and experiences God's love. The people of the church should be such a compelling witness of Christ's love for the spiritually, socially, and physically needy of their societies that all who see them will say: "What a loving and great God these people have!"

---

[48] Ro, 36-38.

Thank You!

Many of my pastoral colleagues in the Two-Thirds World serve in churches founded by evangelical missionaries of previous generations. Often, their heritage does not include ministry to God's big agenda. When we discuss the information in this chapter, they express relief. They have sensed God's call for balanced ministry, but were not adequately discipled in it.

I do not intend to judge the courageous missionaries of the past. I praise God for them! When servants of the next generation reflect on our activities, they will see gaps of which we are now unaware, as well. I am thankful for the sacrificial servants of the last generation who brought an awareness of God's saving grace to thousands of communities around the world.

Father,

Thank you for those who have gone before. Millions of people owe them the debt of knowing You. We also plead with You that the church of this generation be given a clear and compelling vision of Your full agenda.

Give us, please, a portion of the zeal and courage of our forebears. May we be empowered by Your Holy Spirit to courageously advance into territory occupied by Satan, drive him out, and "occupy" it until Jesus returns. In Jesus' Name. Amen.

Characteristics | 8
of the Church That
Fulfills God's Purpose

The church has a grand purpose--to advocate for and advance God's agenda for the restoration of *all things*. This is no little task! Churches that fulfill God's purposes need to have God's power and character. They need to be useful. They need to care for the things that would be on Jesus' heart and agenda as Mayor. In an earlier chapter, we had seen how the Apostle Paul instructed the Ephesians about the key role of the church. Now, as we rejoin him in his letter to the Ephesians, we uncover four necessary characteristics that we—the church—need if we are going to be effectively used in the Mayor's service:

- Humility
- Love
- Works of service
- Unity

These are "characteristics of usefulness." With them, the church is useful and effective in God's agenda. Without them, the global and local church will miss the mark.

The Characteristic of Humility (Ephesians 2:1-9)

In the second chapter of Ephesians, Paul reminded us of our origin. We—and the rest of the broken world—were disobedient objects of God's wrath. Because of God's great kindness, we have been rescued. Our rescue had nothing to do with our worthiness or works. Whatever role God has for us, it is something we should receive and pursue with great humility. There is nothing we have done, are doing, or will do to deserve the role God gave the church— and we are still able to stumble, treat others selfishly, and reflect poorly on our God. In the midst of its task, the church must wear the cloak of humility. We have not earned our role—it is the gift of God. We are absolutely unqualified to boast, wrote Paul:

> *For it is by grace you have been saved, through faith—and this not from yourselves, it is the gift of God—not by works, so that no one can boast.*[1]

Humility will keep us from seeing leadership positions in the church as our primary calling. A teaching colleague in South America explains:

> When I ask my students at the seminary about their calling, some of them refer to their leadership positions. And I ask the question again, using different words to lead them to where their heart is. "Ah!" they usually say, "I have a heart for broken families." "I have a heart for children." "I have a heart for drug addicts."[2]

This heart for people is a gift from God. Those who are called have no reason to boast, but to serve with the heart God gives them! Humility also helps the people of the church serve others with unconditional love:

❖ In Asia, a Christian doctor and a nurse wanted to treat patients in a notorious prison hospital. They met with prison hospital authorities, who reluctantly gave approval but ordered them not to talk about Christianity. They arrived to treat the prisoners. The smell was unbearable. The toilets and ward were filthy. The doctor and nurse only stayed one hour, appalled by the conditions and frustrated that they could not proclaim the Gospel. Later, they attended our conference and began to think what Christ might have done. They decided that, on their next visit, they would simply clean the toilets and the ward. They asked churches to help. The first two churches declined, but the third church—a congregation of former drug and alcohol addicts—agreed. The prison authorities once again granted permission and again told them not to talk about Christianity.

---

[1] Ephesians 2:8-9
[2] Ruth Concha, manuscript review (Peru: 2003).

Cleaning supplies, gloves, gowns, and masks were assembled. The work began. Everything was scrubbed clean, including toilets. The Gospel had not been proclaimed in words. The authorities were overwhelmed! They now allow the volunteers to treat the prisoners anytime, with complete freedom to speak of Christ. The premise is so true—their humility made them useful![3]

The Characteristic of Love   (Ephesians 3:17-19)

The church, wrote Paul in Ephesians 1, is *"the fullness of him who fills everything in every way."*[4] You might think, "Not the churches I know—they're filled with strife! How could that be true?" Paul clarified this when he wrote of fullness in Ephesians 3:

> *And I pray that you, being rooted and established in love, may have power, together with all the saints, to grasp how wide and long and high and deep is the love of Christ, and to know this love that surpasses knowledge—that you may be filled to the measure of all the fullness of God.*[5]

Paul knew that love is the fullness of God. This love is very high, deep, wide, and long. It surpasses our ability to understand it. Because it is God's love, it is an enormous love. It is the cornerstone of His agenda to restore His broken creation. In fact, *God so loved the world that he gave his only begotten Son.*[6] This love is an encompassing love. Paul prayed that we, the church, would be rooted and established in God's grand love in order to express the love, or the fullness, of Christ.

> ## The church progressively becomes the fullness of Christ—as it obeys.

---

[3] Sources for stories marked by ❖ are listed in the Bibliography at the end of the book.

[4] Ephesians 1:23

[5] Ephesians 3:17-19

[6] John 3:16 (KJV)

The church does not always reflect this grand love, but it has the potential, through its obedience. The church is saved through faith, but it is sanctified by obedience. Jesus said: *If you obey my commands, you will remain in my love, just as I have obeyed my Father's commands and remain in his love.*[7] We are to obey Christ, as he obeyed His Father. As we do, we reflect the fullness and love of God and Christ. This is the same love that was reflected in creation. This is the same love that was lavished on us when Christ redeemed us. When the church reflects this love, God's power is unleashed, available for the mission of the church.

The church reflects God's love and fullness when its members intentionally touch others with the love of God:

❖ A hairdresser in Asia goes to a home for mentally disabled children, where she volunteers to cut and style the children's hair. She is also learning to reflect the love of Christ as she serves the clients who come to her shop.

❖ An African widow's home had been demolished by a strong wind. Church members brought building materials and rebuilt her home, stronger than before. She has come to know the Lord, impacted by people who showed her that God is love.

❖ Church members in Africa visited homes in their community and asked if anyone in the household had AIDS. The residents in one home pointed to an animal shed where they had put their kin to die. The sick man was kept with goats and chickens in a dark room! The church members relocated the animals, bathed the man, made a bed for him, and put in a window. The relatives asked the church members why they bothered, and the Christians explained that the man was made in God's image. After the man died, several relatives came to know the God whose love they had seen.

---

[7] John 15:10

The Characteristic of Good Works (Ephesians 2:10, 4:11-12)

"Proclamation" and "demonstration" are both needed to communicate the Gospel in its fullness. "Proclamation"—preaching or teaching—is essential. Yet, the message is hindered unless there is also "demonstration." "Demonstration" is practical expression of the Gospel of God's love. It "demonstrates" the reality of God and validates the message. We, the church, were made alive in Christ to do specific good works that God prepared for us from the dawn of creation. Incidentally, the church is to do the good works that *God* has ordained for it—not the good works that the church itself chooses and then asks God to approve and bless! The Apostle Paul wrote:

> *For we are God's workmanship, created in Christ Jesus to do good works, which God prepared in advance for us to do.*[8]

Good works are an essential component of the Gospel. They are the practical ways in which the church will be used by God to accomplish His agenda to reconcile *all things*:

- They are discovered as the church stays in communication with its head, Christ.

- They are identified as churches seek and work at God's agenda.

- They do not originate from an analysis of perceived needs in or around the church. They are identified through revelation from Christ, who knows the difference between perceived needs and real needs.[9]

> **Works are given by revelation, not chosen through analysis.**

---

[8] Ephesians 2:10

- They are not the good works that the church decides and then asks God to bless.

- The works that *God* identifies, directs, and empowers are the works He will bless and use to accomplish His agenda.

Paul wrote of five ministry classifications for church leaders— apostles, prophets, evangelists, pastors, and teachers. He wrote, though, of only one overarching job description for them all: *"to prepare God's people for works of service."* [10] Whatever a church leader's ministry gift or calling is, it must result in God's people being equipped for good works. The implication of this passage is both clear and challenging: *If the work of church leaders does not result in equipping the members to serve, they have not fulfilled the task they were assigned.*

> An evangelist who does not prepare God's people to serve has not done his job.

The Gospel is not complete unless we reflect Christ's servanthood. Paul wrote: *"For we do not preach ourselves, but Jesus Christ as Lord, and ourselves as your servants for Jesus' sake."* [11] A Gospel that does not include works is not the complete Gospel. It may have the power to convert individuals, but it will lack the power to transform societies. Only the complete Gospel has power to do both. I encourage you to ask yourself:

- Does our church *equip* its people for good works?
- Is our church known for its good works?
- Do we allow God to direct us to the good works we choose?

---

[9] Needs analysis can be useful, but should not be the driving force behind the church's decisions.

[10] Ephesians 4:12a

[11] 2 Corinthians 4:5

Here are some reports from local churches that answered "Yes!"

❖ Church leaders in a local church in Myanmar made small micro-enterprise loans to people who had previously been employed in the community's drug trade. Many Buddhists became followers of Christ as Christians treated them with love and fairness.

❖ A woman from a church in Brazil decided to clean the land around four houses in the slum. Twelve people came to help and committed to help the community begin a garden.

❖ Church members visited orphans in their Rwandan neighborhood. The children live alone, as do many children whose lives were forever altered by AIDS and civil war. The church group took food to the orphans, as in the past. This time, though, they asked if the children had food for the rest of the week. There was none. The pastor urged the church members to give something of more lasting benefit to the orphans. He urged them to bring their hoes and handfuls of grain, beans, or maize. The church members soon returned to plant a garden, with the help of the orphans.

Service-Based Unity

More than 1500 years ago, St. Augustine said:

> In essentials, unity.
> In non-essentials, liberty.
> In all things, love.

I recently found great disunity about this unity statement! So, let me say what happens—and what does not happen—in service-based unity . . .

In service-based unity, the servant-churches share a common vision, heart, and understanding of God's intentions for the need. They serve together, despite doctrinal differences.

However, service-based unity does not require churches to give up truth in areas where Scripture is clear. They hold these truths dear, whatever the cost.

As churches carry out service-based unity, let's focus on Augustine's final statement: "In all things, love." Nothing could be more biblical!

The Characteristic of Unity (Ephesians 4:1-6, 12)

The healing potential that God has built into His church has incredible power to bring together the world's peoples who have been otherwise divided by racial, tribal, cultural, religious, economic, and political differences. The power of the church to heal these divisions is part of God's agenda, and it is part of His purpose for the church. That purpose can be realized only if the church itself lives in oneness and unity. Paul begged the Ephesian church to live in unity:

I urge you to live a life worthy of the calling you have received. Be completely humble and gentle; be patient, bearing with one another in love. Make every effort to keep the unity of the Spirit through the bond of peace. There is one body and one Spirit . . . one hope . . . one Lord, one faith, one baptism; one God and Father of all.[12]

He then explained the relationship between unity and works of service. Church leaders, wrote Paul, are to *"prepare God's people for works of service, so that the body of Christ may be built up until we all reach unity in the faith."*[13]

Christian unity has been described as both a gift and a task.[14] How true! I have longed to see unity in the body of Christ. For years, I saw churches attempt unity by holding meetings to gain consensus on doctrinal issues. Sometimes, greater division resulted! In our training conferences, however, God has shown us that one of the surest ways to achieve unity is for His people to do works of service—together.

Our training conferences are designed to equip local churches to demonstrate God's love in their communities. Local church leaders attend the conferences, and they come from a wide spectrum of denominational backgrounds. As they sit across the table from each other, I hear, "We know each other by reputation, but we have

---

[12] Ephesians 4:1-6
[13] Ephesians 4:12-13a
[14] Bloesch, *The Reform of the* Church, 181.

never met. We are conservative Plymouth Brethren. Because you are liberal Baptists, we haven't seen a reason to get together, even though we've ministered in the same city all our lives." Yet, there they are. Learning how the church can demonstrate God's love in a broken world brought them together, despite their theological differences.

❖   This was especially powerful at a conference we held in Central Asia. It was the first time in that nation that all denominations had gathered to pray, worship, strategize, fellowship, and eat. During this time, past hurts and denominational barriers were openly confessed and forgiven. The same thing was happening in the kitchen! As members of different churches prepared the afternoon meals, they repented and confessed religious pride. At first, they were hesitant to work together. When the Holy Spirit convicted them, they asked forgiveness and started to pray together. On the final day they saw a miracle. They had run out of money for food. They prayed, and God provided the meat and rice for them to make the best dish of the week. At the end of the time, pastors from five ethnic groups and fifteen different churches and denominations held hands, prayed, and wept for their nation. Later, we heard that this may have been *the single most important event in the history of the national church!*

To be useful, the church needs the characteristic of unity! After all, the church itself is formed by individuals who were once alienated from one another—Jews from Gentiles, citizens from aliens, excluded people from included people. In Christ, though, we have been created as one new community, members of God's household, joined together as a holy temple, a living structure in which God Himself lives. Paul gave us word pictures of unity: *"two into one," "one new man," "fellow citizens," "built together."*[15] He urged the church to live in unity. We have a model of unity in the original community, the Trinity—God the Father, Son, and Holy Spirit.

The watching world rightly judges Christians' lack of unity as hypocrisy. Satan loves it when those outside God's family use the lack of unity as an excuse to dismiss the Lord, the church, and the

---

[15] Ephesians 2:11-22, selected.

church's good works. If there is a lack of transforming power *outside* the church, the first place to look for an answer is *inside* the church. Biblical unity must begin within each church. An expression of unity *inside* the church will lead to unity *between* local churches.

Here is an amazing story of unity that furthered God's agenda in the Balkans:

❖ The Muslim populations of Albania and Serbia have been historically resistant to the Gospel. The Christian God is the God of the enemy! However, when Muslim Kosovar refugees returned home from Albania to Serbia following the 1999 conflict, a missionary friend related that "hundreds upon hundreds" of Serbian Muslims came to Christ.[16] He related, "Nobody knows how many turned to Christ because it happened so fast!" My friend and his colleagues were amazed! What had been bringing such radical openness to the Gospel? They soon discovered that the Albanian church—the church of the country of refuge—demonstrated God's love to the Muslim refugees in their midst. A United Nations official said that, in the beginning days of the Kosovo refugee exodus, up to eighty-five percent of the half-million Kosovar refugees were helped with food, clothing, or shelter by the Christian community in Albania. The Christians were only a tiny minority of 6,000 in a population of more than three million! Their demonstration of God's love encouraged the Muslims to hear and accept the Gospel. Not only did the Christians demonstrate God's love, but they did so in unity. My friend was amazed by the wide range of people who worked together in Kosovo. Fundamentalists and liberals worked as one body. Their doctrinal differences did not keep them from serving. When they saw a need, they responded, together. What were the consequences? There were many. Refugees were served. God was honored. The church was strengthened. And, in my friend's words: "Hundreds upon hundreds of the historically hardest people to reach for Christ responded to the Gospel."

---

[16] I have had this confirmed by other Christians who served in Albania, too.

Unity is a necessary characteristic for usefulness. What a powerful demonstration of unity when the church obeys Christ's call to His service! The potential of the church united is more powerful than any other entity in the world!

The Four Characteristics—Powerfully Linked

There are keen connections between the four characteristics—humility, love, works of service, and unity. They are more powerful together! Let's see how they relate.

1. *There is an overarching need for humility in the church.* God has given the church the awesome privilege of administrating His big agenda. It is an undeserved privilege. It is a choice of God's amazing grace. There is no room for pride. It is not by our power or strength that this task will be accomplished. The Lord emphasized the same truth in the Old Testament: *"Not by might nor by power, but by my Spirit."*[17]

2. *Humility enables love.* When the church is consciously aware that it does not deserve its privileged position, pride evaporates. A humble church receives God's love. It moves into a broken world with humility and God's love. It actively, obediently does the works God created. This love, too, comes from God. Paul wrote that *"God has poured out his love into our hearts by the Holy Spirit, whom he has given us."*[18] He gives us His agape love, which then enables us to minister to the brokenness of others. Even the love that we give away was given to us!

3. *Humility motivates our works of service.* As we serve the world, we do not do it to look good or make others think we are good servants. We serve not because we are better than others but because Christ gave us a servant heart. This is not a heart that we are entitled to have—it is a gift. We are God's workmanship, and He prepared works of service in advance for us to do.[19] In the

---

[17] Zechariah 4:6
[18] Romans 5:5
[19] Ephesians 2:10

Greek language, Paul described us as God's poem, or masterpiece. The watching world needs to encounter the masterpiece of God as we carry out the works of service He created for us to do. Again, there is cause for humility. He is the Master; we are the masterpiece. He even prepared the works of service beforehand! As we do them, people will see God's glory. Jesus emphasized: *"Let your light shine before men, that they may see your good deeds and praise your Father in heaven."*[20]

4. *We experience unity in Christ as we work together to demonstrate God's love.* God is glorified by our works of service. Amazingly, something else happens when churches do acts of loving service—*unity.* God has shown us that one of the surest ways to achieve unity is for His people to do works of service—together. When people of different churches join in service, they no longer view each other as impersonal "different theologies." Rather, they see each other as brothers and sisters who are working toward a common purpose. As they work, they are not protecting doctrines or recruiting members for their own churches. Their focus is to love the people God loves and wants

> # Maturity is like the strength of a man at the height of his development.

in His family. This service-based unity does not require uniformity of doctrine, but it also should not cause churches to surrender or dilute the biblical truths they hold dear.[21] On the other hand, deep unity requires more than a common function—it also entails a common faith and a common Lord.

---

[20] Matthew 5:16

[21] Because of that, there may be groups with whom cooperative service is not possible or wise.

Moving toward Maturity

Ephesians tells us that *maturity* is another by-product of humility, love, and service. This maturity is more than "head knowledge," intellectualism, or doctrinal understanding. Mature church people are more than knowledgeable about God's truth. They are deeply rooted in Christ, and they demonstrate the message and relevance of His Kingdom.

Discipleship programs are intended to develop Christian maturity, but many such programs focus solely on the "vertical" aspects of following Christ—Bible study, prayer, Christian character, and holy living. They omit good works—the essential "horizontal" components that Paul said were necessary for maturity. Discipleship materials often imply that maturity comes from spiritual knowledge and spiritual activity, without an equal emphasis on works. Very likely, the developers of these discipleship programs know the importance of works. They know that loving God and neighbor is the summary of *"the Law and the Prophets."*[22] Yet, I have found that their written materials have little, if any, emphasis on practical demonstrations of God's love to others—a very unfortunate oversight.[23] As we have seen, though, the Bible says that church leaders must *"prepare God's people for works of service."* Thus prepared, God's people *"become mature, attaining to the whole measure of the fullness of Christ.*[24]

The Greek word for maturity relates to the strength of a man at the height of his development. The Holy Spirit, through the Apostle Paul, told the church how to have this kind of strength and maturity. It is a by-product of doing the works that God has prepared, made possible through humility and love. The end results

---

[22] Matthew 22:40

[23] We have since found materials that refer to "wholistic care," where small group members are urged to offer practical service to one another. This is good, but ministers only *within* the small circle. We also need to minister wholistically *outside* our Christian circles, particularly in our spheres of influence.

[24] Ephesians 4:12-13

are unity, maturity, and the fullness of Christ. I like to summarize this in a mathematical equation:

$$
\begin{aligned}
&\textbf{Humility} \\
+\ &\textbf{Love} \\
+\ &\textbf{Works of service} \\
\hline
=\ &\textbf{Unity} \\
+\ &\textbf{Maturity} \\
+\ &\textbf{The fullness of Christ}
\end{aligned}
$$

An Internally Consistent Lifestyle—Humility, Love, and Service

Let's continue as Paul concludes his letter to the Ephesians, describing practical applications of love.

Paul wanted his readers to embody an internally consistent lifestyle. The principles of love and service must operate *within* the body of Christ, as well as outside the church walls. They must be part of the consistent lifestyle of the people of the church. If the church's internal life is devoid of God's love, there will be little transforming effect on *all things*. Having written of lifestyle *principles*, Paul then gave practical *applications* of the principles—so his readers might grow in unity, maturity, and the fullness of Christ as they operate in humility, love, and service. Here are his instructions to them—and to us:

- Reflect God's righteousness and holiness. Do not seek to satisfy the sensual desires of the flesh.
- Speak truthfully. Do not lie to one another.
- Forgive one another daily.
- Work hard and give to those in need. Do not take what is not yours.
- Say only what builds up others. Do not say things that diminish others.
- Respond to the Holy Spirit. Do not grieve the Spirit of God.

- Forgive others with kindness and compassion. Do not harbor grudges against them or contemplate harm.
- Imitate the God who is love and reflect the sacrificial love of Christ.
- Avoid any hint of sexual immorality or greed.
- Let your conversation be flavored with thanksgiving.
- Avoid conversation that is obscene, crude, or joking that diminishes others.
- Remember that impurity and greed are idolatry and that those who choose them have no inheritance in God's family.
- Do not choose actions of disobedience. Instead, expose them.
- Steward every opportunity God gives you to seek to do His will in each instance.
- Do not abuse alcohol. Instead, be filled with God's Spirit.
- Share Scripture with each other. Sing spiritual songs together and in your heart.
- Do this with a spirit of thanksgiving for God's blessings in every area of your life.
- Do not insist on your plans. Submit to one another out of reverence for Christ. Families, exemplify this. Wives, submit to your husbands. Husbands, model Christ's sacrifice of His life for His bride, the church. Children, submit to your parents. Fathers, make your expectations reasonable and train your children to live as children of Christ's Kingdom.
- Workers, serve others as if you were working for Christ Himself. Your ultimate compensation will come from Christ. Supervisors, be like God. Do not treat people with favoritism. God will judge you—and those you supervise—by the same criteria.[25]

As Paul prepared to close his letter, he reminded his readers that the privilege of being the church of God's plan will not be without challenge. The enemy knows that the church is God's uniquely

---

[25] Ephesians 4:17- 6:9

chosen instrument to carry out and administer His grand plan. The battle rages between the forces of Light and Darkness. The result in each generation depends, in great measure, on the church and its passionate commitment to God and His intentions. Every force and cunning device that the enemy can wield will be used against the church. Satan knows that if he can divert, divide, or corrupt the church, God's ordained purpose will be temporarily thwarted.

To help the church get ready for the inevitable battle, Paul prepared for defensive and offensive war. He instructed his readers to put on the whole armor of God:

- Defensive armor—truth, righteousness, faith, confidence in our salvation
- Offensive armor—the Word of God, the Holy Spirit, and prayer

The Reason for Hope

The church of our generation should heed the last message written to the church of Ephesus. This message was not written by Paul, but comes from Christ Himself. It is recorded in Revelation, the last book of the Bible.

The Lord affirmed the church at Ephesus for its deeds, hard work, perseverance, intolerance of ungodly behavior, ability to discern between truth and falsehood, and endurance under hardship. Christ also warned the church at Ephesus that it had lost its first love. Possibly, it had lost its strong love for Christ that would cause it to tirelessly pursue what pleased God—His agenda to restore *all things*. Christ warned the Ephesian church that, if it did not return to its first love, He would remove its lampstand—its usefulness.[26]

May God help the church today when we turn from our first love. May He renew our passion to love and obey God. Scripture is clear. The

---

[26] Revelation 2:1-7
[27] Matthew 16:18

church *will* prevail, and the gates of Hell *will not* stand against it.[27]

Yet, generations of God's people who do not respond to His orders will miss the blessings He intends. The generation delivered from slavery in Egypt did not receive the inheritance God promised Abraham. They feared involvement with the enemy, and they were inattentive to God's command to occupy.[28] Every generation of the church—and each local church—is responsible to "occupy" until He comes.[29] It is a choice. We stay where we are, or we move further into obedience to God's purpose for us.

The task may seem impossible. But because of His power working within us, it is not:

Now to him who is able to do immeasurably more than all we ask or imagine, according to his power that is at work within us—to him be glory in the church and in Christ Jesus throughout all generations for ever and ever! Amen.[30]

This is an eloquent expression of praise to God! It reminds us of the incredible power of God's work through us, the church. Notice that the "glory in the church" is the same glory that is in God's Son!

What is this glory? It is God's image, perfectly reflected in Jesus. How was it reflected? It was reflected through the doing of His Father's will. God's glory in the church is reflected in exactly the same way—through the doing of God's will.

God's glory is also related to His power. God's power comes with the reflection of His image—the doing of His will. The same power that raised Jesus from the dead is available to the church today, but only when the church avails itself of it—by doing God's will. His power works within us to achieve His purposes, and the consequences are eternal. They are forever. What a glorious hope! *This* is the reason for hope!

---

[28] Deuteronomy 1:21-34
[29] Luke 19:13 (KJV). The Greek word for "occupy" means "do business."
[30] Ephesians 3:20-21

We often base our reason for hope on the wrong thing—on visible fruit. In the Kingdom, fruit is a gift of God's grace, not a natural consequence of human endeavor. Our hope must be based on the confidence that God fulfills His promises, whether we live to see the fulfillment or not. Hebrews 11 reminds us that many heroes of our faith lived their entire lives without seeing the fulfillment of the promises made to them. We must trust that God is faithful and will fulfill His promises. In the Kingdom, this is the kind of faith that God honors as righteousness—and ultimately rewards.

If we base our hope on visible results, we give up if we see no fruit. If we base our hope on God's faithfulness to fulfill His promises, we will continue to proclaim and live out the Lordship of Christ in the midst of enemy storms that swirl around us. This kind of hope opens our eyes to see life when others see death. It is this supernatural ability to see what others cannot see that gives us courage and hope in the midst of apparent hopelessness. It is the ability of the "eyes to see the flower breaking through the cracks in the street, ears to hear a word of forgiveness muted by hatred and hostility, and hands to feel new life under the cover of death and destruction."[31]

As we cooperate with God's agenda, He does immeasurably more than all we ask or imagine. He has a big agenda, but He is big! His power to accomplish His agenda is far beyond our dreams. God intends to carry out this big agenda, uniting His body, bringing us into His fullness, and healing our brokenness—even the brokenness of our nations! May Christ fill us with His wisdom, His love, and His power—so we may serve His purpose until He comes again. May we, the church, see our role in God's big agenda. May we humble ourselves, repent, and serve. May God heal and restore our lands. May He continue to grant us increasing trust that He will faithfully honor His promise and plan to reconcile *all things*. May we treat those around us with humility, love, good works, and service. May these characteristics of usefulness bring the church of Jesus Christ to

---

[31] Nouwen, quoted in Job, *A Guide to Prayer for Ministers and Other Servants*, 68.

unity, maturity, and the ability to display the fullness of Christ. May we learn to equip our own local churches for their role in changing culture. As we do, may our churches learn to obediently serve and faithfully care for the communities of the world, *as if Jesus were Mayor.* May His Kingdom come, on earth as it is in heaven!

THE CALL TO GOOD WORKS—"I KNOW YOUR DEEDS" *

"**I know your deeds**, your hard work and your perseverance.
. . . **I know your deeds**, your love and faith, your service and perseverance, and that now you are doing more than you did at first. . . . I will repay each of you according to your deeds. . . **I know your deeds** . . . I have not found your deeds complete in the sight of my God. . . **I know your deeds**. See, I have placed before you an open door that no one can shut. . . . **I know your deeds**, that you are neither cold nor hot."

—Jesus Christ, to John, for the churches
(Revelation, chapters 2 and 3, selected)

"I preached that they should repent and turn to God and **prove their repentance by their deeds**."

—Paul, speaking to King Agrippa (Acts 26:20b)

Through him and for his name's sake, we received grace and apostleship to call people from among all the Gentiles to the **obedience that comes from faith**.

—Paul, greeting the Romans (Romans 1:5)

God "will give to each person **according to what he has done**."
To those who by **persistence in doing good** seek glory, honor and immortality, he will give eternal life.

—Paul, writing to the Romans (Romans 2:6-7)

I will not venture to speak of anything except what Christ has accomplished through me in leading the Gentiles to obey God by **what I have said and done**—by the power of signs and miracles, through the power of the Spirit.

—Paul, to the Romans (Romans 15:18-19a)

Keeping God's commands is what counts.

—Paul, to the Corinthians (1 Corinthians 7:19b)

The only thing that counts is **faith expressing itself through love**.

—Paul, to the Galatians (Galatians 5:6b

* <u>NOTE</u>: Emphases were added within each passage.

We continually remember before our God and Father your **work produced by faith**, your **labor prompted by love**, and your endurance inspired by hope in our Lord Jesus Christ.

> —Paul, greeting the Thessalonians (1 Thessalonians 1:3)

Do not merely listen to the word, and so deceive yourselves. **Do what it says**.

> —James, writing to Jewish Christians who had been scattered throughout the world (James 1:22)

Religion that God our Father accepts as pure and faultless is this: to **look after orphans and widows in their distress** . . .

> —James (James 1:27a)

And let us consider how we may spur one another on toward **love and good deeds**.

> —The writer of Hebrews (Hebrews 10:24)

Let us not become weary in **doing good**, for at the proper time we will reap a harvest if we do not give up. Therefore, as we have opportunity, let us **do good** to all people, especially to those who belong to the family of believers.

> —Paul, to the Galatians (Galatians 6:9-10)

In the same way, let your light shine before men, that they may see your **good deeds** and praise your Father in heaven.

> —Jesus, in the Sermon on the Mount (Matthew 5:16)

The King will reply, "I tell you the truth, **whatever you did** for one of the least of these brothers of mine, **you did for me."**

> —Jesus, teaching the disciples (Matthew 25:40)

Our people must learn to **devote themselves to doing what is good**, in order that they may provide for daily necessities and not live unproductive lives.

> —Paul, to Titus (Titus 3:14)

For we are God's workmanship, **created in Christ Jesus to do good works**, which God prepared in advance for us to do.

> —Paul, to the Ephesians (Ephesians 2:10)

PART THREE

Local Churches That Change Cultures

The kingdom of heaven is like yeast that a woman took and mixed into a large amount of flour until it worked all through the dough.

—Matthew 13:33

You are the light of the world. . . .
. . . Let your light shine before men, that they may see your good deeds and praise your Father in heaven.

—Matthew 5:14,16

Local Churches
That Change Cultures

In the Old Testament, Ezekiel is told to ask Israel: *"How should we then live?"*[1] In 1976, Dr. Francis Schaeffer wrote a book by that title, and Chuck Colson followed in 2001 with *How Now Shall We Live?* Both speak of individual Christians' roles within cultures. As important as this is, there is also an urgent need to challenge and prepare the local church to assume its role in its society—both through corporate ministry *and* by equipping its individual members to affect the spheres of society where they live, work, and have influence. We must begin with the agency of God's choice—the church.

In Part Two we looked at God's grand purpose for *the church-at-large*, as defined in Scripture and viewed throughout history. We discussed the nature, history, and role of the church. Part Three now focuses on *local churches* and how they can become agents of change for their communities and nations.

Yeast is an agent of change. Jesus explained: *"The kingdom of heaven is like yeast that a woman took and mixed into a large amount of flour until it worked all through the dough."*[2]

I imagine Jesus as a young boy, excitedly talking to his mother while she worked. He watched as she busily added yeast to the dough. She pounded the mixture again and again and again, working the yeast all through the dough. Jesus watched, as He had many times before. He knew the process well. She would set the dough aside and wait. It was hard for little boys to wait—especially when warm fresh bread tasted so good! But, his mother would explain, the yeast had

---

[1] Ezekiel 33:10 (KJV)
[2] Matthew 13:33

to do its work. As it did, the dough was becoming something new and different—something that would soon be very delicious!

Years later, Jesus was speaking to a crowd, describing the Kingdom to them in parable after parable. He told them it was like planting a mustard seed—when they planted even the smallest of seeds, it would grow into the largest of garden plants. Then perhaps His own childhood scene came into His mind as He explained that "the kingdom of heaven is like yeast that a woman took and mixed into a large amount of flour until it worked all through the dough." Yeast gradually penetrates dough. The entire batch is changed. Yeast is an *agent* of change. Likewise, the Kingdom grows as the power of the Gospel penetrates lives. People who are being transformed into the image of Christ permeate and affect the world around them. David Burnett explained:

> [Jesus] used three very telling metaphors concerning the nature of the Kingdom life within the world: salt, light, and yeast. . . . Each of these elements dynamically penetrates the old order. Salt soaks into the food; light shines into darkness; yeast ferments within the dough. In turn, the Kingdom community will penetrate the old society bringing cultural transformation that will bring wholeness to the people.[3]

The local church and its members are transformed. They then become activating agents of transformation for others. United and serving, the people of the church are agents of change, permeating and changing their cultures. This is the growing, penetrating yeast of the Kingdom! Jesus could have been describing the "yeast" of a large church in the capital city of Uganda as it brings His transformation to its culture.

❖ The city police of Kampala, Uganda, work in difficult circumstances and are often ridiculed and criticized by the public—

---

[3] Burnett, *The Healing of the Nations,* 130.

which further affects job performance and morale. Several church members in Kampala have a desire to restore community values, and they recognized the importance of the police for the community. Rather than focus on the police force's shortcomings, however, they decided to provide encouragement. The church members staged a major, stirring all-day event which honored and rewarded the police. At the close of Police Appreciation Day, the Inspector General of Police remarked: "You do not know what amount of energy and inspiration you have given to the police by standing up publicly to say thank you." The police were indeed motivated to do a better job amid difficult circumstances, and a bridge was built between the police and the church. Members of the police force even expressed interest in contacting the church for counseling and ministry.[4]

Even more exciting, though, is the ongoing opportunity to mentor the police in biblical principles! Here's what happened:

❖ Long before Police Appreciation Day, a few women from a cell group approached the police department and said, "We'd like to do something to serve the police." The police asked them, "What can you do?" "Well," they replied, "we're able to teach values and moral principles." "Then why don't you teach them to our police cadets?" For one whole year, every week for two hours, they taught the cadets. The cadets did not even know they were being taught by the church! When the women came to the graduation exercises, the police commissioner said, "This is the first year we have had no discipline problems with the cadets. We want you to do this every year." Imagine! The church was invited to "disciple" the police cadets of the capital city of a distressed nation, using biblical principles.[5]

What an extraordinary opportunity to influence a society! What an opportunity to penetrate a culture, as yeast penetrates and changes

---

[4] Police Appreciation Day was one of seven community ministry stories captured on a video that Harvest produced, titled *The Church as a Window*. Together, the stories illustrate the powerful impact that a few dedicated followers of Christ can make on their communities.

[5] Sources for stories marked by ❖ are listed in the Bibliography at the end of the book.

an entire batch of dough! What a remarkable opportunity to act on behalf of the Mayor! Local churches *can* bring transformation to cultures. Followers of Christ *can* disciple nations.

In Part Three

- We will see that God uses local churches to bring biblical transformation to their cultures, to bring people into the freedom of His good intentions.

- We will examine the meaning of biblical transformation and see that evangelism and church planting are only the first steps of cultural transformation. Transformation is a process which will not be completed until Christ returns, yet the church must model the future by demonstrating God's intentions here and now—doing what Jesus would do if He were Mayor.

- We will explore how to make God's broad agenda the vision, practice, and DNA of the local church. We will discover how pastors and leaders identify vision, impart it to the church, and implement it in the community—through the people of the church.

- We will understand that, if the church is to represent God's full agenda in its society, its approach must be comprehensive. It must penetrate every part of church life, from the public sermon to every member's personal lifestyle. The transformation that the church represents must first be visible in the lives of its leaders and members.

- We will see how God calls all His children—rich and poor— to faithfully and sacrificially give Him what we have. As we do, He uses what we offer Him, multiplies it beyond our imaginations, and advances His purposes on earth.

Premises for Part Three

Although I enjoy reading theology and history, my perspective comes primarily from studying Scripture, working within the church, and watching it in action. From both observation and study, I have gleaned premises about the church. We have already reviewed some of them, but I will present them here again as premises for Part Three:

<u>*Premise 1*</u>: *Jesus established the church to disciple nations, teaching people everywhere to obey all that He commands. The church promotes the Kingdom of God on earth by teaching obedience to all Jesus commanded.*

As we know, Jesus told His disciples to disciple nations, baptize them, and teach them to follow His commands.[6] In other words, the church was being sent out to train and transform entire cultures. The people of a discipled nation would not only know Christ's commands, but would live by them. Their lifestyle would be reflected throughout their societies. Nations would be baptized in His name—and would be fully immersed in His will. Entire cultures would be discipled and transformed. Jesus related the Kingdom to God's will being done on earth—here and now.[7] The Kingdom of God exists on earth to the extent that God rules and His will is done.

<u>*Premise 2*</u>: *The local church is the principal institutional expression of the church Jesus ordained to carry out His purpose. When the local church fulfills the role God designed for it, God involves Himself in healing and restoration.*

The church—through its corporate activities and the actions of its individual members—is to transform all areas of personal and community life. In order to accept and promote God's full agenda, the church itself must also be transformed.

The body of Christ is a clear New Testament picture of the church. As a body, the church should carry out the intentions of its head, Jesus Christ.[8] Each member has a unique function in

---

[6] Matthew 28:19-20a
[7] Matthew 6:10
[8] Ephesians 1:22

this body.[9] Members come from all sectors of society—God's love does not show favoritism. Membership in Christ's body is based on personal acceptance of God's grace and forgiveness for our sins through Christ's death. When genuine, this results in loving obedience to Christ as Lord.[10] God equips the church with leaders, who are to further equip His people for works of service.[11] He has chosen to use the church (corporately) and its individual members to demonstrate His love, intentions, and purposes to the world.

Premise 3: A lack of material resources does not exempt the people of God from serving the world in which God places them.

As the people of the local church—whether rich or poor—obey His commands to lovingly and sacrificially serve others, God multiplies their efforts, resources, and effectiveness. Resources are not only financial. As God's people make available to Him all that they are and have, He multiplies the impact on the people they are serving.

Premise 4: The church on earth is both visible and invisible. It has at least three contemporary expressions.

The church is both visible and invisible. The visible church is composed of individuals and institutions that have identified themselves as Christian. The invisible church is composed of all who have been reconciled to God through Christ, regardless of religious affiliation.[12]

The church on earth has at least three contemporary expressions:

- *The universal church* includes all Christians and their institutions or fellowships.

- The *local church* is a fellowship of Christians who identify themselves as such. It may be a small group or have a

---

[9] 1 Corinthians 12:7-11

[10] 1 John 2:3-6

[11] Ephesians 4:11-12

[12] The true church—visible or invisible—is known only to God, who knows each heart.

membership of thousands. It meets regularly for corporate religious expression. It is headed by pastors and local leaders, and its members are from the same general geographic area.

- The *parachurch*, a more recent development, is not mentioned in Scripture. By definition, parachurch organizations come alongside the church. They generally offer a more specialized ministry and have a narrower focus than a local church.[13]

Premise 5: The church is far more than an agent or tool used by God to accomplish His purposes.

The Christian community is unique and of infinite worth to God. God *loves* the church with an infinite love. The church is Christ's bride. The earth and its societies will end, but the church is eternal.[14] This love does not exempt the church from its earthly role in God's transforming agenda. On the contrary, the intimate relationship between Christ and His bride provides high motivation for the church to do His will.

———

May these thoughts encourage and impel you as you and your church catch a vision and carry out God's broad agenda, *as if Jesus were Mayor.*

———

[13] See Appendix B for a discussion of local church and parachurch roles.
[14] Snyder, *The Community of the King*, 57-58.

Transformation through the Local Church | 9
Moving toward Biblical Transformation

When tens of thousands of people at a giant crusade raise their hands and declare that they want to follow Christ, this is not transformation. When fifty percent of a nation's citizens are listed as "born again," this is not social or cultural transformation. When eighty percent of the Ugandan population call themselves "Christian"[1] but the United Nations lists Uganda as the second most corrupt nation in Africa, transformation has not occurred. When there is a church within walking distance in every community of the nation, this is not the healing and restoration of which the Bible speaks. It can be good, but it is not biblical transformation. It is not the coming of biblical *shalom*.

As we discuss transformation, let's look at what happened recently at a large university in the United States. The university had a bad reputation. It was labeled as the nation's second biggest "party school," and many students "entertained" themselves by abusing alcohol, drugs, and sex. But then an evangelistic effort came to the campus. Within three years, thousands of students had met Christ, and they now had sufficient political power to elect Christian leaders. Christians were elected to positions of leadership—student body president, officers of fraternities, and leaders of campus organizations. After three years, the university was not even listed among the top ten "party" schools. The pastor who worked with the students called this "radical transformation."

I respectfully disagree with his terminology, though the report

---

[1] Forty percent are listed as evangelicals, according to Pastor Gary Skinner of Uganda. (The category would include all conservative Christians, including the Pentecostal/charismatic church he pastors.)

is wonderful. Transformation is not identified by majority political position. Nor is transformation the same thing as spiritual salvation. It begins with spiritual salvation, but it is more. Transformation comes as people do God's will. God's healing and transformation, then, would occur on the campus as students intentionally seek to do God's will in every aspect of their university and personal lives. It would be visible as they pursue their studies, relate with students and professors, celebrate sports, drive to and from campus, conduct their lives off campus, serve their neighbors, intentionally love others, and purposefully link with God's agency of transformation—a local church.

Biblical Transformation

In a literal sense, "transformation" happens when something is substantially changed in its nature or character. My eating habits would be "transformed" if I ate nothing but vegetables. My typing skills would be "transformed" if I never made another typographical error. But "biblical transformation" refers to the restoration of all that was broken when man rebelled against God. Biblical transformation—an activity of the Kingdom of God— occurs as God's intentions are carried out by individuals, families, communities, societies, cultures, and nations.

This is the kind of transformation we will be discussing. It is God's work, not ours. Yet, God has established a prerequesite to His work of healing and transformation. This condition is more than accepting Christ as Savior. It is *doing* God's will! Spiritual conversion opens the door, but transformation is a life-long process. Even the Apostle Paul, by the end of his life, did not think he had achieved complete personal transformation. He knew he was on a journey and was being transformed into Christ's image. The journey would not be complete until he was in the presence of Christ.[2] Likewise, our societies will not be completely transformed until Christ's return. But, as with Paul's admonition to "work out our salvation," we are to be working for the establishment of God's will on earth until that great day.

---

[2] Philippians 3:12-13

The Transforming Process

Scripture uses the word "transformation" to explain what happens in a disciple's mind,[3] character,[4] and resurrected body.[5] When we speak of the "transformation" of a society, culture, or nation, we extend the word to describe what happens when a multitude of individual transformations work themselves out in families, communities, and societies. Cultures and social systems do not experience spiritual redemption in the same way that individuals become "saved" or "born again." But, individuals who are redeemed should impact the world around them with their changing lives. They speak for truth. They advocate for reformed systems. They represent justice and mercy. They see God's image in people. They carry out the kinds of compassionate activities Jesus would do if He were Mayor.

There is solid biblical evidence to justify this concept. The Old Testament is filled with references to transformation in all aspects of individual, family, community, city, societal, and national life.[6] In the New Testament, Ephesians 4:17-5:20 addresses the character and actions of the new creation, the individual believer. The next passage, Ephesians 5:21-6:5, describes transformation in family life.

Individuals are being transformed as the varied aspects of their lives are guided and ruled by Christ. Paul wrote: *"Do not be conformed any longer to the pattern of this world, but be transformed by the renewing of your mind. Then you will be able to test and approve what God's will is—his good, pleasing and perfect will."*[7] As individuals, we may *know* the will of God. But, unless our pattern of living *conforms* to the will of God, neither our minds nor our lives have been transformed.

---

[3] Romans 12:2
[4] 2 Corinthians 3:18
[5] Philippians 3:21
[6] Deuteronomy 4:5-8; Deuteronomy 11:13-15; 2 Chronicles 7:14; Psalms 2:8; Isaiah 55:3-5
[7] Romans 12:2

This transformation is an ongoing process through which we as individuals understand and obediently respond to the commands of Christ. We are being conformed to His image. This does not happen suddenly. Just as babies do not quickly become teenagers and adults, we cannot become mature disciples after taking our first steps. As we begin to walk with Him, our obedience is immature and unpracticed. As we obey, we grow in understanding what it means to become like Christ. We become transformed to the extent that our lives are brought under His Lordship. Individual transformation is the work of the Holy Spirit, but its prerequisite—practiced obedience—is our work. The Apostle Paul asked God to fill the Colossian believers with knowledge so they could *"live a life worthy of the Lord and may please him in every way: bearing fruit in every good work, growing in the knowledge of God, being strengthened with all power according to his glorious might."*[8]

Transformation begins with individuals and extends to families, communities, and nations. This, too, is a process. When individuals and families obey God's intentions in increasing measure and depth, they influence communities. To the degree that transformed communities influence their cultures, nations themselves are transformed.

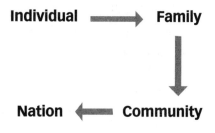

Individual

The Bible says that, in Christ, we become *"new creations."*[9] We are *"born again."*[10] God transforms minds, character, and behavior. God *changes* people! Transformation is a process, and each person's story is unique.

---

[8] Colossians 1:9-12
[9] 2 Corinthians 5:17
[10] John 3:3

Let me give you an amazing example of God's power to change an individual's life. Notice how this man's transformed condition touched the lives of many other people:

❖ A pastor in a "closed" country had been distributing tracts at mosques. To restrict this activity, the government withdrew his official ministry status. His evangelism methods were not welcomed. When he attended one of our training conferences and learned about active demonstrations of God's love, he thought of a new plan. He immediately took four volunteers, bought bread, and asked the head of a local mental hospital for permission to visit patients, share bread, and pray for them. The team received permission, but was assigned to the most difficult ward—a closed unit for incurable schizophrenic patients. One of the patients was a man who had not spoken in many years. Instead of walking, he crawled. His face was swollen and disfigured. One of his ears was greatly enlarged. He had a terrible odor. He was filthy. The visitors laid hands on him to pray and did not want to touch anything else until they washed. The next week, the pastor and volunteers returned. A tall, thin man behind the bars of the psychiatric unit met them. They asked him to take them to the main group of patients. The man announced that he was the man they had prayed for last week—and that the prayers had so changed him that he wanted them to pray again. The group did not recognize him, told him they did not have much time, and again asked him to take them to the other patients. He did, and the staff in the ward confirmed that this was indeed the grotesque man they had prayed for the previous week. The ministry team was amazed! The man had been healed. He walked and talked. He was even able to write. His diagnosis had to be changed from incurable to curable. As time passed, the ministry team kept coming, bringing bread and clothing, and praying for the patients. Other patients began to respond in the same way. The team was next invited to minister to all 800 patients—and the hospital staff. God multiplied resources as others heard of this work. Within three years and with the blessing of local officials, an expanded team was ministering weekly to 2,600 people in five hospitals, five orphanages, two prisons, and a rehabilitation center for drug and alcohol abuse. They also began to minister to street children and the homeless.[11]

Family

Individuals impact families. Scripture confirms it. Parents are to continually teach their children a lifestyle of loving God.[12] Older women are to train younger women to love their families,[13] and deacons and elders must manage their families well.[14] Biblical transformation comes as individuals and families themselves live according to God's ways—and serve others together. Let me tell you about one of our staff families who impact the world around them:

❖ One Haiti staff member and his wife and family routinely invite neighbors to prayer times, meals, and church. Their children are raised to consider the needs of others. Many of the neighbors who are less fortunate have become extended family and are being informally and formally discipled in many areas of life. Sometimes they have been hired to help with household chores or other responsibilities. Sometimes they are given a place to live and food to eat. The family organized their neighbors to discuss what their neighborhood needed. The group decided to hold a community cleanup project—and did. I appreciated a comment in this staff member's annual plan. When he wrote about family goals for the year, he wrote: "We continue to have 'big eyes' for our community."

Community

Transformed individuals and families know God has placed them in their communities for a purpose. They have "big eyes" for their communities! The Proverbs 31 woman is honored for service inside and outside her household. Her husband is respected at the city gate, where he serves as one of the leaders of the community.[15]

---

[11] Sources for stories marked by ❖ are listed in the Bibliography at the end of the book.
[12] Deuteronomy 6:4-7
[13] Titus 2:3-4
[14] 1 Timothy 3:12; Titus 1:6
[15] Proverbs 31:23

Communities are not only impacted by visible leaders, but by behind-the-scenes networks. Paul had trained Timothy, and Timothy was to train men who would then train still others.[16]

Service in a community can even affect a nation, especially when it is lovingly offered to those on the opposing side of long-standing hostilities:

❖ Pastor Boniface influences his community in East Africa through acts of service and forgiveness. After a ruthless genocide, many people had gone into exile. Recently, people of the opposing tribe began to return to their damaged homes. Pastor Boniface wondered, "How do you demonstrate God's love to people who are not trusted?" He mobilized men from his church to repair the damaged home of a returnee and his family. The father of the family could not understand how people from the opposing tribe would provide a home for his family, and Boniface explained they wanted to demonstrate God's love. An African colleague wrote: "People in our country have seen God's love demonstrated in many small actions of this man. The people who have been helped are coming to church to learn more about the Man who triggered the love that Pastor Boniface has shown them."

Nation

Even with such examples, it is difficult to imagine that individuals and communities could actually affect nations. But Scripture again reminds us that it is a process. The progression is not only geographic, but moves gradually through cultures and belief systems, as yeast penetrates dough.

Listen with that mindset to a familiar passage, when Jesus told His disciples they would receive power and be witnesses *"in Jerusalem, and in all Judea and Samaria, and to the ends of the earth."* [17] The city

---

[16] 2 Timothy 2:2
[17] Acts 1:8

of Jerusalem was the disciples' present location. It was the center of their traditional faith and culture, and followers of Jesus were a small minority. Judea was the Jewish "province" in which Jerusalem was located. Samaria was the region north of Judea. Scripture tells us that the Jews felt contempt for the Samaritans, a hated people who had not remained pure before God. Jesus said that His transforming power would progress even into the hearts and lands of enemies! This was radical! "The ends of the earth" were not only places, but peoples, nations, and cultures that were *unimaginable* to the small band of followers who heard Jesus speak that day. Filled with His Spirit, they were to begin the process that would one day penetrate, bless, and transform nations.

The Bible gives us a glimpse of God's plan for the nations, the peoples of the earth. Through the writer of the Psalms, God promised: *"All nations will be blessed through him [Christ], and they will call him blessed."*[18] In another Psalm we hear: *"Ask of me, and I will make the nations your inheritance, the ends of the earth your possession."*[19] God again expressed His will that the nations come under His Lordship: *"Be still and know that I am God; I will be exalted among the nations, I will be exalted in the earth."*[20]

The Africa Working Group is a small but exciting network of African leaders associated with Harvest and our colleagues, Disciple Nations Alliance. It is thrilling to listen to their vision and their strategic plans—not only for one nation, but for a continent. They do not see impossibilities as they look at devastation from AIDS, poverty, civil wars, and drought. They collaborate. They work through the church. They have a plan. They have an enormous vision for the restoration and discipleship of their nations and their continent. Already, they have made numerous inroads. They know the Source of transformation—the hope of the nations.

---

[18] Psalm 72:17b
[19] Psalm 2:8
[20] Psalm 46:10

The Church at the Center of Transformation

We have looked at transformation as a process—individual, family, community, and nation. There is another key component—the Church—at the center of them all!

To accomplish His grand intentions, God planned that the church would disciple nations. Jesus told His disciples to make disciples of nations, baptize them, and teach them to obey His commands. Nations are not transformed at the first steps—going, baptizing, and teaching.

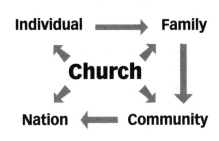

Transformation comes as people obey God's intentions in every aspect of life and every sector of society. Evangelism and baptism open the door; but discipleship—"teaching them to obey"—is the ongoing task of the church.

In God's plan, the church is at the center of all transformation. It administers the process.[21] It is the communicator and facilitator of Christ's agenda at every level of society—individual, family, community, and nation.[22] It equips its members to go into every corner of society and to represent God's will and intentions in every area of life.

Someone asked, *"If your church closed up tomorrow, would your city notice? Would the city protest?"*[23] When churches faithfully serve their communities, the answer is "Yes!" We have seen it. Biblical transformation has taken root in communities as local churches have consistently, creatively, and sacrificially served their neighbors:

❖ After a church and its members have invested several years of physical, spiritual, social, and wisdom ministry, there is visible evidence that transformation is coming to Jose Rissetto, a tiny, impoverished slum community in Brazil.

---

[21] Ephesians 3:9-10

[22] This is not intended to say that the church should *govern* the nation.

[23] Bishop Vaughn McLaughlin, Potter's House Christian Fellowship, www.pottershouse.org.

❖ The same can be said of Carapita, an urban barrio[24] community in Caracas, the capital city of Venezuela. The church has had a powerful, tangible role in the community for a decade, addressing a wide variety of community needs—from drug-prevention seminars to basketball leagues, from Mother's Day celebrations to tree-planting at the hospital, from sidewalks to school repairs.

❖ Several "squatter communities"[25] in the Dominican Republic have been dramatically changed by two decades of wholistic church ministry. Hundreds of local church leaders have taken our Harvest training. They subsequently train others and hold each other accountable for ministry. The churches have intentionally served outside their congregations, even in times of national disasters.

Let's look in greater depth at the growing transformation in another area, a squatter area in Kenya:

❖ Kagishu, a shantytown slum with homes made of discarded sheet metal and broken wood, had a fifteen-member church. This church received an invitation to one of our wholistic ministry training conferences and selected Meshack, a 21-year-old member, to attend. Meshack returned with a new vision: "I learned that obeying Jesus is *not* optional!" So, Meshack, Dismus (an elder), the pastor, and his wife prayed, asking God for a project that might demonstrate the love of God to their community. The answer came: begin a primary school for children in the church.

Immediately, they began talking to church members who have children but could not afford the small fee for public school. Several agreed to send their children to this new "school." With no training, Meshack, the pastor, and the pastor's wife began teaching thirteen children, ages six to twelve, in the one-room church with no desks, books, or equipment. The village people did not want to associate

---

[24] *Barrio* (Spanish): Literally, an area within a city. Often connotes an economically lower-class community.
[25] *Squatter communities:* Areas in which a number of people settle and plan to stay in makeshift shelters on land they do not own.

with the school and came at night to steal building materials. Meshack's first "salary" came during the seventh month—one U.S. dollar, paid by fees and offerings from children's parents. Meschack and Dismus invited neighborhood children, and the school grew. Soon, there were forty-five students of varying ages in one room. A second teacher volunteered by the sixth month, and a third by the eighth month. With 100 students, the teachers stood back to back in the middle of the room, facing their classes. The growing school was soon a disruption to neighbors, who moved out. As they did, the school gained more space. By the time the school was two years old, it had two buildings—more than ten rooms that could also be used for church on Sunday.

The next year, the church bought a parcel of land in nearby Kawangware, purchased a permanent building, and relocated. In its sixth year, there were 17 paid teachers, 5 non-teaching staff, and 445 children! When the newly elected national government made primary education free for all children, enrollment dropped from 600 to 445. Nearly every other private school in the area has closed, but this one still had waiting lists.

This is only the beginning of the story for the community, the school, and the church. As a direct result of this effort, there is a new secondary school in a nearby village, with ten staff and sixty students. Another church in Kagishu started a primary school to fill the gap left by the relocation of Meshack's school. Another congregation started daycare for twenty children whose mothers must work. The original church fellowship grew into a congregation of sixty members and has planted another church of more than forty members. Each of these churches has produced two new churches, in different areas. The original pastor moved to Uganda three years ago, where he began a thriving secondary school. A new grocery store moved into Kagishu to serve the students, teachers, and parents of the school. New small businesses were started around the school's new location. Contractors began to construct permanent buildings.

Six years after the obedient sacrifice of a very, very small church and its members, there is a large, visible effect in the communities and churches of Kagishu and Kawangware. In fact, transformation in Kagishu was verified as community members suggested renaming the community—from Kagishu (which means "the knife," or "stabbing") to Ruita (which means "removing something dangerous").

Though only God knows the full extent of transformation in the community, we were able to tally these evidences of community impact:

> 32 direct, full-time jobs
> 5 schools
> More than 1000 children in school
> 6 new churches
> Uncounted new believers
> New industry in Kagishu and Kawangware
> New economic development in Kawangware

Societal Transformation

Although involvement in civic affairs is not the church's first priority, it is one of the priorities if the church is to represent God's agenda in its society. We see God's concern for government in the Old Testament, where much of the book of Leviticus is a design for civic law and life. God was concerned about righteous leadership for His model nation, Israel. He supernaturally placed His representatives—Joseph, Daniel, and Nehemiah—in pagan nations to rule for the civic good. We have a great deal of detail about Joseph in Egypt and of Daniel and Nehemiah in Babylon, and we see that the Israelites were encouraged to pray for the peace of the pagan nation in which they were exiled: *"Also, seek the peace and prosperity of the city to which I have carried you into exile. Pray to the Lord for it, because if it prospers, you too will prosper."*[26] Jesus was likewise clear that we have obligations of citizenship to God and to the civil society in which we live.[27] Finally, Paul—in his letter to the

---

[26] Jeremiah 29:7
[27] Matthew 22:21

Romans—reminded us that civic governments are God's concern. God institutes them, and they operate under His authority for the good of the society.[28]

It can be hard to imagine something as large as transforming nations! It is not so hard to imagine, though, when we realize that nations are discipled and societies and cultures are transformed when God's people—those who are called by His Name—come under His rule. As we have seen, God told Israel that He would heal the land and forgive His people's sins if they would humble themselves, pray, seek His face, and turn from their wickedness.[29]

Transformation and Justice in Society

Societies are not transformed by good housing or literacy programs, crisis pregnancy centers, or prison ministries. Though positive, these programs address the *symptoms* of societal malaise. Unless root causes are addressed, there will be a continual outgrowth of injustice, social brokenness, and moral malaise.

Isaiah 58 tells us that we worship God as we address both root causes and symptoms. In verse 7 of Isaiah 58, God directs *all* who worship Him to share their food with the hungry, provide shelter to the poor wanderer, clothe the naked, and not turn away from their family.

But, some people are positioned even more strongly to affect the root causes of social injustice. Verse 6 speaks of worship in these ways: *"loose the chains of injustice;" "untie the cords of the yoke;" "set the oppressed free;" "break every yoke."* These words—"loose," "untie," "set free," and "break"—are words of authority. Followers of Christ who have influence and authority in government, politics, or business are strategically positioned to address root causes of injustice. Here and also in Isaiah 59, God commands people in authority to exercise godly influence. If our societies ignore root issues, we will face a continual harvest of injustice, social brokenness, and moral malaise.

---

[28] Romans 13:1
[29] 2 Chronicles 7:14

The church should encourage those in leadership to work for changes that reflect God's agenda and urge its young people to prepare for positions of influence, in order to represent God's intentions in the next generation. Here is what one Christian civic leader does:

❖ A Christian woman who directs a community-wide networking agency said of her leadership position: "This is a sacred trust." She keeps an empty chair at the table at every meeting she leads, reminding her that Jesus is present. Jesus "comes" to community planning and agency networking meetings—*as if He were Mayor.*

Charles Colson, a Christian radio commentator, author, and founder of the Prison Fellowship ministry, personally abused political power and went to prison for doing so. On his radio program, though, he discussed how Christians who want to make an impact on the world may be best positioned to do so if they pursue power—the right kind of power—in business, culture, and political and public affairs. Pursuing power, Colson said, is not contrary to Scripture. The Bible tells us to serve, and positions of power provide great opportunities for significant service. If power is an end goal itself, though, it is dangerous. Colson urged Christians in public life to be firmly planted in a church and surrounded by friends who will hold them accountable.[30]

Generally, the church can deal most effectively with root causes of injustice when there are godly people in positions of influence and power. On a local-government level, city council members and mayors have the kind of authority to battle deep-rooted injustices in social structures. The church should encourage its members who have callings for community affairs to take on political responsibility. Then, do not abandon these members. Surround them, pray for them, encourage them, and hold them accountable.

As we actively address both root causes and human suffering, we will see God's promised healing in Isaiah 58:

---

[30] Colson, *BreakPoint.*

Then your light will break forth like the dawn, and your healing will quickly appear; then your righteousness will go before you, and the glory of the Lord will be your rear guard. Then you will call, and the Lord will answer; you will cry for help, and he will say: Here am I. [31]

In the pursuit of social justice, we must remember:

- If God allows people to be in power, they are to promote His intentions, not their own. All people—even those who come to power for the right reasons—are sinful. Lord Acton's warning is very appropriate: "Power tends to corrupt, and absolute power corrupts absolutely."[32] Christians in power must prayerfully, carefully, and consistently practice humble submission to their King.

- Christians in power need the leaders and members of their local churches to support and hold them accountable.

- All Christians can minister to those who are suffering from the symptoms of injustice. While some people are in greater positions to affect the root causes, all of us have some influence to affect civic change—through our votes, public discourse, letters to newspapers, committed prayers, and practical demonstrations of God's love and principles in our daily lives and occupations.

Let me add another thought. Materially poor churches are not "too poor" to serve their communities. In the same way, local churches and individual Christians are not "too powerless" to care about social justice, whether godly humans are currently in power or not. As God's embassy, the church has His power and His authority for the tasks to which He calls it. As His ambassadors, we work as His representatives—in His name.

---

[31] Isaiah 58:8-9

[32] Lord Acton was a British historian of the late nineteenth and early twentieth centuries.

Cultural Transformation in Morality, Ethics, Worldview, and Faith

We have been looking at political process, but this is neither the only nor even the best means for cultural transformation. Our communities and nations will change as the people of God faithfully examine: *"What would Jesus do if He were Mayor?"* His people, empowered by Him and representing Him wherever they are, humbly introduce the kind of transformation He intends.

Clearly, our societies and cultures need to be transformed. All things, said Paul, are to be reconciled to Christ—and we are His agents. The people of our societies need spiritual regeneration. Our cultures need biblical transformation in order to operate according to the values, morality, and ethics that reflect God's intentions and biblical principles. As the Kingdom of God permeates our lives and churches and as we obey His ways, our nations and cultures will be discipled—in justice, morality, ethics, worldview, and faith.

It does not take long to list the ills in any society. I can think of many in my culture. Traditional family values have declined. There is little respect for authority. Consumerism is rampant. The media demeans Christians. The populace claims to be spiritual, but the prevailing worldview is godless. Sexual immorality is the norm. Decisions in government and business are not made by biblical standards. Violence, crime, drugs, and ethnic animosity are in nearly every community. Respect for life—unborn, sick, and aged—has diminished. The entertainment industry promotes promiscuity. The work ethic suffers. People prefer their rights and choices over the interests of God and others.

Not surprisingly, researchers found that only nine percent of born-again Christians in the United States hold a biblical worldview, and only four percent of the overall population holds a biblical worldview. The researchers found that people with a biblical worldview were much less likely to accept, engage in, or condone people living together outside of marriage, drunkenness, homosexuality, profanity, adultery, pornography, abortion, or gambling. These researchers commented:

If Jesus Christ came to this planet as a model of how we ought to live, then our goal should be to act like Jesus. Sadly, few people consistently demonstrate the love, obedience, and priorities of Jesus. The primary reason that people do not act like Jesus is because they do not think like Jesus. . . . Most Americans have little idea how to integrate core biblical principles to form a unified and meaningful response to the challenges and opportunities of life.[33]

You, too, can likely make a list of ways your society deviates from God's intentions. You, too, can likely see where your culture's worldview is less than biblical. I trust you are encouraged to hear what churches in an African capital city decided to do to communicate their Lord's thoughts about one of their nations' leading social ills:

❖ Organizers from many denominations planned a city-wide demonstration against pornography and obscenity. One Sunday morning, all across the capital city, church people signed a petition. They were also urged to come to a public demonstration against the vices in society. On the day of the demonstration, 1,000 people from all walks of life attended a rally in the city square. Church leaders attended and gave full support. Rally participants marched peacefully to the Parliament Building, where dignitaries waited. Downtown traffic was brought to a standstill. At the Parliament building, the demonstrators sent six representatives to submit their petition to the Speaker of Parliament, Ministers of the Government, and ten Members of Parliament. The room was packed with journalists. The archbishop handed over 12,000 citizen's signatures. Various dignitaries spoke, promising to look at the grievances. It was the first time that the churches of the country united to speak as one body about an issue that touched the nation. There was a strong sense that history was made that day. Our colleague commented:

---

[33] Barna Research Institute, "A Biblical Worldview Has a Radical Effect on a Person's Life," Internet.

"The organizers were amazed to see how easily the churches could mobilize people for an issue. Church people expressed that the time had come when the church in that nation could no longer be ignored when it takes a stand."

We—the church—are to be the salt of the earth and the light of the world today.[34] We have the responsibility and opportunity to bring the Mayor's flavor and illumination to our societies and cultures. How now shall we live?

Societal Transformation—Does It Last?

Why do societies that have experienced biblical transformation in the past not continue to enjoy its fruits? An article by Rabbi Daniel Lapin titled "Equal Earthquakes with Unequal Results" sheds light on the answer. Rabbi Lapin cited the vast differences between the numbers of people killed in natural disasters of equal magnitude and circumstance in countries with and without biblical worldviews— countries *with* biblical worldviews have far fewer fatalities in similar disasters. He summarized his conclusions:

> Western societies originally shaped by Judeo-Christian values enjoy an enormous advantage in this area. Unlike most of the world's other religions, many of which stress fatalism over faith, both Judaism and Christianity, each with its utterly distinctive theology, impart a framework of faith to its adherents. Other cultures believe they please their god by submissively accepting his wishes. But societies sculpted by biblical ideas have faith that tomorrow can, and must be improved, and that it is morally worthy to bring about that improvement.[35]

Rabbi Lapin concluded that, when cultures move away from a biblical worldview, they do so at great risk to themselves. As the

---

[34] Matthew 5:13-16
[35] Lapin, "Equal Earthquakes with Unequal Results," Internet. Radio talk show host Rabbi Daniel Lapin is president of Toward Tradition, a Seattle-based voice for Americans who defend Judeo-Christian values.

Israel of Solomon's time moved from following God's instructions, it descended from the most prosperous nation in the world into defeated captivity. As reformed nations in Europe and North America turned away from their biblical roots, they also began to decline. Each generation of a nation either adds to or subtracts from a commitment to know, love, and obey the Creator. Each generation's decisions and actions regarding God's instructions for life have an impact on the generations that follow. Turning to God and His design leads a generation and its descendants upward. Turning away from that plan begins a downward spiral.

Yes, societal transformation can last, but each generation carries the responsibility for activities that lead to life or death. The church, because it transcends generations, is the perfect tool to "interrupt" culture—to *stop* the passing of unbiblical principles from one generation to the next and, instead, lead its community and nation to life.

Six Reasons the Local Church Impacts Society

As the rabbi indicated, Christians have the ability to think God's thoughts and live by His design. This gives the local church a unique and strategic position from which to impact its society! Our greatest strength is that Christ is the head of the church. But, in addition, there are at least six logistical reasons that explain why the local church impacts the society in which it serves:

1. *The local church has a wholistic mandate.* If the local church is true to God's broad agenda, it is involved in all aspects of individual and community life. It carries a vision for its community and the individuals who live there—for their physical, spiritual, social, and intellectual needs. It does not limit itself to the care of its own members or the cares of its community. It does not limit itself to one or two areas of God's concern. If the church is infected by God's broad agenda, it intentionally ministers in all areas of life.

2. *The local church continually equips its people.* The congregation comes together regularly and voluntarily to be instructed, encouraged, and equipped through sermons, Bible studies,

Sunday schools, small groups, and more. These ongoing gathering times help members learn to live as God intends wherever they are—in their homes, communities, work places, and schools. The Apostle Paul said that church leaders equip and prepare God's people for works of service. "Equipping" is far more than knowledge. It provides preparation and experience. It develops people's skills, attitudes, understanding, abilities, spiritual gifts, faith, and faithfulness.

3. *The local church represents a broad spectrum of society.* The local church in a community represents all socio-economic classes, ethnic groups, educational levels, and vocations. Church members reside in urban slums and large estates. They come from educational institutions, the business community, the service industry, the media and arts, the world of sports, the medical community, the social service sector, agriculture, sales, manufacturing, factories, law, manual labor, and government. Where else but the church could we find such a diverse people with one allegiance?

    The complete spectrum of the community may not be present in a single local church. If there are local churches in all sectors of a society, however, the church of Jesus Christ has representatives *throughout* society. Together, local churches have the opportunity to represent God's intentions in many sectors—where their members live, work, gather, shop, study, recreate. The church's cumulative impact on its culture is most visible when the church exists throughout a society. It is less visible when the Christian church is marginalized. Even when marginalized, though, the church can penetrate its culture, just as light penetrates darkness.

4. *The local church is indigenous.* The local church is often planted by people or groups from outside the local community. After an initial "mission" stage, it becomes indigenous—its members and leaders come from the community in which it ministers. This is especially true of local churches not governed by a denominational or ecclesiastical hierarchy from outside the community.

5. *The local church's ministry is sustainable.* Because the local church is indigenous, it is generally able to support itself and its outreach with local resources. Many other institutions and programs designed for community transformation come from outside the community—especially in communities among the poor. Examples include orphanages, schools, hospitals, and agricultural programs. While many such programs cannot continue to exist without outside support, the ministry of the local church is sustainable without the ongoing support of outside personnel and resources.

6. *The local church is designed for life-long involvement with its members.* There are few other institutions where people come voluntarily, regularly, throughout their lives, to receive instruction about how to live. The local church has the mandate to equip believers of all ages for life-long service—children, teens, young adults, adults, and seniors. Few institutions in a society have such a privilege! Educational institutions speak to the lives of their students, but only as long as they are students. Businesses impact employees' lives, but only as long as the employees work for them. Politicians speak to citizens, but primarily when they are in office.

Parachurch organizations do not have the same advantages. Even the smallest local church has a larger mandate than large parachurch ministries with global outreach and large budgets. The Navigators—which began as a ministry to the armed forces and college campuses—is now involved in evangelism and discipleship in many different contexts around the world. Even so, its focus is narrower than that of the local church. The Business Men's Fellowship-India (BMFI) has a goal "to reach businessmen everywhere with the Good News of God through testimonies."[36] The organization starts chapters in India cities, is

---

[36] Alex Branco, "Business Men's Fellowship – India," Internet.

part of a larger network outside India, and has auxiliary chapters for women and youth. Yet, its mandate is much narrower than that of the local church. Parachurch institutions are temporarily involved in people's lives. Their contact with members lasts only as long as the members fit the specialized focus of the organization. I thank God for many parachurch organizations, but they can never match the potential impact and mandate of the local church.[37]

The local church is a place where members can form lasting relationships, where help is given and received, and where members are matured and equipped to minister outside its walls. It is an amazing entity! God fills us with His fullness, His power works within us, and His glory is in the church—for all generations![38]

A Note about Church Growth

There is a false assumption in many churches today—an assumption that societies will automatically be changed as more people

Kingdom Growth!

This topic reminds me of an embarrassing statement I made years ago at a national conference of international relief and development leaders. I had been speaking about the role of the local church in relief and development. I had poured my heart into this message, and I did so with considerable passion.

Toward the end of my presentation, I said something I had not planned: "We are all familiar with the emphasis on church growth in the AD 2000 efforts—I believe this is straight from the Pit!" I had just tied people's sacrificial church-planting efforts to Satan! You can imagine the silence and glares that came my direction—and rightly so. Immediately, I knew that I had crossed a sensitive line. I did not say what I wanted to communicate, and it certainly gave my audience an opportunity to exercise Christian forgiveness.

What I intended to say is what I still passionately believe: church growth is not equivalent to Kingdom growth!

---

[37] See the Appendix for a discussion on the local church and parachurch.
[38] Ephesians 3:19-21

are evangelized and churches grow numerically. But the primary goal of the church should not be numerical growth! Sometimes, numerical growth comes at any cost, including softening the message to not offend or challenge the ungodly aspects of our cultures. The Apostle Paul wrote that we are in a war.[39] This is a high-stakes war, not a skirmish. We must defend our stance and challenge our opponents. We do not need to entice people to join us by softening the requirements of discipleship.

One of my colleagues showed me an apt comparison of two kinds of churches—lake and river churches. These are not physical locations, but philosophies of ministries. A lake, though it may be large, is limited by what it can do—it can grow or shrink. It can become stagnant. Rivers, however, go somewhere. They have momentum; they can change course; and they carry people where they are going. A lake church is a place to collect more and more people, and success is measured more by the size of the lake than by whether the people in it grow in character and service. River churches impact people while they are in the channel—and they spill over their banks. "How many people were there?" is a lake question. "What happened to the ones who came?" is a river question. "How many people 'got to' (attended) the program?" is a lake thought. "Did the program 'get to' (affect) the people?" is a river question.[40]

When churches grow according to Kingdom principles, their members are committed to live under the reign of their Savior, to represent His reign in every domain of their personal, family, and community lives. When churches grow like this, society will be transformed. God's Kingdom is made visible as His will is done, on earth as it is in heaven. It is not a matter of numbers, but of obedience. When His will is done, God uses the church to change the culture.

The Power and Potential of Local Churches

More than any other institution, anywhere, the local church has

---

[39] Ephesians 6:12
[40] Brown, *The Other Side of Pastoral Ministry*, 21..

the greatest potential to shape culture. When we glimpse the potential, it helps us understand why Christ instituted the church, specifically the *local* church, as the administration of His grand agenda. The church announces and advances the Kingdom. It helps carry out God's will on earth as in heaven. Many local churches do not yet have this kind of influence, but the primary reason is that they do not yet understand the task, and they do not know their God-given potential. They have great potential, with His mandate and His power.

It has been said that totalitarian governments fear the potential of the church. After the fall of Saddam Hussein, an Iraqi pastor commented: "[Saddam] wiped out anyone who was a threat, but he didn't consider the church to be a threat at all. After all, we were just a bunch of different squabbling communities too scared to evangelize." This doesn't sound like this dictator feared the potential of the Christian church! But, look at a comment from another Iraqi pastor: "We just learned to survive under Saddam. He stamped out all ambition and daring. It was forbidden to dream under him."[41] Saddam may not have feared the church, but he feared its potential. He knew to keep it weak, fearful, divided, and without dreams! The church is inherently powerful. Its potential is enormous. Jesus said that even the gates of hell will not prevail against it.

There are thousands of local churches in my metropolitan area of 3.5 million people. By itself, my church has little influence. It is unlikely that any single local church will transform an unjust social system or a morally and ethically debased culture. Yet, God uses the combined efforts of community churches to introduce societal transformation that reflects His will. The churches of my city, united with a common vision and determination to seek God's justice and will, can touch our city and reach our world!

When churches unite in works of service and ministry to disciple their nations, their potential is powerful. Unity was of supreme importance to Jesus, who prayed for His disciples and for those of us

---

[41] Boyd-MacMillan, "TheCry of Iraq's Church," Internet.

who would follow Him in coming generations: *"May they be brought to complete unity to let the world know that you sent me and have loved them even as you have loved me."*[42] The world will understand Him and His love when it sees unity among us, His church.

God is calling churches and individuals to represent Him in our societies, to minister to hurting people and to be beacons for social, moral, and ethical virtue. Churches must act, but with God's power, not their own. God is powerful. He could bring about transformation without us, but He has chosen to use us. He does not command us to do the impossible and abandon us. He equips us, empowers us, gives us the people and gifts we need, and leads us in the task. The church is His tool, His agency of reconciliation. For a reason too large for us to fully comprehend, the Lord of the universe has chosen to use His people to carry out His plan—to be His hands, arms, legs, and mouthpieces in a hurting world.

Where else but in the church do we find this kind of potential? Where else but in the church could a young child begin a life in Christ, grow up in the church, serve Him faithfully throughout life, and make an impact on the world? Where else but in the church could this child leave the faith, return, be forgiven, and be restored to Kingdom usefulness? Where else but in the church could an elderly person enter the Kingdom for the first time and be as fully received and valuable as the young child or repentant adult?

God intends the local church and its people to serve, impact, and bring biblical transformation to individuals, families, communities, and nations. In the next chapter, we will see how wholistic ministry becomes part of the DNA of a local church. We will look at several ways that God's vision can be identified, imparted, and implemented in the community by local churches that are equipped and mobilized to serve, *as if Jesus were Mayor.*

---

[42] John 17:23

Equipping the Local Church for Wholistic Witness

10

For more than twenty years, I have watched God liberate churches in the Two-Thirds World, taking them from a narrow focus on spiritual ministry to the broader agenda of the God of Scripture. A narrow focus obscures the rest of God's concern for a broken world. It stands in the way of the church being an embassy of God's full intentions. But when a church mobilizes its members to do the kinds of transformational acts Jesus would do as Mayor, the results are dynamic and exciting!

Let me emphasize that a focus on wholistic ministry in no way diminishes the need for proclamation of the Gospel—expressing God's love and redemption in verbal and written communication. Proclamation is an equal partner in the fulfillment of God's intentions for His church, but we are focusing here on the other partner—the demonstration of God's love. We are examining how wholistic ministry becomes a deeply ingrained characteristic in the lifestyle of local churches and their members.

In one Africa denomination, each local church made "Love One Another" its theme for the year. This is good! Yet, we must be careful never to say, "Oh, that was *last* year's theme!" When wholistic ministry is our church's DNA, loving our neighbors is our theme for all years, forever.

Planting DNA

A basic question was asked of me when I was teaching at a cell church conference. One of the leaders of the global cell church movement kept probing:

Bob, as you look around the world at many local churches,

what is different about the ones that make wholistic ministry a part of who they are? What are the elements that have caused them to "grab" this teaching and live it? We've held a conference at our church. Our cell church has done a few Seed Projects. But I want this to be much more for our churches! I want this to be a part of who we are! *What are the elements that make wholistic ministry part of the "DNA" of local churches?*

What a challenging question! Science tells me my DNA carries my unique "code." My DNA describes me, my appearance, my abilities, and my characteristics—the unique things I pass on to my children and grandchildren. A local church's DNA would be a description of its identity, qualities, and values—the unique and defining characteristics it passes on to its members.

My friend wanted to learn how a local church could become so infused with wholistic ministry that it was a foundational part of its identity. I laid awake much of the night looking for just the right response. By morning, I had five characteristics, which I then discussed with the pastor of a large church in Uganda. His church has wholistic DNA, and I wanted his opinion. In fact, when people are interested in joining the church he leads, he tells them, "We are wholistic. This is who we are. If you are going to be part of us, you need to get ready for this. You will be doing wholistic service if you are part of us." When they join the church, they already know its DNA. They know the expectations—that they will be in a small group, that they will provide service to the community, and that they will be held accountable. They understand the corporate personality of the church. The pastor from Uganda agreed with the five elements. Since then, colleagues have pointed out two more elements—a total of seven.[1]

---

[1] Each church is unique. Sometimes there is not a separate time of repentance, or a church's accountability structure is less formalized. Yet, each deeply impacted church has somehow experienced these elements.

Elements of a Local Church's DNA

1. *Conviction: The church's top leadership is absolutely convinced that it is not negotiable to demonstrate Christ's love.* If the leaders are not convinced, then wholistic ministry will not be part of a church's DNA—though the church might still do occasional wholistic projects. The church leaders should also be convinced that it is *God who produces fruit* as they love their neighbors. They do not need to see the fruit—it may come in the next generation.

> ### DNA Elements
> 1. Conviction
> 2. Repentance
> 3. Commitment
> 4. Application
> 5. Ongoing teaching
> 6. Accountability
> 7. Acknowledgement

2. *Repentance: A wholistic church repents of past disobedience, turns away from the detour it traveled, and walks whole-heartedly with God on a new path.* In most places where we teach, the Spirit has already begun to open the eyes of the church to God's broad agenda. God has already created in pastors and leaders a genuine hunger for Kingdom answers to the brokenness of their societies. They see the distance between their church's ministry and God's intentions for their societies. They recognize the church has fallen short of God's full intentions. Falling short of God's will is sin—even though it is unintentional. Repentance is the answer, but let me explain. To "repent" means to turn around and change direction. It is turning and allowing God to change us, as the Holy Spirit directs. The Bible tells of ceremonies that commemorated and reinforced significant events. A church may want to hold a service or, in some other way, commemorate its repentance of past blindness and its commitment to change and move forward.

3. *Commitment: Pastors and leaders are committed to do whatever it takes to lead their congregations in wholistic ministry.* They work with vision for the *church,* and they are *personally* committed to lives of loving service. Their commitment requires sacrifice, risk, time, and effort. They may need to reorganize. They may need to

give up some church activities. They may lose church members. They may lose funds, or they may need more funds for some endeavors. Their denomination or colleagues may question their loyalty. But, church leaders are completely committed to make wholistic ministry the normal, natural lifestyle of their church.

4. *Application: Local church leaders stress application of wholistic ministry in their teachings and personal lives.* There are visible expressions of wholistic ministry in the activities of the church. Church leaders are not only thinkers and speakers of wholistic ministry, but doers. They use and apply tools like those we introduce in later chapters—Discipline of Love and Seed Projects. Nearly every sermon or study has a wholistic dimension that is stated, practiced, and applied.

5. *Ongoing Teaching: Church members need to be reminded of the mandate for good works.* Wholistic ministry may be introduced through a conference, but it must not be abandoned thereafter. That would be like bringing someone to Christ with the basics of the Gospel; never again reminding them; and expecting them to know, understand, and live it. Wholistic ministry is woven into the teaching fabric of the church—in sermons, Bible studies, liturgy, small groups, and mentoring. Wholistic ministry is one of the church's most often-repeated themes. In fact, every biblical theme has wholistic implications. The congregation receives ongoing and regular preaching, teaching, and mentoring in wholistic ministry.

6. *Accountability: When a local church has wholistic DNA, there is genuine accountability—individually and corporately—for faithful and loving service.* Church leaders hold themselves and their members responsible for acts of service. People expect to be asked. Small group leaders report on the ministry activities of their groups. Every person is accountable; and the church itself accounts to its membership. Just as a church reports on finances, attendance, membership, baptisms, or commitments for Christ, it reports on wholistic ministry.

7. *Acknowledgement*: When wholistic ministry is part of a local church's DNA, the church celebrates the acts of service carried out by the church or its members. This is not to celebrate people's goodness—but that God has empowered people with His Spirit to be the kind of ambassadors He wants. There are several ways:

- *In the worship service:* The church allows opportunity for testimonies in the weekly worship services. Care is taken not to exalt the person, but to glorify God through His people. Matthew 5:16 says, *"Let your light shine before men, that they may see your good deeds and praise your Father in heaven."*

- *In small groups:* In Sunday School, Bible study, or cell group, as an expected part of the meeting, each person shares how God has used his or her obedience in service since the last time the group met.

- *In the communication tools:* The church includes stories or photos on the church's bulletin board, in the bulletin, or in a church newsletter.

When we are born again, we receive the "DNA" of Christ—the ability to be conformed to His image. It is already there, but we need to appropriate it.

The wholistic message is already in Scripture, too. It is already in our DNA—but it is not always in our theology. As local church leaders utilize it, it becomes part of their church's DNA. The stories on the following pages illustrate how conviction and repentance help build the wholistic DNA of the local church.[2]

---

[2] Sources for stories marked by ❖ are listed in the Bibliography at the end of the book.

Stories of Conviction and Repentance

❖ The Old Testament contains an important lesson. The Book of the Law had been lost for many years. It was finally found in the temple. King Josiah heard it and wept when he realized the great difference between God's expectations and how he and his people were actually living. They repented and turned.*

❖ In 1986, Harvest's international leadership held a conference to evaluate our ministry strategies. After much discussion, we decided to work only with local churches—not day-care centers, orphanages, or Christian medical societies. The next month, we had a regional staff conference in Port-au-Prince, Haiti. During an extended time of prayer, the Holy Spirit convicted each person that our ministry had been ignoring the bride of Christ, the church. It was a holy moment, a pivotal time in the life of Harvest. Since then, we have always said that our repentance in Port-au-Prince was when we changed our focus. Recently, we wrote our history and read communications from that era. To our surprise, we saw that our decision to change courses had been made and announced in writing one month earlier. Our turning point was not engraved in our hearts and memories until the meeting in which the Holy Spirit convicted us—and we repented.

❖ For two decades Pastor Thomas, a shy man with a primary school education, had thirty members in his Nicaragua church. A handful of people gathered every night for services, and the church maintained a severely judgmental attitude toward its community. Then, God began to open members' eyes and hearts. They called a community meeting and publicly repented of their lack of compassion for the community. Pastor Thomas changed his leadership style and began working with small groups. Within eighteen months, the church grew to over two-hundred members. Seven-hundred children attend home Bible clubs. The church began an adult literacy program, a micro-enterprise loan program, three neighborhood

* Leviticus 4:13 and 2 Chronicles 34

> preschools—and recently purchased land for a Christian school. Pastor Thomas credits this amazing turn-around to a radical change in his understanding of the mission of the church and its relationship to the community.
>
> ❖ Immediately after leading his church in a Bible study on "A Christian Response to Human Need," a pastor in the Dominican Republic called the church to repent. Members realized they had not been responding to the physical needs of the poor in their community. Many church members committed to volunteer two hours of their vocational skill each week. The church coordinated and scheduled the skills with community needs. If their services were not directly needed, the members agreed to contribute financially what they earn in two hours, and those funds would be used for community outreach.

Identifying God's Vision for a Local Church

As local churches transition to a wholistic vision and equip their members for wholistic ministry, they must take steps to *identify* a wholistic vision, *impart* it to their people, and *implement* it in their communities.

Equipping is more than teaching. It is modeling, training, providing tools, instilling character and attitudes, enhancing vision, providing knowledge and experience, mentoring, and discipling. It is broad-scale preparation.

To help church leaders gain a wholistic vision, we like to ask them: *"If Jesus were mayor, how would your community change?"* Vision is key. The Bible says: *"Where there is no vision the people perish."*[3] A church without a vision does little more than maintain the status quo. It has little, if any, chance of making an impact for the Kingdom of God in its community. A church with a vision, however, has great potential for temporal and eternal significance.

---

[3] Proverbs 29:18 (KJV)

God's vision for the church usually spreads from the shepherds to the sheep. It is then communicated and promoted everywhere in the ongoing life of the church—the mission statement, the pulpit, Bible studies, Sunday schools, small groups, and service projects. It is vital to communicate the vision, act on it, and reinforce it as the lifestyle of the church.

Pastors are most effective in communicating the vision church-wide when they first communicate it to all the church leaders—pastors, elders, teachers, and staff. Pastors and leaders need to catch and implement the *same* vision and, together, shepherd the people toward God's intentions.

Further, preaching is far more effective when the same message is integrated throughout the church. The congregation hears God's vision during sermons, and the same emphasis is communicated in Sunday schools, Bible studies, home fellowships,

The Power of Vision

In the early days of my ministry, I directed an alternative school for delinquent young people. They were near the bottom of our community's social structure. They felt rejected and insignificant. They were unaware that God created them for significance. They rebelled against authority. They got into trouble. They were known for all kinds of antisocial behavior.

One of our staff arranged for our students to volunteer as helpers at a local institution for the mentally disabled. He told them they would receive name badges and be official volunteer staff. Their task was to talk to the inmates, push wheelchairs, wipe saliva from mouths of drooling patients, and be companions to people who otherwise had little interaction with people.

On the day their service was to begin, a miracle took place! The usually unkempt and stooped kids came to school neatly dressed, standing tall.

What made the difference? They caught a glimpse of God's vision for them! God affirmed their significance —their likeness to Him and His Son—in their service to others.

discipleship groups, worship, youth work, counseling ministry, and outreach teams.[4]

It is vital to have wholistic ministry as part of the church's mission and vision statements—and well worth the work to develop them. One noted church leader described the *mission statement* as a clear summary of a church's ministry, a *broad* explanation of why the church exists—for example, a combination of the Great Commission[5] and Great Commandment.[6] A *vision* statement, then, would define a local church's *unique* calling—its geographic area, people served, methods used, or end-goals.[7] Personally, I usually think of "vision" as broad and "mission" as unique! Either way, it is key to be intentionally wholistic in both the general and specific callings of the local church. It is important that the church's mission and vision statements refer to God's whole agenda—spiritual, physical, and social. They may feature such concepts as the following, which I have deliberately integrated:

- Preaching Christ as Lord and serving others for His sake (2 Corinthians 4:5)
- Going into the world, discipling nations, teaching God's ways (Matthew 28:19)
- Doing God's will, extending the Kingdom of God (Matthew 6:9-10)
- Restoring all things (Colossians 1:20)
- Teaching, fellowship, communion, prayer (Acts 2:42)
- Being salt, light, and yeast (Matthew 5:13-16; 13:33)
- Doing justice, loving mercy, and walking humbly with God (Micah 6:8)

---

[4] See interactive Bible studies, group lessons, and instructional aids on the Harvest Web site: www.harvestfoundation.org.

[5] Matthew 28:19-20a

[6] Matthew 22:37-39

[7] Barna, *A Fish out of Water,* 70. This book helps churches identify their general and specific callings.

[8] Ephesians 4:12

- Worship, especially through music and praise (Colossians 3:16)
- Equipping the saints for works of service (Ephesians 4:11-12)
- Doing to "the least of these" as unto Christ (Matthew 25:40)
- Meeting and encouraging one another in love and good deeds (Hebrews 10:24-25)
- Caring for one another (Romans 12:13)
- Loving God above all things and loving our neighbors (Matthew 22:37-39)

Our organization, Harvest, has mission and vision statements. We review them every year during our staff conference to remind us of the purposes to which God called us and to keep us from doing good things that are not part of our calling. If mission and vision statements do not exist, they should be developed by the pastor and a team of dedicated leaders. Those in denominations may need to adopt the mission statement of the denomination and clarify their local church's wholistic calling in a vision statement.

Imparting and Implementing the Vision

After a wholistic vision has been caught by the pastor and leaders, it must be imparted to—and implemented by—the individuals, families, and small groups of the church. Sometimes at this point, pastors and church leaders are starting to think: "Wait! Our church is small! We have no money! The people won't do this!" What I propose is not about grand-scale projects that require large investments of time and money. No, it is about a grand-scale vision, accomplished through small projects and small, sacrificial investments of time, talent, and other resources! Small applications may seem insignificant in the grand scheme of advancing God's agenda, but distant destinations are reached one step at a time. God's will is reached one application at a time. I like to ask: "What is the best way to eat an elephant?" The answer: "One bite at a time!" Now, please understand that I do not really eat elephants. But, as I look at very large tasks, this helps me remember that small-scale actions, one by one, fulfill large visions.

At one of our conferences in Myanmar, we divided several hundred pastors and church leaders into many small groups. We told each group to plan a small project for the community and be prepared to introduce the plan to the entire conference. A medical doctor attended that conference. She was very aware of the overwhelming needs in her country, and she thought her group's simple project was insignificant. Then, thirty other groups finished planning and presenting their projects. When she saw all of them together, the doctor was astounded at the potential power of their combined witness!

Following are some ways to mobilize the church and implement the vision through both traditional and nontraditional teaching forums of the church—one bite at a time.

Wherever They Are!

The first place God calls His people to represent His agenda is—wherever they are! Local churches often neglect to equip their people for the most transformational activity available—the witness of their individual lives! Equipping and mobilizing individual saints for service is the job description of each church leader—*"to prepare God's people for works of service."*[8] As followers of Christ, we are to obey God in the arenas of service where we spend *most* of our time—not our extra, donated time. This might be the home, factory, print shop, office, clinic, or Parliament. All Christians are Kingdom ambassadors, representing God's purposes in the areas we best impact.

Hebrews 10 affirms the same message: *"Let us consider how we may spur one another on toward love and good deeds. Let us not give up meeting together."*[9] These verses are linked. The people of the church are to gather to be instructed and encouraged for compassionate service, and they are to disperse to do what they learned. I believe God knew we would need encouragement, instruction, and accountability to serve Him well.

---

[9] Hebrews 10:24-25
[10] 1 Thessalonians 4:3-12

Let's look at a few people who were not only encouraged by their churches, but were equipped to serve—wherever they were:

❖ One Saturday, two nurses in Africa were visiting relatives in a nearby town. They decided to gather nursing mothers and pregnant women for a discussion about health care, delivery, child care, eating habits, family planning, and basic hygiene. Great amounts of new knowledge were imparted to one-hundred young mothers!

❖ A retired Christian engineer in Asia organized the repair of the community road on which he and his neighbors lived. The primarily Buddhist neighborhood also included a mosque, public elementary school, Buddhist temple and orphanage, and Baptist church. Each of these neighbors contributed funds, and the retired engineer organized the road repair. The gentleman freely credits the Lord for the road and continues to reach out to serve his neighbors.

❖ Several Christian nurses in Myanmar decided to stop overcharging for prescription medications, a common method of supplementing low wages. Instead, the nurses started a fund to provide free medications to the neediest patients.

Personal Applications to Sermons and Lessons

Mobilizing the entire local church for wholistic service can be as basic as making a way for all who heard a sermon or lesson to apply what they learned—wherever they are! Near the end of *each lesson, small group meeting, or sermon*, those in leadership can:

- Encourage applications that are realistic, specific, and immediate.
- Challenge listeners to choose an application.
- Urge them to pray for another person's application.
- Ask them to report or testify at the next meeting or service.

1. *Encourage applications that are realistic, specific, and immediate.* (See examples in the box.) Speakers often suggest broad applications that people forget, see as irrelevant, or are not willing to try. Instead, they should encourage their listeners to think of applications that are realistic, specific, and *immediate.* It is helpful when pastors and leaders share how *they* freshly applied the lesson—in ways that are realistic, specific, and immediate.

   - The application must be *realistic* in relationship to other obligations.

   - It should be *specific.* "What will I do?" "When?" "With or for whom?"

   - It is best if it is *immediate*—completed before the next service or meeting.

   - Applications may cost the person doing them a meal, leisure, or sleep. They should not be done at the expense of other biblical priorities (family, work, or church).

> ## Applications Should Be Realistic, Specific, and Immediate
>
> You have just learned that we are to forgive those who have offended us. You need to plan an application. Which application is more likely to be completed?
>
> *Option A*: "I will look for an opportunity to forgive all who have offended me in the past."
>
> *Option B*: "Next Monday, I will invite my coworker for coffee. I will say I would like to improve our relationship and ask for forgiveness. I will suggest we leave our disagreements behind us and begin a new level of friendship."
>
> *Option A* is too general. It is not realistic to forgive everyone. It is not specific. Nobody was identified. It is not immediate. There is no time frame. It would be hard to know if it was done.
>
> *Option B* meets all the criteria. It seems realistic to have coffee together during a workday. It is specific. The broken relationship has been identified, and a plan has been established. It is immediate. Within the next week, the application will have been attempted.

2. *Challenge listeners to choose an application.* Pastors and group
    leaders should, after each sermon or lesson, challenge listeners to
    choose a personal application. Remind them to avoid the habit
    of knowing something, but doing nothing. Encourage them to
    prayerfully ask God for His direction. It may help people to think
    of several applications and then ask God to guide their choice.

3. *Urge participants to pray for another person's application.* Near the
    end of a meeting, pastors or group leaders ask participants to
    relate their choice of application to another person and then pray
    for each other. This is easier in a small group setting, but can also
    be done during an altar call or after a service. Telling another
    person how they plan to apply the lesson helps participants
    clarify and reinforce their decisions. It also provides motivation
    when another person is aware of the planned application and
    has prayed for it.

4. *Ask people to report or testify at the next meeting or church service.*
    Pastors and leaders provide accountability by asking members to
    testify or report. In a group, there can be quick reporting from
    everyone as the meeting opens. In a church service, there can be
    a testimony from one member, or the congregation can divide
    into groups of two or three for quick reports. This confirms that
    applications are being done; reinforces the importance of taking
    action; and allows people to encourage and pray for one another.

A building cannot be safely enlarged and extended unless it has
a strong foundation. In the same way, Christ's followers must have a
strong foundation if the reign of Christ is to extend firmly into their
societies. This foundation is more than correct theology—it is the
character of God, demonstrated in their daily lives. As individuals
are trained by their churches to touch their communities, their lives
must reflect the character of Christ. The Apostle Paul told us that
we are to lead holy, pure, quiet and productive lives[10] and that we
are to be sober, Spirit-filled, singing, and thankful.[11] Unless we are

---

[11] Ephesians 5:17-20
[12] Micah 6:8b

moving toward God's character in our personal lives, we have little to say to others about God's agenda. I believe quiet, sacrificial, holy, individual demonstrations of God's love are even more powerful influences for the Kingdom than corporate church activities, as this example illustrates:

❖ Let me tell you about the shoemaker! Our wholistic training materials were taught in a Brazil church. Jose, a shoemaker, attended all the sessions. When our staff member visited the shoemaker in his store, he was surprised to see that Jose was mentoring Maikon, a young man from a poor family, in the business and in the faith. Jose already had a desire to help people, but the studies and personal applications opened his eyes even more. He is an enthusiastic Christian, doing work and sharing faith with a young boy who might otherwise have been "mentored" by the streets.

Families can be encouraged to carry out ministry applications together. They have natural contacts with many community institutions—schools, the urban work force, the farm, the neighborhood, apartments, and multiple social services. God wants His will to be done in each one of those places! Families can be trained to open their eyes, to see and meet needs around them. Further, local churches can mobilize multiple families to serve God *together.* When the church mobilizes families, it not only meets current needs, but equips future generations. Children who are raised to serve others will likely become adults with vision, purpose, and servant hearts.

The Sermon

If God's grand vision truly consumes the pastor, this passion will be reflected in what is taught to the entire congregation and will become contagious. The sermon is an obvious and important place to impart the vision of God's full agenda. Every time Scripture is explained, pastors should ask themselves, "How can I refer to this

> If God's vision consumes the pastor, the vision will be contagious.

passage's implications for wholistic service?" As pastors prepare to study and preach familiar passages, I encourage them to humbly ask God to open their eyes to His full intentions for the church.

The communication of the vision should be grounded in Scripture, so church members understand that this is more than a nice, new idea. They need to hear through God's Word that this is God's intention for His church—for *their* church. Sermons can help the congregation see that God has used His church around the world, throughout history and in this generation, to transform societies.

Sermons must be illustrated by the lives of those who preach

Do Sermons Change People?

Preachers assume that the Word and Spirit will produce conviction and change. It's not automatic!

My wife and I recently visited a church. The sermon was about honoring God by stewarding His creation. The message was solid, and the pastor suggested applications, but a critical element was missing.

There was no time for response. There was no time for each listener to prayerfully consider a personal, specific, realistic application. And there was no invitation to commit to a specific action.

. . . And few of us will change the way we steward creation!

---

and live them. Are pastors involved with broader concerns in the neighborhood, community, town, or nation? Do the church people know this? When Jesus washed His disciples' feet, He led by example. When I teach, I use stories from the past and from other parts of the world, but people respond best when I relate how God worked in and through me last week—or yesterday.

I often challenge pastors to take a survey—to ask the congregation to write down the theme of last week's sermon, then two weeks ago, and finally three and four weeks ago. I suggest they be ready for disappointment as they see how people's ability to remember drops sharply as time passes.

But sermons *can* be remembered, and they will be if they are intentionally applied! Here are some suggestions:

- Sermons should be *designed* to be lived—not just heard.

- At the end of the sermon, each person should be challenged to make an application commitment that is specific, realistic, and immediate. If sermon applications are not specific, people are left with a warm feeling that, yes, they will live in a better way—in general, in the future. This resolve evaporates in the coming week—or when the service is over and conversations with other church members begin.

- Unless the Holy Spirit speaks through the message, nothing of eternal significance transpires. We must be sensitive to His guidance as we prepare and preach.

The Small Group

Small groups are probably the best place to encourage applications that are specific, realistic, and immediate. Here are some key principles to equip and mobilize small groups with a wholistic vision:

- Churches can use existing small group meetings to equip members for wholistic service. This focus can easily be incorporated into Sunday schools, Bible studies, prayer meetings, home fellowships, and cells.

- Small group leaders should be equipped to see wholistic implications in everything they teach. They should be trained to facilitate meetings in such a way that group members discover and immediately apply lesson principles in their own lives.

- Small groups enforce individual applications. At the close of each meeting, group members tell each other how they plan to individually apply the lesson in the coming week and then pray for each other. At the beginning of the next lesson, a few minutes are taken to review applications. They could use the Discipline of Love tool in Part Four.

- As small groups learn of their potential and responsibility to touch their community and culture, they can be mobilized to seek and plan ways to demonstrate God's love to the world around them. They could use the Seed Project Planning Guide in Part Four.

- Small groups can then carry out small-scale wholistic ministry projects together. It is easier to equip and mobilize small groups and cell groups than it is to engage one large, traditional church body in community service. Small groups are good contexts for group service.

- Any kind of small group can encourage wholistic service. Two small group models are family groups and affinity groups. Family groups meet regularly, encourage individual applications, pray and praise God, and plan to serve together. Affinity groups are comprised of people at a common point in life—medical professionals, businessmen, teachers, mothers of young children, or people who like photography. They witness to God's concerns in their specialized spheres of influence. A business affinity group, for example, might address such issues as tax fraud, bribes for jobs or contracts, or ways to help low-wage earners support their families.

Here is an example from several small groups in one Korean church:

❖ A Korean church has twenty-five cell groups. Each group executed a small-scale project in its community, paid for by a weekly offering in the cell group. Several groups went to the county assistance office to identify neighbors who needed assistance. One group made food and brought supplies for an elderly couple; the group noticed the disorderly state of the home and returned later to help. Another group visited two people suffering from disabilities—one person had been confined to bed for thirty-seven years and appreciated help taking a bath; the other person was a Christian, and they had a wonderful time of worship and fellowship. Another group helped a handicapped boy celebrate his birthday. They took gifts and a card. The parents of the boy are not Christians and were very pleased with this act of kindness toward their son.

A church or small group might look at its neighborhood—looking for older people who are no longer able to clean their homes, cut their lawns, care for their gardens, do laundry, cook, or recover from illness. Or, perhaps loneliness is their greatest burden. The elderly may not have family or friends who can help them, but a church family or small group of families can "adopt" and care for them. God used these two local churches to serve elderly widows:

❖ In a small church in the Dominican Republic, church members identified seven widows who lived in a lower-economic neighborhood. These widows had no extended families helping them. The church "adopted" them and cared for them as part of the church family. The widows received practical help from the church families—and more. They personally experienced a powerful witness to the goodness of God's intentions and love. Although the church intended to serve the widows whether or not they were Christians, all seven widows put their faith in Christ as a result of the compassion they saw in the Christians who served them.

❖ Wholistic ministry students in Korea were assigned to demonstrate Christ's love to nonbelievers in their community. The church staff members decided to work as a small group and do the same. The church staff visited the local government office to get names of the community's neediest people. They were eventually directed to an old woman who, they discovered, was a traditional shaman—a spiritualist medium. She lived by herself among her idols and religious paintings. Her home was in disrepair. The people talked for awhile and then helped with housecleaning. Promising to return, they began a relationship which God honored and blessed. The next month, the church staff recruited two other groups to help refurbish the woman's home. Donations resulted in significant repairs to the home. A few months later, these students had another assignment—to share something they learned with one other person who needed to hear it. An assistant pastor chose to talk with the shaman woman, which led to a full discussion about faith in Christ. She committed her life to the Lord. They immediately searched her house for statues and shamanistic items and disposed of them. The following Sunday, she attended church for the first time. She began to tell everyone who would listen that they, too, need to give their lives to Jesus Christ.

The Congregation

A local congregation can be transformed when it sees a community "problem" through God's eyes:

❖ The assistant pastor of an Ethiopian church attended a training conference. His congregation had been debating what to do about a great problem—the street children who were living on the church property. After the conference, the children were no longer a "problem," but an opportunity. The pastor went back to his church and relayed his new conviction. The church formed a committee of twelve members whose hearts were stirred by what they had heard. They began to coordinate a ministry to the children. They raised money and helped the children with food and clothing. They helped them generate their own income, too—washing cars, shining shoes, or peddling small items. Most of the children have since been reunited with their families and continue in their small businesses. The parents have become involved in the ministry as guarantors, responsible for their children's income-generating activities.

There are many ways to mobilize a local church for involvement with community needs. The tools in Part Four can be used to help churches discover God's intentions and demonstrate His love in their neighborhoods. The congregation should be encouraged to participate not only in community service, but in civic activities that represent justice, righteousness, and God's intentions, as understood through Scripture. The church itself should address these matters in ways that honor God. The prophet Micah gave us a good standard:

"And what does the Lord require of you? To act justly and to love mercy and to walk humbly with your God."[12] Here are several suggestions for a congregation's civic involvement:

- When there are civic or political concerns the church should address, church leaders can speak about them from the pulpit, encourage focus groups to form, and participate in meetings to express the church's stance on an issue.

- Congregations can join with other churches or existing community networks to address critical civic issues, working with existing collaborative structures, if possible.

- Local churches can make civic concerns a standard part of the prayer life of the church in worship services, prayer bulletins, and small groups.

- Church members can be encouraged to become informed about civic issues—to gather facts and search the Scriptures. They can be encouraged that there may be more than one godly perspective. They can be helped to learn to listen to others and intentionally trained to represent Kingdom principles in civic issues.

- Churches can offer an accountability group for members involved in civic leadership, praying for them and holding them accountable for their decisions and actions.

- Congregations can encourage young people who have an interest in government to prepare for vocations—to be Kingdom representatives in the civic/political arena.

"Grass-Roots" Efforts and Civic Involvement

Sometimes, an individual in a church catches a specific vision for wholistic service or civic involvement and starts doing it—perhaps privately first and then promoting it to others in the church. More people become involved. It eventually becomes a ministry that the church adopts—including the leadership.

Churches should also encourage their individual members to

---

[13] 2 Corinthians 5:20a

be personally engaged in civic activities. Suggestions for individual civic involvement include the following:

- Individuals can be encouraged to attend neighborhood, community, city council, or local school meetings.

- They can participate in public dialogue on important issues, writing letters to editors and elected representatives, where possible.

- Individual Christians can visit local civic leaders, thanking them for their service, inquiring how the church can help, asking the civic leaders to list the major problems they face, and asking how they can pray. They can pray with them during the visit if the leaders wish. Finally, they can carry the leaders' concerns back to the local church for assistance and prayers.

- Individuals can vote in local and national elections.

- They can run for political office or volunteer in a city or community position.

- Finally, they can speak about the specific issues that have impacted their own lives in unique ways.

Discipleship Training

Followers of Jesus are not automatically prepared to be representatives of God's purpose in the world. When Paul spoke of Christians who purposefully represent God's agenda, he called them "ambassadors."[13] The people of the church must be *equipped* to become effective ambassadors of God's intentions. Their discipleship training should teach them about the basic beliefs of the faith. It should also encourage them to intentionally act on what they learn, obey Christ's commands, and daily advance God's purposes in their spheres of influence.

This kind of discipleship training is best communicated individually or in very small groups. Discipleship training should be an intentional program of the church. Disciplers should be individuals

[14] Colossians 1:20

who are experienced in God's broad agenda before they disciple others. Disciples then learn from those who have more maturity, experience, and knowledge. Discipleship training that prepares Kingdom ambassadors should impart *three key characteristics*:

- Passionate vision
- Strategic intention
- Appropriate contextualization

1. *The first task in "ambassadorizing" a disciple is to impart a passionate vision of God's intentions for the restoration of "all things."*[14] This includes the following:

   - The grandness of God's purpose, especially the discipling of nations
   - The connection between an individual's obedient action and the discipling of that individual's nation
   - The high privilege of giving one's life to God's cosmic purpose, above any other
   - A passion to pursue this vision

2. *The second task is to train the disciple to be intentionally strategic as an ambassador of God's intentions.* Disciples must be equipped to be both intentional and strategic.

   - Ambassadors are more than citizens—they act intentionally to advance the agenda of the government they represent. In the same way, Christians are to be *intentional* about our task—to go, preach, make disciples, and teach obedience.[15]
   - We must not only be intentional. We must also be *strategic*. There are many opportunities to advance God's will daily— more than our capacity. The opportunities we select should be strategic. While others may yield results, it is the strategic opportunities that produce the richest results. We should look for and seize opportunities with the greatest possibility to advance God's agenda.

---

[15] Matthew 28:19-20a
[16] Read about Meshack in Chapter 9.

3. *The third task is to train disciples to be appropriately contextual.* Disciples need to know how to present God's agenda in such a way that it has the greatest chance to be understood and welcomed as the Good News that it is. Contextualization is the process of adapting, shaping, or fitting something to its situation. For example, God who is Spirit contextualized the message of His love for the human race by sending Jesus in human form. One way Jesus contextualized His message was by telling agricultural stories to people who lived in an agrarian society.

Two Discipleship Scenarios

Scenario 1: A professional—a social worker—has become a believer. She has entered the discipleship program of a local church. How should she be discipled?

- *Passionate Vision*: As this new believer learns about the basic beliefs of the Christian faith, she needs to encounter more than cold facts. The Bible, her discipleship textbook, is the narrative of a glorious and true story of God's salvation for broken people. It must be communicated to her in such a way that she catches a vision of—and develops a passion for—the profound beauty of God's plan. Specifically, the social worker should be encouraged to envision her clients' lives—as if Jesus were providing and managing the social services they receive. She should be urged to develop a passion for this vision and to pray that it will be realized. She needs to be trained to ask God for the courage, strength, and tenacity to pursue her role in helping her clients move toward God's purposes. This is the *vision* toward which the social worker should work—and work with *passion*.

- *Strategic Intentionality*: Disciples must also be trained to remain continually, intentionally aware of their role as ambassadors. As such, this disciple must be helped to look for opportunities to advance God's kingdom—every day, every hour, in both the large and small events of her life. Her intentionality doesn't need to be mechanical. (A hunter doesn't keep repeating, "I am looking for an antelope, I am looking for an antelope," but he is keenly aware of his surroundings and is intentional about where he goes, how he walks, and what sounds he makes.) This disciple must be encouraged to be on an *intentional* "hunt"—for opportunities to advance God's intentions.

Disciples must be trained not only to be intentional, but *strategic*. The social worker will have many opportunities during a day to advance God's purpose. She may share God's comfort and hope with a client. She may arrange for needed client services. She may speak up for justice in a staff meeting. She may pass beggars on the street. She may get an urgent phone call from a friend. There are usually more opportunities to advance God's purpose than can be accomplished in a day. She needs to be trained to pray for wisdom to discern which opportunities are most strategic.

Let's say that the most strategic opportunity in this instance is the social worker's staff meeting. The issue being discussed is the distribution of condoms to client families. The social worker knows that this is an emotionally-charged issue in her society and that the agency's policy leans toward distributing condoms in order to promote safe sex. The meeting and discussion would take time away from her clients. But because of her discipleship training, the social worker would likely decide that the staff meeting is a more strategic use of her time.

- *Appropriate contextualization:* The social worker should be discipled to represent God's agenda in various situations. To be an effective ambassador at the staff meeting, for example, she should have been trained to see how God's agenda could be contextualized—adapted, shaped, or fitted—and appropriately communicated to other staff members in such a way that they are able to understand and consider it as a wise alternative. Her discipleship training should have equipped her to assess her team members' opinions about a given issue and prayerfully select an approach that would help them consider and adopt a biblical solution.

Service . . . Now

As new disciples are learning basic truths about the faith, they must also be intentionally putting them into practice—in their own lives and in service to others.

A major weakness in many discipleship programs is that the demonstration of God's love to others is omitted or postponed until a later stage of training. Many Christians who have not been thoroughly trained feel exempt. They wait for more training—and they never begin to serve.

But Paul told us that we are saved to serve! Service is not the responsibility of mature Christians. It is a mandate for all believers—from the babes in Christ to the most mature saints. We need to disciple new believers to begin to serve . . . now.

One approach to the meeting's topic would be to say something like, "I'm a Christian. The Bible says that sex outside of marriage is sin. I'm sorry, but I won't be a part of promoting sin among our clients!" This approach may crudely represent God's agenda, but it would most likely alienate non-Christian team members and push them away from considering a godly alternative. This would not be an appropriate contextualization of God's intentions. A more contextual approach might be to recommend a pamphlet that promotes a biblical understanding of sex and ask if the group would be willing to discuss it at the next meeting. There are other approaches, too, that would better advance the biblical position to nonbelievers than saying, "The Bible says . . ."

Scenario 2: An unemployed young man, a secondary school graduate, has become a new disciple at the church. How should he be discipled?

- *Passionate Vision:* This new disciple also needs to be instructed in the basics of the faith and helped to carry out applications of what he is learning. What kind of specific vision can be imparted to this unemployed youth? His discipleship training should challenge and inspire him with the beauty of work. He should understand that he was created to work—to do good works—with or without pay. What would Jesus do if he were unemployed? I think He would devote time to look for work, but He would also keep His eyes and heart open to help others in His community. The young man could be encouraged to do something that would express the servant heart of God. He might organize sports for other unemployed youth, befriend a young person with AIDS, or help his parents with younger children at home.

In these pages is the story of another young man in a similar situation.[16] Meshack had a Kingdom vision for children who could not go to school. He dreamed of them learning to read. For seven months, this unemployed young man and his friends taught slum children without pay. Each day they asked each other, "Did you eat today?" If one had not eaten, the others shared what they had. This young man's vision was passionate because he saw God's great intentions for the unschooled children in his community—and he knew he was an ambassador for God's purpose.

In these pages is the story of a similar young man. Gizachew.[17] He was one of ten children from a poor family. His Kingdom vision was for the street kids of his city. Beginning with very meager resources, he and his friends shared their food, provided baths, and held Bible studies for street children. God blessed their faithful obedience. Today, they lead a thriving ministry to street children.

Unemployment can be a curse. It can also be a gift. If it is involuntary, it needs to be seen as a temporary gift that God intends to be creatively and productively used to extend His Kingdom. Discipleship for this unemployed young man needs to impart a vision for what God can do through his present difficulty. Let's say in this instance that he gains a passionate vision for the kind of ministry that God gave Meshack and Gizachew. (Imagine the difference that could be made by an army of unemployed Christian young people with a vision to serve the Kingdom of God in this way.)

- *Strategic Intentionality:* I have seen many unemployed young men around the world—simply sitting, playing cards, talking to friends, getting into trouble. But an "unemployed" Christian

---

[17] Read about Gizachew in Chapter 5 and Chapter 11 (in the box).
[18] Stott, *Involvement,* 81-83,89.

is not to be unproductive or unoccupied. Christians, with or without paying jobs, are ambassadors of the King of Kings. They have a very important job to do. This young disciple is no exception. He must be discipled to be both intentional and strategic in how he chooses to use his time. He needs to be discipled to be intentionally occupied doing good, looking for the most strategic ways to advance God's purpose. As he does, like Meshack and Gizachew, he may also discover his life work—the calling God has given him.

- *Appropriate contextualization:* In this example, let's say that the unemployed young man has developed a passionate vision and strategic intention for ministry to the other unemployed youth of his city. I have observed that nobody is as good at appropriately contextualizing the message of God's compassion for needy youth as other unemployed, discipled young people, especially those with God's vision. Those I have seen are energetic and creative. They have learned to trust God. They are better prepared than their teachers in communicating with those who are enduring hardships similar to their own. Because of his own background, then, let's say, that the young man in our example does not need to be discipled to contextualize the message to the youth—but he does need his pastor and mentor to encourage, pray for, and support him to be courageous and strategic. He also needs to be discipled to wisely contextualize his message for other settings— perhaps as he seeks funds from city authorities, organizes volunteers, solves problems, or establishes new programs.

Persuasion and a Note to the Oppressed Church

Many of the churches with which Harvest ministers are in non-Christian settings, where Christians are limited in their civic participation by anti-Christian governments or by secularized societies. Yet, churches must still represent God's agenda in their societies. One way is through individual service. Another is persuasion.

Persuasion is God's way of relating to us. He does not coerce us into doing the right thing. He presents us with options, the consequences of options, and leaves the decision to us. Here are several principles of persuasion:

- People must speak up—and not remain silent.
- Christians should not rely solely on biblical assertions to make their points.
- They should study the issues in order to make an informed case for a biblical position.
- They must work to help the non-Christian community see that God's way is the better way.
- Finally, they must be sure that their own lifestyles are consistent with the biblical position. [18]

The church must help the public see that God's agenda will bring greater benefit to the community than other options. The church cannot disciple its nation or community unless it teaches and promotes God's intentions for all aspects of life, including civic life.

Some governments do not permit the church to engage in social outreach. They want the church to limit its activities to "spiritual" needs, in order to prevent the "buying" of converts. The real reason may be that churches have a powerful influence when they are engaged in meeting people's physical and social needs. Anti-Christian governments are afraid of the cumulative power that churches develop through such service. Yet, civil governments cannot prohibit individual Christians from demonstrating God's love to others. The Bible says it best: *"But the fruit of the Spirit is love, joy, peace, patience, kindness, goodness, faithfulness, gentleness and self-control. Against such things there is no law."* [19]

I have observed that individual demonstrations of God's love are more powerful influences for the Kingdom than corporate activities. Government restrictions against corporate outreach can actually release energy and resources that would otherwise be given to group activity. Quiet, sacrificial, individual demonstrations of God's love—especially to those with whom church members are naturally in relationship—are always possible. This is powerful!

---

[19] Galatians 5:22-23
[20] Romans 10:14,15

❖ An Indian pastor ministers in rural villages. In one village, thirty percent of the people had converted to Christianity. Other villagers perceived this as a threat and plotted to kill the pastor if he did not stop holding meetings. After he attended wholistic ministry training, he commented that he had "learned to connect people to Christ without using actual words." Listen to his account:

> I found I could show love to the people who hated me. Some of the people who had been my enemies were in a village that had no water. By God's grace and through the teachings, we were able to put in a well. Because of the well, I was allowed into the village. I have been able to teach the people how to take care of their surroundings, in addition to sharing the Gospel. The people who had plotted to kill me now began to speak to me. They said: "You are an evangelist for Jesus and have done what the government could not do. Thank you." Fourteen families in this village have been drawn to Christ, and many Hindus in the village want to participate in our Seed Projects.

Sending and Commissioning the Church

Christians talk about bringing unsaved people to church— "churching the unchurched." Yet, the most effective way to reach people is by sending members *out* of the church and into the world. We need to "unchurch the churched"! We need to cross the bridge that separates the church from the community. People should not have to belong to the "club"—the church—to find out that God loves them.

The following verse has traditionally been used for cross-cultural missions. It also needs to be understood as a charge to the local church as it sends its own people into their world to "preach" that Jesus is Lord—with their words and their lives:

> *How, then, can they call on the one they have not believed in? And how can they believe in the one of whom they have not heard? And how can they hear without someone preaching to them? And*

*how can they preach unless they are sent? As it is written, "How
beautiful are the feet of those who bring good news!"*[20]

Most pastors want their members to be "sent." I would like
to suggest here that the church not only preach, impart vision,
train, mentor, and encourage applications—but that it formally
commission and "send" its equipped members into their worlds. We
memorialize and mark other faith journeys in church. New believers
testify and are baptized. New members are formally welcomed.
New couples are joined in marriage ceremonies. Newborns are
dedicated. Pastors are ordained. The journey from earthly life is
marked by a memorial service. One event is usually overlooked,
though, and it may be the most important milestone in disciples'
faith journeys—when they and their congregations acknowledge
that Christ and His church have sent them into the world around
them, wherever they are, as His ambassadors and witnesses. This
is the grandest commission that human beings could receive! Why
not commemorate this with an intentional, formal commissioning?
Just as church membership may be accompanied by a letter and
marriage by a ring, perhaps being "sent" could be accompanied by
a towel—the symbol of Christian servanthood. Or perhaps there
could be a foot-washing ceremony. However it is done, I encourage
pastors and church leaders to formally acknowledge the "sending" of
their church members as ambassadors of Christ's Kingdom.

In Conclusion

In conclusion, I encourage churches not to "play" with wholistic
ministry and not to treat it as optional. The whole Gospel has its
greatest effectiveness when it is part of a local church's foundational
identity, or DNA. It is an essential part of what God has called His
church to be as we express Christ in our communities, serving them
as if Jesus were Mayor.

A wholistic vision must be *identified* by the leaders, *imparted* to
the church, and *implemented* in the community. The church must

be equipped to minister outside its walls—through individuals, families, small groups, and congregations.

God has given His people the opportunity to participate in the grandest purpose in history. He allows us to be stewards. Our actions impact eternity. Nothing we do in accordance with His will is insignificant. The widow who gave her two coins at the temple never imagined the 2000-year impact her gift would have. We, too—the church of Jesus Christ—make an impact that will reach into future generations, far beyond what we can know or see at this time.

If the people of our churches could understand the relationship between their lives and the wonderful intentions God has for mankind—both in the present and the future—they would see that there is no greater cause for which they could live or die. The people of our local churches need ever-increasing clarity of their roles in God's grand vision.

In this chapter, we have looked at how the local church motivates its people to wholistic service. In the coming chapter, we will see how the Mayor asks us, His citizens, to give Him everything we have. We will watch His amazing multiplication at work to fulfill His purposes.

Kingdom Mathematics
Multiplication for Service

11

❖ Gizachew and his friends had been Christians most of their lives.[1] They had grown up in a solid church with good teaching. However, they were part of a culture that believes poverty in its society can be significantly reduced only by outside resources. Of course, they had heard of God's power to multiply resources, but could not apply it to their setting. It conflicted with the societal belief that only outside material resources can address poverty. See the box on the right to see how God changed their belief and practice. (Thank you for teaching me, Gizachew.)

---

[1] Sources for stories marked by ❖ are listed in the Bibliography at the end of the book.

Teaching the Teacher

I will never forget visiting a group of young men who are ministering to street people in Addis Ababa, Ethiopia. I had met two of their leaders a few years before, when they attended one of our conferences. At that time, they were struggling to befriend a handful of street boys.

During the conference, they had heard that God would multiply the willing sacrifices of His children. Now, two years later I was meeting with Gizachew, the leader of the ministry. In the two years since the conference, the work had greatly expanded. Gizachew showed me a sophisticated organizational chart that represented forty staff and volunteers who provide ministry to hundreds of clients. Their multiple programs ranged from the rehabilitation of prostitutes to working with families to prevent children from leaving home to live on the streets.

I was amazed. I asked, "How did this happen? Gizachew looked at me quizzically. He said, "Why are you asking me? You're the one who taught us Kingdom Mathematics—that God would multiply if we give Him what we have! This is the fruit of that teaching."

In the last chapter, we looked at *mobilization* for witness. In this chapter, we look at *multiplication* for service. The multiplying agent is God, Himself. This is a simple but powerful message. I enjoy teaching it because I know God uses the truths of this message to free church leaders around the world—especially those who are materially poor—to do the kinds of things in their communities that Jesus would do if He were Mayor.

A mentality of dependency imprisons much of the church in the Two-Thirds World today. God wants to use His church as a channel through which He releases His transforming power to heal brokenness—but He does not do so when the church trusts primarily in resources other than God. God may use outside resources, of course, but the church needs to look to God as its primary resource. When we look anywhere else, we move perilously close to worshipping something other than the Creator—unintentional idolatry.

When we teach Kingdom Mathematics at a conference, we examine familiar biblical stories and turn them into mathematical equations. The first passage we translate into an equation is Isaiah 40:29: *"He gives strength to the weary and increases the power of the weak."* I invite five volunteers to the front of the room. I give each person a large piece of paper to hold, showing words or symbols from the verse. Then I ask the audience to arrange the people holding the papers into a sequence that represents the Isaiah 40:29 passage. Here is how they should arrange the elements:

$$\text{Our weakness} \times \text{God} = \text{Strength}$$

The message of Kingdom Mathematics is summed up in this brief passage. It tells us that, when we give our weakness to God, He multiplies it. He turns our weakness into strength.

The rest of the passage tells us: *"Even youths grow tired and weary, and young men stumble and fall; but those who hope in the Lord will renew their strength. They will soar on wings like eagles; they will run and not grow weary, they will walk and not be faint."*[2]

---

[2] Isaiah 40:30-31

This is not an ordinary transformation. It is not something that we do ourselves, nor is it something that comes from inside us. It is miraculous. It is God. Kingdom Mathematics is not a philosophy that says, "If you believe enough in yourself and in the power of positive thinking, you can change your circumstances." It begins with an acknowledgement that we, ourselves, are weak. Even youths grow tired and young men stumble! When we are ready to admit our weakness, we are in a position to come to God and offer our weakness to Him. It is then that He performs the miracle of Kingdom Mathematics and transforms our limitations into His strengths.

In our conferences, I like to describe four biblical accounts as if I were a storyteller. I then ask the attendees to work in small groups and form mathematical equations that tell the story. After they finish the equations, we summarize the truths they learned—truths that free people from dependency on anyone or anything but God.

Biblical Equations

Here is how I like to tell the first story:

> Once upon a time, there was a boy named Barak. He was about ten years old. He had heard from neighbors that, this very morning, a famous teacher had come to the lake and was speaking to the people. Barak went to his mother.
>
> "Mom, can I go down to the lake and listen to the teacher?"
>
> "No, son. It's too far. Your father isn't home, and I'm afraid to let you go so far away. It's at least an hour's walk."
>
> "Oh, Mom, please! I'll be okay. I *am* ten-years old, you know!"
>
> "Son, it's meal time, and you haven't eaten."
>
> "Mom, I'm not hungry! Please, please, let me go!"
>
> "Okay, but you have to take something to eat."
>
> So, Barak's mother spread a napkin out on her kitchen table. She reached into a pottery jar and took out one, two, three,

four, five bread rolls she had baked that morning and two little baked fish she had purchased at the market. She put the rolls and the fish in the napkin, tied it, and gave it to Barak. The boy tucked it into his belt and raced out the door.

Barak ran most of the way to the lake shore. When he got there, he found such a large crowd of people gathered around the teacher that he could not hear a word. An adult would have politely sat at the edge of the crowd, but not a ten-year-old boy! Barak moved through the crowd until he was right in front.

Barak did not understand much of what the teacher said, but the boy was drawn to this man in an unusual way. Like many preachers, this teacher talked a long time! It was about four o'clock before Barak felt his stomach growl. When it did, he immediately thought of the lunch his mother had made. But, he wondered, how would he eat it in front of all these people? He thought, "If I'm careful, perhaps no one will see what I'm doing."

So, Barak slid his little pack of food to the ground and carefully opened it. He was hungry, and it looked good! He was ready to reach for the first roll when he heard some of the teacher's disciples say something to the teacher. They suggested, since it was getting late, that the teacher send the people away so they could get something to eat in the nearby villages. He heard the teacher say, "The people don't need to go away. You give them something to eat."

One disciple, Philip, grumbled that even eight months' salary would not buy enough to give everyone even a small bite of food.

Another disciple, Andrew, happened to be sitting next to Barak and had seen him open his little pack of food. Andrew said to the teacher—who, of course, was Jesus—"Jesus, all we have here are . . ." At that, Andrew looked into the napkin and counted, ". . . five rolls and two little fish." Jesus said, "Bring them to me."

I wonder what was going through Barak's mind. "I'm hungry. This is all I have. What will I eat if I give my lunch to the teacher? Oh well, I like him. He can have it."

We know the rest of the story. Barak gave his lunch—all he had—to Andrew, who gave it to Jesus. Jesus gave thanks for the little lunch and then began to break it into pieces and distribute it to the crowd.

You can imagine the conversation between Barak and his mother when he got home that night:

"Mom, Mom! Guess what happened! The teacher took my lunch!"

"He did what?"

"Yeah, Mom! He took my lunch, and he broke it up and fed all those people. There must have been *thousands and thousands and thousands* of them. And when everyone was done eating, there were *twelve* baskets left over!"

"Barak! How many times do I need to tell you to stop exaggerating!" Barak, of course, was not exaggerating.

I then ask the people at the conferences: "How would you have felt if you had been the little boy? What if all you had to eat was packed in your belt, and Jesus asked you for it?" Surely, Jesus could have fed the crowd another way! He healed the blind. He calmed the storm. He walked on water. He could have turned stones into bread. Yet, He did not. Instead, he asked a young boy to give him all He had.[3]

We then discuss how to express this story in the form of an equation. Each small group at our conferences is given a package

---

[3] John 6:1-14, Matthew 14:13-21

of cutouts that they can discuss and arrange as a mathematical summary of the biblical account. Here is one possibility:

```
  Boy
+ 5 loaves and 2 fish
x Jesus
_____

= Food for 5,000 men
+ Food for women and children
+ 12 baskets
```

Assuming there were at least 1,000 women and children, this was a multiplication of at least 6,000 times!

Now we have come to our second story:

> Jesus was sitting in the temple with His disciples, observing people as they came to deposit their offerings. We can imagine the rich people walking to the treasury box to deposit their gifts. They were standing tall, chests extended. They held their silver coins high enough so, when they fell into the box, they would make an attention-drawing *clink*. Can you imagine Jesus' disgust?
>
> Then a widow entered. She was not standing tall. In fact, she hoped nobody would notice her. Her gift—the two smallest coins made in that day—was tiny. No matter how high she held the coins, there would be no *clink* when they went into the treasury box. That was not important. Though what she had was small, the widow wanted to give it to God.[4]
>
> Jesus knew exactly what was going on. He could have gone to the woman and said, "Dear woman, God appreciates your sacrifice. But, He owns the cattle on a thousand hills. He really doesn't need your money. I know these two small coins are all you have. You are excused from this offering.

---

[4] Mark 12:41-44

Please, go to the market and purchase something to eat. God cares about your physical need. Thank you, but—please, with my Father's blessing—feed yourself."

Yet, that is not what Jesus did. On the contrary, He allowed her to give all she had. He did not even say to her, "On behalf of My Father, thank you." She walked away, hoping no one had seen her. Jesus had seen her, though, and He said something profound: *"I tell you the truth, this poor widow has put more into the treasury than all of the others."* [5]

Let's see what Jesus meant—that she gave more than all the others. Of course, the widow gave *proportionally* more because she gave all she had. The rich gave out of their wealth; the widow gave out of her poverty. The rich did not sacrifice; the widow sacrificed. The rich would eat after their gift; the widow would still be hungry.

These are all true, but I propose that the widow *literally* gave more money than the rich. You might say, "No, she gave only two worthless coins, and the wealthy gave what was worth a hundred or a thousand times more." That is what I thought until I applied the principle of Kingdom Mathematics to the widow's gift.

As the small groups at our conferences work with the elements of the equation, they usually determine that this arrangement best summarizes the story:

$$
\begin{array}{l}
\textbf{Widow} \\
+\ \textbf{2 coins} \\
\times\ \textbf{Jesus} \\
\hline
=\ \textbf{2,000 years of inspiration}
\end{array}
$$

---

[5] Mark 12:43

How many millions of times has the widow's gift been multiplied in 2,000 years? Christians throughout generations have given more—much more—because of her example. This may be the greatest story of multiplication in all of Scripture!

Now for our third story:

> The famine in Israel was very long. Actually, it lasted more than three years. Elijah had asked God to send a famine to punish unrighteousness in Israel. King Ahab was angry and was looking for Elijah. God sent Elijah to hide in a ravine with a stream. He fed Elijah bread and meat brought to him by ravens, and Elijah drank from the stream. The drought got so bad, though, that the stream dried up. God told Elijah to go to a Gentile town called Zarephath, where God would take care of him. The journey was more than 90 miles—145 kilometers—and Elijah walked. That's a long way in a drought-stricken land. By the time Elijah arrived at his destination, he was *thirsty!*
>
> As he came toward the gates of the city, he saw a woman—a widow—gathering sticks for fuel. Elijah was well-known in this area. After all, people wanted to capture and kill him! From the way the woman spoke to him, it is likely that she knew who he was. I imagine she was a bit intimidated by this infamous prophet of God as he asked her for relief from the famine—the famine that he himself had asked God to send! Their conversation might have been something like this:
>
>> "Excuse me, ma'am, but I'm very thirsty. Could you get me a jar of water?"
>>
>> "Yes, sir (with fear in her voice). Please wait here."
>>
>> "If you don't mind, would you please bring me something to eat?"
>>
>> "As the Lord your God lives (with understandable anxiety in her voice), I only have enough flour and oil for one small meal for myself and my son. It is our very last food. After we have eaten it, there will be no more and we will die."

"Don't be afraid. God will provide for you. Your flour and oil will last through the drought."

In faith, the widow returned to her home. She took her last remaining flour and oil, made it into bread, and baked it with the sticks she had gathered at the city gate. Even though she used all she had, there was still oil and flour in her jars! She ran to tell Elijah about this miracle—and the supply lasted and lasted. In fact, it fed the widow, her son, her family, and probably Elijah throughout the famine.[6]

As the small groups at our conferences work with the elements of the equation, we presume that the widow, her son, three more family members, and Elijah ate together for the remaining two years of the three-year famine. Here is a possible equation to summarize this lesson:

Widow
+ 1 cake
x God

= 2 cakes (meals) per day
x 6 people (widow, son, Elijah, and 3 other family members)
x 365 days
x 2 years

= 6,570 cakes (meals)

If the approximate numbers are close to reality, this would be a multiplication equivalent to that in our first story—a multiplication of more than 6,000. That is amazing. What is most amazing, though, is the way God fed His prophet—He used a widow who

---

[6] 1 Kings 17:1-16; 18:1

was as poor as anyone can be. She, her son, and family were ready to starve to death for lack of food.

Isn't this amazing? Is this the God we know? Our God is compassionate toward the poor. He could have fed Elijah another way. God could have fed the 5,000 another way, too, but He chose this way. Just as He did with the boy and his lunch, God looked at a widow who only had enough for herself and said, "Me first." Interesting!

These three stories can be summarized in a Kingdom equation, expressed below:

Kingdom Equation

All people (even the poor)
+ Faith in God
+ Sacrificial giving
x God
_____
= Great multiplication
+ Blessing to others
+ God is praised
+ Personal blessing (sometimes)

The lessons of these stories are consistent with the life Jesus lived. He had little of this world's goods. He once said: *"Foxes have holes and birds of the air have nests, but the Son of Man has no place to lay his head."*[7] Yet, He made the greatest sacrifice anyone ever makes—He gave His life.

There is one last story. This one does not have a happy ending. It is a story Jesus told to illustrate His Kingdom:

> A wealthy man was going on a long journey, and he called his servants to give them instructions before he left. He had

---

[7] Matthew 8:20

three servants. He told each of them he was going to entrust them with a portion of his resources. He wanted them to invest what he gave them so he could have a profit when he returned. According to their abilities, he gave one servant five talents, another servant received two talents, and the third servant got one talent. Then the wealthy man left.

On his return, he called his servants. The conversation might have gone something like this:

"Well, Simeon, how did you do?"

"Master, the market was very good! I bought and sold and doubled the talents you gave me. Here are ten talents from the five you gave me when you left."

"Great job, Simeon! Because of your good work, I'm going to put you in charge of much more. Actually, I am going to consider you as a member of my own household!"

Then, the master called his second servant, Joshua:

"Joshua, how did you do while I was gone?"

"Master, the market was very good. I invested and doubled what you left me. Here are four talents for the two you gave me."

"Well done, Joshua! I'm proud of you. You have done well with what you had. I want you to consider yourself a member of my own household."

The third servant was called by the master:

"Ananias, welcome! How did you do with the talent I left you?"

You could almost predict what Ananias was going to say by looking at him. He was clearly uncomfortable in the presence of his master and the other two servants.

"Master, you only left me with one talent—just one."

Ananias glanced with jealousy at his two colleagues. He spoke with a quavering voice:

"As you know, sir, you have a reputation for being a tough

businessman. Because I was aware of that, I was afraid to take chances. So, I didn't. I buried your talent in the ground for safe-keeping. It was protected there. I didn't lose it. I humbly give you back the talent you gave me."

As Ananias was speaking, the face of the master changed. He responded to Ananias, but he did not even call him by name:

"You wicked and lazy man! If you knew I was a hard businessman and expected a profit from my resources, why didn't you at least take my money and put it in the bank where I could have received interest? . . . Guards! Take the talent from this worthless man and give it to Simeon. Throw him out of my household to where it is dark and where there is sorrow and regret!"[8]

What a harsh response! Is this the God we know? God has compassion for the poor, and the third servant was clearly the poorest. Could God not have shown him some mercy? Not only did the fearful servant lose what he had, but he was thrown out of his master's kingdom!

The small groups at our conferences then work with the elements of this equation. Here is one suggestion to summarize the parable:

$$
\begin{array}{l}
\textbf{Servant} \\
+ \ \textbf{1 talent} \\
\times \ \textbf{0} \\
\hline
= \ \textbf{0} \\
+ \ \textbf{Servant thrown} \\
\quad \ \textbf{into darkness}
\end{array}
$$

---

[8] Matthew 25:14-30

Implications for the Kingdom

These four stories have important implications for all Christians, but especially for those who believe they have only enough resources to take care of themselves. The stories and equations teach the following:

- All people, regardless of their material possessions or positions in life, are called by God to give Him what they have. There are no exceptions, even for the poor.

- There are no circumstances in which what we have is "too little" or "too insignificant" to be used by God.

- We need to give to God when He asks, regardless of our own circumstances.

- Faith in God and love for God should be our motives for giving. Material gain should not motivate us. Gain and provision may come, but giving should never be based on the expectation of receiving something in return.

- Sacrificial giving leads to multiplication. God always multiplies what we give Him.

- The greater the sacrifice, the greater the increase.

- The last lesson is perhaps the hardest: If we do not invest what God has entrusted to us, we not only lose it, but risk being thrown out of the Master's household.

As we consider these four biblical accounts in our conferences, people sometimes wonder why a God of love would require such large sacrifices of people—but they also see that the power of God's Kingdom is released when people act with loving and obedient sacrifice. God wants us to be like Him, and loving sacrifice reflects the character of God Himself. As we become like Him, His power is released, we flourish, and the world around us flourishes. The call to sacrifice is indeed from a God who loves us—from a God who is Love.

"What Is That in Your Hand?"

Many Christians look at themselves and say: "I can't do anything for the Kingdom. I don't have charisma. I'm not a leader. I can't preach and teach. I don't have enough to help needy people." They feel inadequate. One of the first examples of this in Scripture was Moses.[9]

God met Moses at the burning bush and said, "Moses, I want you to go to Pharaoh and lead my people out of Egypt into the land that I promised their forefathers." We can imagine what is in Moses' mind: "God, You don't understand! I have a price on my head in Egypt. I killed a man. I've been out of Egypt for forty years. I don't know the culture or what's been happening there. I'm truly unprepared to do this." Moses basically said: "Who, me?" He asked, "Who am I that I should go to Pharaoh and demand to bring the enslaved people of Israel out of Egypt?"

God answered: "But, Moses, I will be with you." Moses then made a series of excuses: "God, I don't speak too well. I'm not very charismatic. My brother is better at this than I am."

Then God said to Moses (and I can almost hear the disgust in His voice): "Moses, what is that in your hand?" Moses replied: "It's just a stick—a staff." God told Moses to throw it down. Moses threw it down, and it became a snake! God told Moses to pick it up. Amazingly, Moses did. It was once again a stick. God used that stick to demonstrate his power before Pharaoh. He used it to divide the Red Sea so the Israelites could cross ahead of the Egyptian army. He used it to strike a rock and provide water for a thirsty nation in the middle of a desert. He used it in sustaining the power of Israel's army to defeat the enemies. It was only a stick, until God used it. Moses thought he was incapable of doing what God asked, and he thought the stick was insignificant. In asking Moses to throw his stick down on the ground, God was saying, "Moses, give me whatever you have in your hand, and I will take it and use it to extend my Kingdom."

We need to remember that God wants us to give Him whatever we have in our hands, for His use! This can seem risky. In a modern-day African nation, Gizachew and his colleagues risked. They sacrificially invested in the Kingdom as they ministered to street children and others in need. God has blessed their efforts!

---

[9] Exodus 3 and 4

Implications for Local Churches

There are compelling implications for local churches:

- Local churches—even those with few members or few material resources—are not powerless. God will use what they give in loving obedience, and He will multiply it to glorify Himself. When God is glorified, His Kingdom is extended.

- It is dangerous for local churches to keep what they have for their own use. Churches should also use resources to demonstrate God's compassion for the needs of others.

- When people outside the Kingdom receive help that was given sacrificially, the impact is far greater than if it comes from someone's surplus.

- Churches need to teach their people to give. We must teach principles of Kingdom Mathematics. To not teach these truths robs the people of the blessings God wants to give them.

- Local churches should mirror the sacrificial giving of its people, not using resources only within the church but gladly and sacrificially investing them in service outside the church.

- Churches must not be afraid, but have confidence in God, the multiplier. One difference between the servants in the parable of the talents was how they spelled "F-A-I-T-H." The first two spelled it "R-I-S-K." This was not blind trust, but trust in God. The third servant spelled it "F-E-A-R"— the fear of losing the little he had.

God has not changed! Here are several "Kingdom Mathematics" stories from today's local churches:

❖ A cell church meets in a neighborhood that is eighty percent Muslim. At first, the church was scorned by the neighborhood, but the members started tutoring Muslim neighborhood children every Saturday morning. (Many children in the neighborhood had been abandoned by their fathers and were too poor to go to school.) The cell group started teaching five children. In a short while, more than fifty children came! One of the church members moved the furniture out of her apartment so two rooms could serve as classrooms, while a third group met on her porch. The cell group members decided, instead of buying nonessentials for themselves, they would send some of the children to school. The mostly Muslim community openly embraced this group of young, dedicated Christians. One of our staff asked the cell group members: "What relief agencies from the West did you approach to financially support your project, and how much money did they give you?" They laughed! "No," they said, "you don't understand. We did this with what we had. Nothing from the outside—just our own resources." They threw down what was in their hand—and God multiplied it.

❖ La Verdad is a church in a slum area of Guatemala. The church building was made of wooden planks, a tin roof, and a dirt floor. There were about eighty church members. When the church heard the teaching on serving their neighbors by sharing what they had, they said, "We are so poor; we cannot do that." Their pastor challenged them: "You may not have much, but you can share a small amount of sugar, rice, soap, or something else with those who have less than you." Each week, the members brought small amounts of food and put them into a common basket. Each week, the church gave the food basket to a poor, non-Christian family. Each week, God multiplied individual sacrificial gifts into an adequate supply of food for a needy family.

❖ God even multiplies resources so children can have fun! An Arizona church had a clothing drive to help a ministry that works with the poor. This ministry operates a summer day-camp program for hundreds of poor children. One of their favorite activities is going to a city swimming pool, but few of the children own a swimsuit, which is required at the city pool. The need for children's swimsuits was announced at a church, and an out-of-town visitor was moved by the Lord to donate $1,000 to purchase swimsuits! David, a church member, went to several stores, trying to find where he could get the best value for $1,000. He chose the store that offered the best discount, carefully selected 150 children's swimsuits, and piled them all in front of the cashier! Several people behind him reacted with dismay, knowing that this big purchase would delay them. An older woman who was directly behind him, though, asked him if he had a large family. He laughingly said, "No" and explained that the swimsuits were to be given to poor children who were going to a Christian summer day-camp. The woman continued to watch while the clerk totaled the cost. Finally, the total reached $1,000. This paid for 125 suits, leaving 25 unpaid. David told the clerk he would put the extra swimsuits back on the sales rack in the store. The woman behind him said, "No, I would like to pay for the extra twenty-five suits." David was astounded by this unknown woman's generosity and by the goodness of God. He was sure he had just seen another example of Kingdom Mathematics.

❖   We first conducted a training conference in the Democratic Republic of Congo in 2002. Here is a report received by the trainer only a few months after the first conference:

> The conference is beginning to bear fruit as people learn to provide for their needs. Already, we have planted a field of four hectares (ten acres) with vegetables. We also have developed small pens for raising ducks and chickens at our homes. We also had the opportunity of procuring two cameras, and they are now being used in a small photo studio. All of this is to say that the projects are bearing fruit. Long-term, we hope to open a small bakery in our neighborhood. Our project is called "Amukeni," which means "Wake up!" You came to wake us up from our ignorance.

Now, let's move up to February of 2004. The same trainer was speaking at a conference in another part of the D.R. Congo. People from the first conference traveled a great distance over dangerous roads to participate in the second conference. Our trainer reported:

> The men arrived from [the far-away city in the D.R. Congo] yesterday. Praise the Lord! They are astounding us with stories of how the people are learning to care for themselves after the war, thanks to the teaching. The work with people in the fields outside the city is progressing well. People generally are afraid to show they are prospering because

of fear of witchcraft, so they will plant only tiny plots for food and wear clothing that looks like they are in distress. When they can be freed from these lies of Satan into the truth of God, they can grow larger plots of food and care for their families. One area is a refugee camp. Now that the war is over, there is no more assistance for displaced people, so the group from the conference taught them to care for themselves without outside resources! They even rebuilt a medical clinic and organized themselves to man it. They are now looking for medicine. This amazes me! Our great God is able to do so much with so little!

A few days later, the trainer sent another e-mail about Kingdom Mathematics—true stories that were told at the same conference:

Having the men from the D.R. Congo with us is a plus. They have lived through a similar situation to the one here, and God has SO GREATLY multiplied their resources during the last one-and-a-half years. For example, they are raising pigs, having purchased two pregnant sows. The pigs are multiplying, and the group is able to distribute pigs to people in need. They had no money to buy food for the pigs—but by-products from the brewery next door make great pig food! Another Kingdom Mathematics story is about a one-hectare field they purchased to help a village raise food. After receiving the land title, they discovered that the soil is rich in cobalt and copper! The government recently signed a bill giving small miners permission to mine by hand. They are preparing to do just that. If they can make enough this way, they will have seed money for other projects. For example, they are helping the people of this same village prepare to build their own elementary school by teaching them how to make their own bricks. They can even cut their own timber to make the rafters. The only thing lacking will be laminated roofing, but perhaps with mining proceeds they will be able to help the village even with this.

Just a few days later, these hardy Christians returned to their city from the conference, and the trainer soon received another e-mail from them:

> As soon as I arrived back home, I began a marathon program. Every Saturday, I bring together Christians and those who live in a neighborhood near our city, to give them the teachings. This neighborhood for a long time has lacked electricity. As I write to you, we are in the process of putting up poles and purchasing electrical wire to deliver electricity to the neighborhood. We are taking old, unused posts from an old railway that is no longer viable. Our hope is that, at the end of three months, this neighborhood will be lit up.

We have not heard the end of the story from these brothers, nor have we heard the end of how God multiplies what people sacrificially invest. As children of the Creator, we have reason to risk in the midst of apparent lack. This risk is not blind trust, but trust in God. It is important to recall, as we risk for the Kingdom, that what we risk is not our own. What we risk is the "talent" God entrusted to us. The Bible explains: *"His divine power has given us everything we need for life and godliness through our knowledge of him who called us by his own glory and goodness."*[10] He has already given us all we need to honor Him. There is hope. There is certainty that God honors the faithfulness of His children. The church must be courageous in its expression of God's love. Real sacrifice takes courage. However, "a life incapable of significant sacrifice is also incapable of courageous action."[11]

In Conclusion

In Kingdom Mathematics we saw that God calls all of His children—rich or poor—to sacrificially give Him what is in their hand for the extension of His Kingdom. The motive is not to receive, but to allow God to use our gifts to glorify Him. When

---

[10] 2 Peter 1:3
[11] Holmes, quoted in Ruben, *A Guide to Prayer for Ministers and Other Servants*, 204.

we respond in loving obedience, He uses our sacrifice beyond our imaginations—whether or not we see the results. God calls us to give him whatever we have, wherever we are. The task is truly cosmic, but so is the multiplying power that God has released through His church to accomplish the task he has given it!

Many materially poor churches look first to the outside world for resources in order to minister wholistically. They develop a mentality of poverty, not realizing that looking to a primary source other than God is idolatry. God may indeed bring us resources from outside our communities, but our trust needs to remain first in Him.

We have seen stories of courageous men and women of the church, followers of Christ, who are representing and serving Jesus the Mayor in various sectors of their societies. We will meet still more of them. How we thank God for our brothers and sisters whose lives and actions illustrate the truth of His Word and principles!

Also in the next part are useful tools that enable local churches and church members to be doers of the Word, to represent Christ in their communities. The tools have been used all over the world for many years, helping followers of Christ pray, strategize, and demonstrate God's love to the world in which God has placed them. I pray you will find them useful, as well.

PART FOUR

Tools for Transformation

I tell you the truth, unless a kernel of wheat falls to the ground and dies, it remains only a single seed. But if it dies, it produces many seeds.

—John 12:24

Tools for Transformation

Part Four presents some of the planning and reporting tools that have been used by individuals and churches around the world to demonstrate God's love and agenda.

First, let me introduce the four categories of human need that we will use frequently in the tools in the coming chapters.

In the early 1980s, Harvest began to use a simple paradigm to help churches in Latin America think about balanced ministry in their materially poor communities. We used the statement that the Holy Spirit directed Luke, a Greek doctor, to write as he described Jesus' growth: *"Jesus grew in wisdom, in stature, and in favor with God and man."* [1] This passage gave us a simple, usable way to think of human development—and God's concerns. People were never commanded in Scripture to develop as Jesus did—yet He was the eternal God in human form. He was the only person to fully reflect God's intentions for a human being. We decided to use Luke's description of Jesus' growth as a model.

This short verse lists four categories of human development:

- Growth in "stature" represents physical development.
- Growth in "favor with God" indicates spiritual development.
- Growth in "favor with man" represents social development. [2]
- Growth in "wisdom" represents learning about and obeying God's ways, instructions, intentions, commands, and desires for all of our physical, spiritual, and social relationships.

---

[1] Luke 2:52

[2] Note that "social development" deals with God's intentions for interpersonal relationships. This differs from the concept of social transformation, which deals with deep change in an entire society or culture.

We have found Luke 2:52 to be a good model for individual, family, church, community, and societal growth. When we first began to use it as a paradigm for ministry, however, we were accused of being simplistic. We knew that universities devote entire departments to discover the factors that cause people and societies to flourish or flounder. We understood that human and social development can be described in more complex terms. But we did not believe it was necessary to master complexities in order to minister to the whole person—or introduce transformation to a nation. Complex academic methods of studying human and social development are useful in the right context, but these methods were unnecessarily complicated and abstract for the local churches that worked with us. We believed that Scripture—while deep enough to be mined by generations of skilled theologians—is also simple, realistic, and useful.

We were also accused of stretching the biblical text beyond its intention. We were told that such abuse of the text would fail, but two very early experiences convinced me that this little verse from Dr. Luke's pen would make a positive difference. The first happened in an impoverished neighborhood within Tegucigalpa, Honduras. I had been there the previous year and had taught about Luke 2:52 in a community meeting. Here's what happened one year later in the same neighborhood:

❖ As I was walking down a dirt road, a man I did not recognize came up to me with a big smile. In Spanish he said, "Jesus grew in wisdom, stature, and in favor with God and man. And so we should grow that way, too." I asked, "You are a Christian?" He said, "No, but I was at the meeting where you taught last year, and I remember that we need to develop like Jesus did." I regretted he was not my brother in Christ, but I was encouraged that this model had stayed in his mind all year.[3]

---

[3] Sources for stories marked by ❖ are listed in the Bibliography at the end of the book.

The second experience was in Brazil:

❖ I taught Luke 2:52 to a group of Brazilian missionaries with Youth With A Mission. They subsequently spread out all over Brazil. Two of the students were single women who ministered to a remote tribe of indigenous river people along the Amazon River. The literacy level was low, so they taught the message using stories and pictures. After teaching the tribe, the missionaries asked them to choose one of the four areas in which they wanted to work. Leadership emerged. The river people caught the vision so clearly that the missionaries appointed and discipled four elders and assistants to lead and manage village life according to the categories of Luke 2:52!

- Wisdom: The man in charge of wisdom became the leader of the community. He became a missionary himself, teaching this broader view of ministry to his tribesman up and down the river. A woman was trained to be the teacher. The community initiated a preschool, adult literacy class, and sewing classes.

- Physical: The man who led this area organized a community work project each Saturday. This was already a tradition, but it was never organized. He divided the people for their tasks, such as planting rice and preparing pasture land for cattle. Another person became a trained health-care worker for the village. Another was in charge of the community kitchen to provide food for the work projects every Saturday.

- Spiritual: The man in this position was the leader of the church, along with others. Another became a trained counselor. Another became a deacon. Another was put in charge of praise.

- Social: The man who led this area organized the villagers into sporting teams. He included women in community recreation—something new in their culture. The events were great sources of unity.

Local churches have appreciated this model for ministry. The Luke 2:52 paradigm has been easy to comprehend, remember, and put into practice. It has been used for over twenty years in thousands of churches, in multiple cultures, and on nearly every continent. Now, the tools presented in Part Four incorporate the same four areas of Jesus' growth—helping individuals and local churches carry out ministry to their neighbors. I have used them myself and have seen them used in thousands of applications around the world. I can heartily recommend them!

In Part Four

- We will examine tools to help individuals and local churches carry out small projects and intentionally impact their worlds with God's purposes and agenda.

- We will look at the *Discipline of Love*, a tool that helps *individual* believers develop the habit of service as they undertake acts of love for their families, churches, and communities. Real-life examples and reports are included.

- We will study *Seed Project Planning*, a planning tool that enables *local churches* and *small groups* to plan and to serve outside the church with small demonstrations of God's grace. Seed Project stories and reports are included.

- We will examine Planning for Community Transformation. This chapter includes real examples and tools to help local churches plan their community service over a period of time.

- We will also look at several tools that measure obedience and faithfulness in individual and corporate service.

Premises for Part Four

Premise 1: *Seeds have great implications for service—especially as they illustrate sacrifice—and the impact of our service is often proportional to our sacrifice.*

Seeds are one of the word pictures Jesus used in Scripture, and they have great implications for service. In fact, we have chosen to implement something we call "Seed Projects," based on the lessons we learn from seeds.

The most significant lesson about seeds comes from Jesus' prediction of His own death: *"I tell you the truth, unless a kernel of wheat falls to the ground and dies, it remains only a single seed. But if it dies, it produces many seeds."*[4]

Seeds illustrate sacrifice. Seeds must die in order to do what they were created to do! Unless they die, they cannot produce fruit. When they die, they produce great multiplication. Death is the ultimate sacrifice—for seeds, for human beings, and even for the Man who was God. Jesus made it clear to His disciples that the cost of discipleship was a denial of themselves—a death to everything except following Him. In the economy of God's Kingdom, it is this ultimate sacrifice that releases the power of healing, the power of salvation, and the power for transformation.

One of my favorite illustrations of sacrifice comes from India, where I had the privilege of sharing with a group of pastors:

> "Unless a kernel of wheat falls into the ground . . ."

❖ One pastor was from a very poor rural area. His congregation lived as an oppressed minority. He was not sure how to implement what he had heard, but he was convinced that he and his people needed to demonstrate God's love to the people among whom they lived. After the training, the Indian pastor taught his congregation what he had learned. The pastor suggested that the church women look for needs among their Hindu neighbors—needs that the Christians could meet. The women did just that.

---

[4] John 12:24

They found several Hindu women in the neighborhood who each had only one sari, the traditional dress for women. This was summertime. Summers are very hot and humid in that region, and saris must be washed after even one day of hard work and sweat. After she washed her only sari, a woman had to stay indoors all day while it dried in the sun.

The women reported their findings at church the next Sunday. The pastor then asked how many women in the congregation had three saris and would be willing to give one away. One by one, the women of the congregation raised their hands. The next morning, the women from the church visited their needy neighbors and gave them each a sari. The Hindu neighbors were deeply touched. Some even asked the Christian women to pray to the Christian God for their unborn babies. The director of the denomination told me that this action had a profound impact—not only on the Hindu community, but on the church. The Christians had previously seen themselves as a powerless, oppressed minority. After this, they realized they could make a difference in the community.

I have often wondered. Would the impact be different if a Christian NGO[5] came to the same village and distributed free clothing for everyone? The gift would have been larger. It would have met a greater physical need. But, I doubt if it would have had nearly the impact that was made by the few saris from the church women. The NGO's action would be appreciated, but people would think: "That's the job of an NGO, isn't it?" What came from the Christian women represented real sacrifice. It was their sacrifice that made a huge impact. Small initiatives, when they represent sacrifice, have great influence.

The seed principle is true. When our demonstration of God's love is sacrificial—when we die to ourselves in loving others—the impact will be far greater than if our service comes from our surplus. The kernel of wheat needs to "fall into the ground." It needs to die before it can make its intended impact.

---

[5] *NGO:* A non-governmental organization.

I also believe that the impact of service is most often proportional to sacrifice. I would state it this way:

- Less sacrifice results in less impact for the Kingdom.
- Greater sacrifice results in greater Kingdom impact.
- Impact is proportional to sacrifice.

Scripture supports this principle. Paul told us that sowing generously enables us to reap abundantly: *"Remember this: Whoever sows sparingly will also reap sparingly, and whoever sows generously will also reap generously."*[6] Generosity is a relative term. How it is defined depends on the resources of the giver—but we cannot truly sow "generously" without sacrifice. Even the smallest of seeds—sown sacrificially—can produce something mighty. Jesus taught:

The kingdom of heaven is like a mustard seed, which a man took and planted in his field. Though it is the smallest of all your seeds, yet when it grows, it is the largest of garden plants and becomes a tree.[7]

> ## Impact is proportional to sacrifice.

<u>*Premise 2*</u>: *It is God who brings the harvest. We must obediently plant the seeds, but it is God who makes projects fruitful.*

Jesus reminded the disciples that the impact of their service was not something for which they could take credit: *"I sent you to reap what you have not worked for. Others have done the hard work, and you have reaped the benefits of their labor."*[8]

It is the same for us. God has already been at work in the hearts of those to whom we minister, long before we begin. To take credit for what God has done is naive. It is even dangerous. It robs God of

---

[6] 2 Corinthians 9:6
[7] Matthew 13:31-32
[8] John 4:38

credit and glory. (Malachi asked: *"Will a man rob God?"*) When an impact for the Kingdom appears to come through our obedience, whom do we credit, both in our minds and with our mouths? Paul confirmed this: *"So neither he who plants nor he who waters is anything, but only God, who makes things grow."*[10]

The ultimate purpose of our obedient service is the expansion of Christ's reign! Jesus taught His disciples to pray that God's Kingdom would come and His will would be done, on earth as it is in heaven. Our purpose is to do His will and serve His Kingdom on earth—not to boast that great numbers came forward to accept Christ, that we taught a good Bible study, that our church is growing, or that we built a school or hospital or clinic.

> The objective is the extension of the Kingdom, not the growth of our church.

We need to remember that it is God who draws people to Himself. When I teach pastors in our training conferences, I often ask those from charismatic or Pentecostal churches to raise their hands. I then ask those from churches that are not charismatic or Pentecostal to raise their hands. Soon, everyone has been "classified." I first address those who identified themselves as neither Pentecostal nor charismatic:

> Suppose you are the pastor of a Baptist church. You work hard for months, even years, planting the seeds and sowing the soil in a new community. You proclaim and demonstrate the Gospel with energy, passion, and sacrifice. Then, a new ministry comes to town. The people you worked hard to win to Christ join the new Pentecostal church. How do you feel? What would you do?

[9] Malachi 3:8
[10] 1 Corinthians 3:7

In the conferences, pastors often laugh uncomfortably. Sometimes, they confess serious jealousy. They see the point. If it is God who draws people to His Kingdom, we must be concerned with the growth of His Kingdom, not ours. The same principle applies everywhere. Our sacrificial works of service must be done with the motivation and objective of building Christ's Kingdom—not taking pride in the fruit of our labor or the growth of our church.

A trainer of pastors in South America voiced a similar concern. "A church that is focused on numerical growth," she explained, "turns into an activist church, full of programs and methodologies, but missing the focus of the real purpose of the church of Christ."[11] She pointed to another analogy that relates seeds and church growth:

> Don't worry about the growth of your church. Focus on the purposes of your church. Keep watering and fertilizing and cultivating and weeding and pruning. God will grow His church to the size He wants it, at the rate that's best for your situation. . . . God may allow you to labor for years with little visible results. Don't be discouraged! Underneath the surface things are happening that you can't see. Roots are growing down and out, preparing for what is ahead. Even if you don't see the wisdom of what God is doing, you must trust God. Learn to live with the assurance that He knows what He's doing. . . . If you are building a ministry on God's eternal purpose, you cannot fail. It will prevail. . . . Just as with a bamboo tree, when the time is right God can change things overnight. What is most important is that you remain faithful to His purposes."[12]

Seeds are small and, at first glance, insignificant. They even experience sacrificial death. Then, directed by the Master Gardener, they produce a harvest. It is our task to continue to plant sacrificial seeds and cultivate obediently, as the Gardener directs—for His sake, not for our own.

---

[11] Ruth Concha, manuscript review (Peru: 2003).
[12] Warren, *The Purpose Driven Church,* 395.

Premise 3: Individuals and churches need discipline if they are to reflect the love of Christ as a lifestyle.

As I was reading *My Utmost for His Highest,* I was challenged by Oswald Chambers' insights on 2 Peter 1:5-8, which reads:

For this very reason, make every effort to add to your faith goodness; and to goodness, knowledge; and to knowledge, self-control; and to self-control, perseverance; and to perseverance, goodliness; and to goodliness, brotherly kindness; and to brotherly kindness, love. For if you possess these qualities in increasing measure, they will keep you from being ineffective and unproductive in your knowledge of our Lord Jesus Christ.

Chambers explained:

We are to "add" to our lives all that character means. No one is born either naturally or supernaturally with character; it must be developed. Nor are we born with habits—we have to form godly habits on the basis of the new life God has placed within us.[13]

We need discipline to reflect the love of Christ as a lifestyle. This is as true for local churches as it is for individuals. Peter wrote that character is developed by adding, and we rarely add to our character without intentional effort. The call in Peter's passage is to add the kind of discipline that leads to a lifestyle of love and maturity. As we know from Kingdom Mathematics, it is God's role to multiply— and He does.

Premise 4: Church outreach needs to include both individual and church-wide expressions of God's love, as a way of life.

Part Four presents two principal tools—Discipline of Love and Seed Project Planning. The more I have watched churches respond to our training, the more I have become aware of the danger of focusing *only* on Seed Projects, the second tool in this section.

---

[13] Chambers, *My Utmost for His Highest,* July 15.

Let me issue a word of warning. People are attracted to Seed Projects. Seed Projects produce visible, immediate, tangible results. They are appealing and powerful. They bring change. They engender enthusiasm. They are exciting—even dramatic. They make sense. I am concerned, however, that people seem less convinced of the importance of personal applications, as in the Discipline of Love. Both are exciting. Both are worthwhile. Both must be done.

Consistency is the key. If the church does corporate acts of love for its neighbors but its individual members do nothing, the world notices. If individuals serve their neighbors but the church does nothing, the world notices. Seed Projects might *seem* more impactful than an individual Discipline of Love. Yet, individual obedience—each believer's response to Christ's command to love his neighbor—yields far greater power for overall transformation.

There are other dangers if Seed Projects are the only expressions of wholistic ministry in a church:

- Seed Projects, by their nature, involve a small percentage of people. Perhaps thirty percent of the people in a church may do four Seed Projects a year. Yet, those who are *not* involved can think: "I'm involved—I attend a church that is wholistically engaged!" They assume they are actively serving. The "Seed Project excuse" may actually inhibit individuals from loving their neighbors!

- Those in the church who are involved in Seed Projects may see them as the only means by which they express God's love. They may think: "I've done my Seed Project, so now I'm finished." It's like saying: "I'm a Christian on Sunday, so I don't have to act like one the other days of the week!"

If I had to choose between the two tools, *I would choose to use the Discipline of Love.* I would encourage each and every person from a local church to be engaged in a disciplined lifestyle of service and love. When the individuals of a congregation are passionately demonstrating God's love in their community, the church—corporately—will do the same. The community will be touched.

Fortunately, we do not have to choose! The church can use both tools to reflect the Kingdom of God. In Discipline of Love, the individual is the Kingdom *ambassador*. In Seed Projects, the church is the *embassy* of the Kingdom. As the church plans its outreach, it needs to include *both* individual and church-wide expressions of God's love.

Doing both is more than coordinating two parallel programs. Doing both is a way of life that impacts the church's very DNA. It says: "This is who we are. This is what we do. We love our neighbors as ourselves, individually *and* corporately—whether we're at home, on our jobs, or together." It expands biblical transformation wherever people are touched by the church and its members.

These tools are only two methods of wholistic discipleship. Indeed, there are *many* ways for individuals and churches to demonstrate God's love to their neighbors, as we have seen. Yet, as tools, they have proven to be effective starting points, developing people's confidence and experience in ministering the whole of God's Good News. They are aids, like training wheels or a father's balancing hand as a child learns to ride a bicycle. When the new rider develops confidence, the aids are no longer needed for basic bicycling. But the rider must not stop using the balancing skills and techniques to reach greater levels of bicycling proficiency—and to train other new riders.

In the same way, when individuals and churches develop experience, confidence, and lifestyles of wholistic service, they do not need to refer each time to a Discipline of Love chart or a Seed Project Planning Guide. However, they should not forget the skills, techniques, disciplines, and balance learned as they demonstrate God's love to their neighbors—and they should use them to train others.

Service should be a lifestyle! When people at any stage of Christian maturity complete a project or a discipline, they do not have the luxury of smiling with satisfaction and storing their towels and basins . . . or their Seed Project evaluations. No, they are simply better prepared for their *next* demonstration of God's love and service!

If Jesus were our Mayor, I believe He would encourage His people—individually *and* corporately—to continue to plant small, sacrificial seeds. These would be the same kind of seeds of loving service that we see in Scripture and that we plant as we use the tools in this section. If Jesus were our Mayor, He would bless and multiply our sacrificial efforts, just as He did in Scripture—and continues to do today.

Visible transformation grows from small seeds, faithfully and obediently planted by those who love God and neighbor. As we look at the tools in the following chapters, we will continue to meet some of God's seed-planters who serve our Mayor in their local communities throughout the world.[14]

---

[14] See more tools, lessons, and transformational ministry stories on the Harvest Web site: www.harvestfoundation.org.

The Discipline of Love $\boxed{12}$
For Individual Followers of Christ

The church is a community of believers—a body, comprised of many individual members. Therefore, its outreach must include individual and church-wide expression of God's love. The Discipline of Love has been designed to help *individual* followers of Jesus develop the ability to better respond to others with God's love. It asks: *"Just as my community would change if Jesus were its Mayor—how would my family, church, and community change if Jesus were director of my relationships?"* Let me open this chapter with a statement I believe with all my heart:

> If the local church is going to transform its culture, it is much more important that *the individuals of the church* live consistent, *disciplined* lifestyles of *love* and service than if their churches conduct wholistic ministry projects!

Let's look at the italicized words. Just as salt, light, and yeast permeate and transform their environments, it is *the individuals of the church* who best permeate and change their cultures with Kingdom values. William Wilberforce presented legislation to abolish slavery many times, but it did not pass until a groundswell of individuals gained a biblical understanding of life and human dignity.

We also need to define *love*. People have many misconceptions about love—love is a feeling, love is spontaneous, people "fall" in love, love requires warm feelings. If this were correct, it would be impossible to have a "discipline" for love! But this exercise is more about obedient service than warm feelings. It is more about disciplined decisions than spontaneous goodness. It is more about faithfulness to God's commands than following our own desires.

Though our good deeds are worth nothing if they are not done in love,[1] that love is not a feeling. It is a faithful decision to serve others. This exercise challenges us to love God with all of our heart, soul, and mind—and to love our neighbor as ourselves.[2] I believe Jesus was saying that we demonstrate our love for God by showing love to *people*. Loving our neighbor is absolutely important to Jesus—it is showing our love for God!

Why does love require *discipline*? The Apostle Paul told his young protégé Timothy: *"Bodily exercise is all right, but spiritual exercise is much more important and is a tonic for all you do."*[3] There are many spiritual disciplines—such as prayer, Scripture reading, meditation, memorization, or fasting. These disciplines have a *vertical* emphasis and strengthen our love relationship with our Lord. People readily admit needing discipline for these![4] As with other spiritual exercises, we need personal discipline and God's empowerment to love others as He commands. By nature, we are selfish, and our broken cultures further "acculturate" us to love ourselves first. Loving our enemies, for example, does not come naturally. It is a principle of Kingdom culture. It requires commitment, love for God, great grace—and discipline.

Personal Development

God develops characteristics such as these in His people as we practice a discipline of loving others:

- *A broad and balanced response to the needs of others.* Our personalities and gifts cause us to respond to certain needs, but a discipline helps us develop broader sensitivity.

---

[1] 1 Corinthians 13:3
[2] Matthew 22:37-39
[3] 1 Timothy 4:8a (LB)
[4] The Discipline of Love is also a spiritual discipline, but its emphasis is *horizontal*. In some ways, it is both vertical and horizontal. God's love infuses us through our relationship with Christ, *and* we express His love to others.

- *Awareness of God's love.* The more we are aware and respond to others' needs, the more we experience and understand the breadth of God's compassion and love.

- *Creativity and reliance on God.* A discipline requires us to meet needs in new, creative ways that "stretch" us beyond our normal responses—and help us lean on God.

- *Ability to point to God as the source of love.* Those who receive our service can see that *God* is the source of our love.

- *Gracefulness in meeting others' needs.* Disciplined practice makes our service more natural and graceful.

- *Consistency in obedience.* Christ's call to be a channel of His grace to others is a call to a lifestyle of love and obedience. Consistency comes with intentional practice.

- *Intimacy with God.* God's love fills us, and His love flows through us. Intimacy with God is a source and result of listening to Him and doing His will.[5]

- *Loving our enemy.* A discipline gives us the opportunity to love people we normally find difficult to love. The effects are transforming—for them, for us, and even for cultures.

Cultural Transformation

God wants to transform broken cultures through the church— and through the individuals of the church. He has strategically placed us in our specific societies: *"From one man he made every nation of men, that they should inhabit the whole earth; and he determined the times set for them and the exact places where they should live."*[6] He gives us authority and responsibility!

Here are some ways that I believe God allows such a discipline to transform cultures:

- *The big agenda.* God allows us to represent His big agenda to restore *all things* through our daily actions. (Picture many ambassadors consciously representing God in all of life!)

---

[5] John 14:23, John 15:4
[6] Acts 17:26b

- *Agents of change.* We have the opportunity to be salt, light, yeast. Like these elements, we can gradually change our environments—just by doing what we were created to do.

- *Kingdom visibility.* We identify and then model Kingdom values in ways that our culture can observe and understand. Jesus told His disciples that the watching world would observe their love for one another and know they belonged to Him.[7]

- *Director of our relationships.* Cultural transformation begins as individuals honor God in all of their relationships. Jesus is not only Mayor, but director of relationships!

- *A clear message for skeptical people.* As we communicate the Good News by our deeds, we "speak" to cultures that are hungry to see people live by the words they speak.

Areas of Need and Contexts for Service

The Discipline of Love helps us serve four *Areas of Need* in three *Contexts for Service,* as the sample plan indicates. (The sample shows one person's exercises and is only a model.)

Areas of Need are those used by Luke[8] to describe Jesus' growth:

1. *Wisdom* includes learning and applying God's intentions for all of life. It is not the same as intellectual stature, educational experience, mental development, or knowledge.

   <u>*Example:*</u> *Learning God's instructions for social relationships*

2. *Physical* includes any needs related to the physical world.

   <u>*Examples:*</u> *Health, water, shelter, food, sanitation, employment*

3. *Spiritual* includes all spiritually related needs.

   <u>*Examples:*</u> *Need for God, spiritual salvation, prayer, worship*

4. *Social* includes interaction with other persons.

   <u>*Examples:*</u> *Friendship, activity that fosters a sense of community, accountability, relational support*

---

[7] John 13:35
[8] Luke 2:52

Discipline of Love

| | | Areas of Need | | |
		Wisdom	Physical	Spiritual	Social
Contexts for Service	**Family**	**1.** Discuss one Proverb and how to apply it during family devotions each day this week	**2.** Wash dishes after evening meal three times this week	**3.** Ask a different child to lead family prayer each day this week	**4.** Go with my spouse on a date without the children
	Church	**5.** Focus my devotions this week on applying the sermon	**6.** Volunteer to help in the church office on the weekend	**7.** Take 15 min. each day this week to pray for our pastor and elders	**8.** Take a child from church on an outing (a child from a single-parent home)
	Community Jerusalem Judea Samaria	**9.** Visit local leaders to learn about community needs and ask how I can help	**10.** Pick up trash on the streets each day this week as I walk	**11.** Pray with a co-worker about her problems with her sons	**12.** Play football with neighbor-hood kids

Contexts for Service are Family, Church, and Community:

1. *Family* includes spouses, children, parents, brothers, sisters, in-laws, extended family, roommates, and close friends.

2. *Church* includes our own church leaders, members, small groups, and church building—but goes beyond our own local fellowships to include *all followers of Christ.*

3. *Community* includes people who are not believers—those who are *outside the church.*

   Most Community exercises should serve people in "Jerusalem," the place we spend most of our time—at our work, school, daily activities, or neighborhoods.

   Other Community exercises should impact *"Judea"* and *"Samaria,"* where we go beyond our own environments to influence city or regional issues or to serve people with special needs—the sick, prisoners, homeless, immigrants, or lonely.[9]

---

[9] Acts 1:8.

Discipline of Love Stories

The following real Discipline of Love accounts come from many corners of the world.[10] They will encourage and challenge you as they help you see how to use the tool for service. The tool is intended to be a flexible categorizing system. Enjoy it!

Family

Box 1   Family/Wisdom: An American family met to study *BASICS*, Harvest's wholistic discipleship material, in order to *learn* about new ways to serve others.

Box 2   Family/Physical: A teacher in Africa reported this story:

One of my student pastors has only one pair of shoes. They are so worn that he fasted until he had enough money to buy shoes. He then saw that his aunt's clothes were almost in rags. He felt challenged to love his neighbor as himself, use the money to buy clothes for her, and trust God for shoes.

Box 3   Family/Spiritual: One lady was reading a book about praying for family members who are not followers of Christ. She arranged for her immediate family to meet together and pray for each family member who is not a believer.

Box 4   Family/Social: Husbands from several countries showed love to their wives with thoughtful acts. One man asked his wife to go to a movie, which was unusual. Another man bought flowers for his wife and wrote a loving note.

Church

Box 5   Church/Wisdom: An American Christian held a group discussion at church about world events and Islam after the September 11 terrorist attacks. The group wanted to *learn* how God wanted them to respond. (*Note:* They also collected funds for shoes for children in Afghanistan.)

---

[10] All exercise sources are listed in the Bibliography at the end of the book. In this chapter, *direct quotes* are indicated by italics.

Box 6   <u>Church/Physical</u>: Notice the variety in this report from South America!

> *The toy library at church is very hot. Gabriela gave one of her wedding gifts—a big white fan. She also fixed a special meal to use the new dishes given to the church. On a hot day, she brought her blender and prepared delicious Swiss lemonade for the adolescents and worship team at church.*

Box 7   <u>Church/Spiritual</u>: An American couple learned of an elderly church woman who could no longer see well enough to read her Bible. They found Bible cassette tapes, delivered them, and spent a delightful afternoon together. They have since found a large magnifying glass to help her read the Word.

Box 8:   <u>Church/Social</u>: One person decided to serve his church staff. He purchased snacks, put them in a basket, and took them to the receptionist's desk at church, with this note:

> *Dear Church Staff:*
> *It is good to celebrate the relationships that God has given us with each other. In this way we can both honor Him and encourage and enjoy one another. I hope you can use these refreshments for that kind of celebration today.*
>
> > *Your brother in Jesus . . .*

Community (Jerusalem, Judea, Samaria)

Box 9   <u>Community/Wisdom</u>: Here is an example from an African colleague:

> *My wife and I live in a rural community. Basic hygiene is lacking. Mothers allow children to drink polluted water; their children suffer from diarrhea, malaria, and cholera. My wife is a nurse. We organized a seminar on basic hygiene practices for community mothers. Fifty mothers attended. I spoke, saying God created us in His image and wants us to care for His creation—and bless our children. Then, my wife talked about staying healthy and preventing diarrhea and malaria.*

Box 10 <u>Community/Physical</u>:

> *Human Physical Needs*—A woman in Brazil met an elderly man selling crafts in her neighborhood. He had been discharged from a hospital and needed money to return to his home state. The woman talked to her neighbors. They collected bus money and accompanied him to the bus.

> *Neighborhood Physical Needs*—An American Christian mowed a neighbor's lawn. The community appearance was improved, and the neighbor was grateful for the help.

Box 11 <u>Community/Spiritual</u>: An African family showed God's love to its neighbors and related the following story:

> *Our neighbors' lives are dominated by the worship of idols. After Christmas, my family decided to express God's love to our neighbors in this very poor community. We decided to have a small party for the community children. We were overwhelmed when 120 children came to our home! In addition, some mothers stayed. They ate, drank, danced, and learned to sing Christian songs. This is the first time some of the children had ever had a celebration. Twenty of them gave their lives to Christ.*

Box 12 <u>Community/Social</u>: A colleague reported the impact made when two seminary students babysat a Buddhist child:

> *A Buddhist woman lived near a Bible school in Asia. One afternoon, she had to leave her young child home alone. Two students from the school saw the child, talked with her, played games, and stayed until the mother returned. The mother was very relieved. Through this demonstration of love, she came to know Christ.*

Discipline of Love Quiz—Classify These Real Exercises

To check your understanding, classify these true examples. Some stories may fit into more than one category. Choose the Box Number that best defines the category of service.

1. ***Meal for Sick Neighbor:*** Here is a report from Africa, but it could happen anywhere:

   My neighbor got sick. My wife and I took our lunch over to the neighbor's home and shared our meal with the family of nonbelievers. It was good, and they welcomed us.

   Box Number: _____

2. ***Prayer Partners:*** One person asked the people at church to write their names on a piece of paper and put the paper in a box. They each then drew out a name and agreed to pray for the person whose name they had.   **Box Number:** _____

3. ***Plans for a Block Watch Program:*** One couple helped organize a Neighborhood Block Watch program, in which neighbors are trained to be alert to danger or crime. To begin, the couple organized a Block Watch party so the neighbors could get to know each oth   **Box Number:** _____

4. ***A Blessing:*** A staff member's husband purchased fabric in a Central American market. The husband uses it as a "prayer shawl." From time to time, he puts it over his and his wife's shoulders and prays a special prayer of blessing for his wife.

   Box Number: _____

5. ***A Pastor Makes Shopping Easier for His Wife:*** A pastor from Asia prayed about how to serve his wife. Shopping with two small children was difficult for her. He could help shop or watch the children, but he wanted a long-term solution. The Lord put on his mind to teach his wife to shop on the Internet, which he did in a two-hour lesson.

   Box Number: _____

6. ***May I Have a Piece of Your Tortilla?*** A Central America colleague related an encounter:

   I was talking with a street boy. Somebody had given him a tortilla filled with eggs. I asked him if I could have a small piece. Immediately, he gave me one. He could not believe that a middle-class person would ask him for food.

*I told him that what he had given me came from God. He
wondered about that! I insisted that it was God who gave
me the piece of tortilla because God first gave it to him. I
explained that God loves him and takes care of him, even
on the streets. After our conversation, I invited him to drink
a glass of orange juice with me. When it came time to say
good-bye, I asked him, "Who gave you the glass of orange
juice?" He immediately said, "God gave it to me."*

Box Number: _____

7. ***Welcome to a New Employee***: It was the first day at a new
job for a young, shy American. A Christian who worked in
the same office bought a potted flower and wrote, "Welcome!
Glad you're here!" He knew the first days on a new job are
stressful and wanted to wish her God's blessing.

Box Number: _____

Compare your answers with those at the end of this chapter.

Using the Tool—Discipline of Love

A blank Discipline of Love matrix is included for you in this
chapter.

We recommend that you do *one exercise a week*. There are twelve
exercises, so it will take *three months* to complete the exercises.

- *Attempt exercises in numerical order.* Begin with Box 1
  (Family/Wisdom) to help your family understand God's
  wisdom for an aspect of life. Continue in numerical order.

- *Exercises may take from 30 minutes to several hours*—or more.
  Begin with short exercises that do not exceed *one hour*.

- *Begin to identify possible needs early in the week.* Ask God to
  open your eyes early in the week.

- *If you cannot identify* service in a category during the week, use
  the time for prayer and meditation. Journal your insights.

- The Discipline of Love tool can be repeated frequently
  until demonstrating God's love in all areas of life becomes a
  spontaneous habit. It is designed to reshape us.

There are *five steps* to each Discipline of Love exercise:

1. *Pray.* Prepare spiritually. Ask God to help you identify a specific need to meet. Listen to the ideas the Holy Spirit gives you, perhaps in a daily prayer time. You are not only identifying a way to help someone, you are also seeking to know the good works that God prepared for you to do.[11]

2. *Identify the exercise.* Write a few words to describe your planned exercise in the appropriate box of the matrix.

3. *Act.* Carry out your service. The exercise should:
   - Point to God's concern—not bring attention to yourself
   - Not impose service that would not be welcomed by the one being served
   - Take you beyond what you would otherwise do
   - Be a sacrifice—but not an excuse from other priorities

4. *Reflect.* Within the next twenty-four hours, reflect and make notes in a journal. (A sample is included.) It also works to e-mail these simple responses to an accountability partner:
   - What did you do?
   - What were the results (for the persons served)?
   - What did God teach you?

5. *Summarize.* Return to the matrix. Check the box and mark the date when you complete each exercise. You can use this summary page as the first page of your journal.

We also encourage people to have *accountability* in place:

- *If you do this discipline with a small group*, the leader provides guidance and accountability.

- *If you do this exercise alone*, meet with an accountability partner once or twice a month for encouragement and prayer.

- At the end, give your leader or accountability partner a copy of your journal, matrix, and a written reflection. It can be helpful if that person writes a short reflection for you.

---

[11] Ephesians 2:10

Discipline of Love

		Areas of Need		
		Wisdom	**Physical**	**Spiritual**	**Social**
Contexts for Service	**Family**	1. Description: ❑ Date_____	2. Description: ❑ Date_____	3. Description: ❑ Date_____	4. Description: ❑ Date_____
	Church	5. Description: ❑ Date_____	6. Description: ❑ Date_____	7. Description: ❑ Date_____	8. Description: ❑ Date_____
	Community Jerusalem Judea Samaria	9. Description: ❑ Date_____	10. Description: ❑ Date_____	11. Description: ❑ Date_____	12. Description: ❑ Date_____

Exercise Steps

- Pray—Prepare spiritually
- Identify the need
- Act—Meet the need
- Reflect and journal
- Summarize

Exercise Guidelines

- Point to God's concern—do not bring attention to yourself
- Do not impose service that would not be welcomed by the one being served
- Go beyond what you would otherwise do
- Sacrifice—but do not neglect other priorities

Sample Journal

Box Number: 8   **Date**: April 22   **Context/Area**: Church/Social

1. What was the need? How did you meet it?

I decided to do something to enhance the staff members' relationships. I purchased snacks and took them to the church for the staff. I delivered them in a basket, with a note:

Dear Church Staff: It is good to celebrate the relationships that God has given us with each other. In this way we honor Him and encourage and enjoy one another. I hope you can use these refreshments for that kind of celebration today-during your break times, during lunch, or whenever you find opportunity.

Your brother in Jesus

2. How did you spiritually prepare for the exercise?

I asked the Lord to use this expression to build staff relationships.

3. Did this exercise help the one(s) you serve move toward God's intentions? How?

If the staff read the note, it pointed to God's desire that they enjoy good relationships. Refreshments could give them more fellowship than they would have had.

4. Did this exercise help you move toward God's intentions? How?

The purchase, assembly, and delivery took two hours. I will need to stay at the office tonight to catch up. This helped me practice sacrificing my personal time for others.

5. What have you learned from this exercise?

I could have been more specific in pointing out the purpose of the service. I should have put a ribbon on the basket with the words "Basket of Joy - Celebrate One Another!"

Advanced Study and Application

Here are options for advanced study, application, and reflection. These work well where a course is being taught and the Discipline of Love is applied throughout the course.

Advanced Pace

- *Option 1* (4-6 weeks): Each week, do four exercises for a different context. The first week's exercises are for the Family context; the second week's are for the Church; the next week's are for the Community. Do only one exercise per day. If unsuccessful, attempt the same area/context the next day. If unsuccessful again, go to the next area/context. Take two weeks at the end to reattempt missing exercises.

- *Option 2* (4 weeks): Attempt four exercises per week. Do them as you naturally encounter them, not in numerical order. Record the exercises in your journal. Note which you did not do—and why.

Advanced Exercises

Select larger exercises, and complete one per week. Each exercise should take from several hours to one-half day. Do them in any sequence. Keep a journal, and be accountable.

Additional Context for Service

Add another *Context for Service,* Distant Community, to serve people who live in other communities, regions, or nations—to respond to needs at *"the ends of the earth." (Examples include unreached people groups and victims of natural disasters or wars.)*

	Wisdom	**Physical**	**Spiritual**	**Social**
Distant Community The Ends of the Earth	13	14	15	16

Biblical Advice and Encouragement

Scripture gives us further insight about discipline and service:

- It is God who compels us to change our priorities: *"It is God who works in you to will and to act according to his good purpose."* [12] He also empowers and equips us.

- God is the source of our sensitivity and love: *"I will remove from you your heart of stone and give you a heart of flesh. And I will put my Spirit in you and move you to follow my decrees and be careful to keep my laws."* [13]

- As we discover His plan for our service, we need to articulate it in practical ways: *"We are God's workmanship, created in Christ Jesus to do good works, which God prepared in advance for us to do."* [14]

Let's also look at biblical encouragement to select the exercises.

- God wants to communicate with us. *"Whether you turn to the right or to the left, your ears will hear a voice behind you, saying, 'This is the way; walk in it.'"* [15] Jesus said: *"My sheep listen to my voice; I know them, and they follow me."* [16]

- Love is our measuring stick. *"Love is patient, love is kind. It does not envy, it does not boast, it is not proud. It is not rude, it is not self-seeking . . . rejoices with the truth. It always protects, always trusts, always hopes, always perseveres."* [17]

- God is at work—join Him:. *"My Father is always at his work to this very day, and I, too, am working. . . . The Son can do nothing by himself but only what he sees his Father doing."* [18] We need to find out what God is doing—and join Him. [19]

---

[12] Philippians 2:13
[13] Ezekiel 36:26b-27
[14] Ephesians 2:10
[15] Isaiah 30:21b
[16] John 10:27
[17] 1 Corinthians 13:4-7
[18] John 5:17,19a
[19] Ideas from Blackaby et al, *Experiencing God*, 14-15.

- God often directs us through His Word. "One Another" verses, listed here, readily spark ideas for service.[20] If we meditate on them or other Scripture, God can direct us to acts of service that honor Him and show love to others.

"ONE ANOTHER" VERSES

1. **Be devoted** to one another in **brotherly love**. (Romans 12:10)

2. **Honor** one another above yourselves. (Romans 12:10)

3. **Love** one another. (John 13:34-35, Romans 13:8)

4. **Accept** one another. (Romans 15:7)

5. **Serve** one another in love. (Galatians 5:13)

6. **Carry** each other's burdens. (Galatians 6:2)

7. **Bear with** one another in love. (Ephesians 4:2)

8. **Bear with** each other and **forgive** grievances against one another. (Colossians 3:13)

9. **Confess** your sins to one another. (James 5:16)

10. **Pray** for each other. (James 5:16)

11. **Be kind** and **compassionate** to one another. (Ephesians 4:32)

12. **Forgive** each other, just as in Christ God forgave you. (Ephesians 4:32)

13. **Spur** one another on toward love and good deeds. (Hebrews 10:24)

14. **Encourage** one another and build each other up. (1 Thessalonians 5:11)

15. **Encourage** one another daily . . . so that none may be hardened by sin's deceitfulness. (Hebrews 3:13)

16. **Build** others up according to their needs. (Ephesians 4:29)

17. **Share with** God's people who are in need. (Romans 12:13)

18. **Live in harmony** with one another. (Romans 12:16)

---

[20] This is a partial list of verses that use the phrase "one another" or "each other" in the New International Version. Verses are not quoted in full. Please read their full context in Scripture. Emphases have been added in each verse.

19. **Encourage** each other with these words. (1 Thessalonians 4:18)

20. **Consider** others better than yourselves . . . look to the interests of others. (Philippians 2:3-4)

21. **Speak** to one another with psalms, hymns and spiritual songs. (Ephesians 5:19)

22. **Teach** and **admonish** one another with all wisdom, and as you sing psalms, hymns and spiritual songs with gratitude in your hearts to God. (Colossians 3:16)

23. **Instruct** one another. (Romans 15:14)

24. **Submit** to one another out of reverence for Christ. (Ephesians 5:21)

25. **Greet** one another with a holy kiss. (Romans 16:16)

Apprenticeship to Jesus

As we carry out the Discipline of Love, God will help us discover opportunities to love Him and others—as apprentices to Jesus. In *The Divine Conspiracy*, Dallas Willard asked: *"How would Jesus lead my life if He were I?"* Willard then suggested that we begin where we spend much of our time—at our jobs:

> Consider just your job, the work you do to make a living. This is one of the clearest ways possible of focusing upon apprenticeship to Jesus. To be a disciple of Jesus is, crucially, to be learning from Jesus how to do your job as Jesus himself would do it. . . .
>
> The specific work to be done—whether it is making ax handles or tacos, selling automobiles or teaching kindergarten, doing investment banking or serving in political office, evangelizing or running a Christian education program, performing in the arts or teaching English as a second language—is of central interest to God. He wants it well done. It is work that should be done, and it should be done *as Jesus himself would do it.*[21]

---

[21] Willard, *The Divine Comedy*, 285-286.

Let me expand on that thought. We need to be alert to the people God brings to us in our local communities. Living and growing as apprentices to Jesus, we must not only do our jobs with excellence, but serve and love the people He has placed there—*just as He would!*

Final Reflections

Here are some suggestions to cover as final reflections:

1. What are your areas of strength and weakness in service?
2. Have you grown closer to the Lord through this exercise?
3. Relate which exercise you believe best served other people.
4. In what specific ways do you hope to develop your ability to demonstrate God's love through your lifestyle?

In Conclusion

As we close the Discipline of Love chapter, allow me to give this reminder. We are not only growing in self-discipline or good works, but we are expressing our love for our great and loving God by loving those He brings to us. May we continually serve our families, churches, and communities—*as if He were director of our relationships.*

Answers to Discipline of Love Quiz

1. Box 10	2. Box 7	3. Box 12
4. Box 3	5. Box 2	6. Box 9
7. Box 12		

Seed Project Planning $\boxed{13}$

Let's imagine that Jesus really is our local Mayor. He has called a meeting of His "Task Force," and we—the local church—are there. He wants us to carry out His agenda. "How?" we ask. He reminds us that seeds work in small, sacrificial ways. We nod in agreement. He sketches out for us something called Seed Projects—and proceeds to tell us that people all over the world use them to serve His agenda. Somehow, we know that He is about to tell us some good stories . . .

"You People Really Know the God You Serve"

❖ A church in West Africa did a Seed Project to demonstrate God's love in one of the country's most densely populated towns—a slum community lacking toilets and garbage collection. Through a local radio station, the church that was planning the project invited the community people to join them in a clean-up exercise. Church members visited the area ahead of time to interact with local people and show the *Jesus* film. On the day of the project, a massive number of community people came, and the church that planned the project brought two bus loads of its members. The interaction between the two groups was unique. It was difficult to know which people were church members and which were not. The people sang together, collected garbage, and weeded together. Within an hour, a vast place had been neatly cleaned!

A Muslim opinion leader of the area actively took part. The next day he met with the pastors of the church and said, "If I ask my fellow Moslem believers in the mosque to come out for this exercise, they will never come. You Christians come from so far away to work with us, joyfully ignoring all these smells. You people really know the God you serve."[1]

---

[1] Sources for stories marked by ❖ are listed in the Bibliography at the end of the book.

Plowing for an Enemy

❖ An Asian pastor went to a training conference. Afterwards, while visiting an area church, he taught the lesson on Seed Projects. He learned of a non-Christian man who had five children. This man could not prepare his rice paddies before the rainy season. He had been ill, and he only had one ox. The pastor discussed this with the church members, who are from a different ethnic group than this man. Historically, their tribes have fought. In spite of traditional inter-ethnic animosity, the church members wanted to do a Seed Project. They took six of their oxen to this man's rice paddies and helped him prepare his fields for planting. The pastor reported that this action of kindness—especially across ethnic lines—had a great impact on the sick man and his family. During another visit to the area, the pastor learned that the man's oldest daughter had become a believer and had been baptized. The rest of the family began coming to church and learning about the Christian faith. The man himself wanted to learn about the Christian faith in his own tongue, so he and some church members constructed a building to hold services in the man's mother tongue. According to reports, there has been a growing unity between the two ethnic groups in the village.

God's Love for Mental Patients

❖ In South America, a local church planned a Seed Project to serve people who live in "shelter homes" for mental patients who suffer from senile dementia, depression, and anxiety. The church members visited two shelter homes, spent time with the residents, talked about Jesus, and shared small gifts prepared by the ladies from the church. They explained that the gifts were an expression of God's love. The team invited people to accept Christ as Lord and Savior. Two people responded—Rosa and Elizabete. The people in the homes were impacted, as were the church members who visited.

Resources for Battered Women

❖ An American Sunday School class planned a Seed Project to sort and organize items donated to a shelter for battered women. The shelter home is a secret location where women and children stay, temporarily, when they have escaped dangerous living situations. They often bring few items with them—and have nothing with which to care for themselves or their children. People from the community donate clothing and useful items, but the shelter staff was too busy to organize and use them. Two storage sheds were overflowing with donations. A Seed Project team from a local church sorted and rearranged the sheds and listed what was available. They found many items the shelter and its residents needed immediately. As they worked, some of the team talked with the women who were staying at the shelter. Others talked with the children. At the end of the day, the team joined hands and prayed with the supervisor of the center. To follow up, one of the team members found donated Bibles for the women to read at the shelter and take with them as they leave.

Seed Projects: A Simple Definition

These were Seed Projects. Seed Projects are **short, small, simple** ministry activities. They are done by **local churches**, use **local resources**, and **demonstrate God's love** to those **outside the church**—whether in a South American shelter home, an Asian rice paddy, a densely populated slum in Africa, or an American battered women's shelter. They are small efforts, but their combined impact has enormous potential.

Seed Projects: Purposes

Local churches can use Seed Projects to demonstrate God's love to their communities. Seed Projects also accomplish three principle purposes within the church, itself:

☐ Wholistic evangelism and lifestyle

☐ Freedom from dependency

☐ Experience and confidence for larger, ongoing ministry

1. *Wholistic evangelism and lifestyle.* Seed Projects are natural components of evangelism and discipleship. They help churches develop a lifestyle of wholistic ministry.

2. *Freedom from dependency.* Seed Projects demonstrate that local churches can do wholistic ministry without reliance on outside resources.

3. *Experience and confidence for larger, ongoing ministry.* Seed Projects provide experience in project planning and implementation. They enlarge a local church's confidence for ongoing wholistic ministry projects. They often lead that church to larger demonstrations of God's love.

This chapter opened with four Seed Project examples—from Africa, Asia, South America, and the United States. The people of these communities experienced God's love and concern through wholistic evangelism. The local churches ministered without seeking outside resources. These churches, like others around the world, are developing lifestyles of wholistic service and are gaining confidence and experience for God to use them in even greater ways.

Seed Projects: Characteristics

The following characteristics are valuable guidelines for Seed Projects. (They are not rigid rules, but should be followed whenever possible.)

1. *Seed Projects should be covered in prayer.*
   - Seed Projects are identified, led, and empowered by the Holy Spirit, through prayer. They are done in conscious response to the commands of Jesus, in the power of His Spirit. Prayer should be a significant focus before, during, and after the project.
   - Ministry projects that are not initiated and sustained by prayer are not likely to be empowered by the Holy Spirit— or have Kingdom Mathematics results.
   - God made Nehemiah aware that the wall of Jerusalem had been broken and the gates burned! From the moment he heard of the problem, he was constantly in prayer—when

he got the king's permission, when the wall was being built, when he faced opposition, and afterwards. Everything he did was bathed in prayer. We need to do the same.

> ## Seed Project Characteristics
>
> 1. Covered in prayer
> 2. Compassionate—not manipulative
> 3. Motivated by God's intentions
> 4. Thoughtfully planned
> 5. Simple and short
> 6. Done with local resources
> 7. Directed toward those outside the church
> 8. Those who benefit participate
> 9. Spiritual impact where appropriate
> 10. Evaluated by Kingdom standards

❖ God still directs projects through prayer! A staff member taught Seed Projects in Mexico. He divided the class into separate small groups to pray and plan a Seed Project of their choosing. He walked quietly from group to group, smiling to hear how God was "assigning" each small group a *different* role in the *same* project—cleaning the local beach for the community.

2. *Seed Projects reflect God's heart of compassion for brokenness. They are not manipulative tools for evangelism.*

- Seed Projects give us the opportunity to obey Jesus' command to love our neighbor, unconditionally. If salvation and church growth are the principal motives for our service, our efforts become manipulative. Jesus did not manipulate. He healed people because it reflected His Father's heart. Some acknowledged Him as Lord, and others did not. We, too, should serve because we are obedient to love our neighbor—and for no other reason.

- There often is a harvest after Seed Projects—but we may not see it. We need to celebrate when we see Kingdom results— and when we do not see the fruit of our faithfulness.

3. *Seed Projects are motivated by God's intentions and are carried out with God's strength.*

    - Traditional projects are often undertaken when a need is seen, felt, or expressed by local people—or when outside resources are available. But this can be a trap—doing good works, carried out in human strength, motivated by human compassion. Christian ministry should be different. It should reflect God's intentions for people, not ours.

    - Seed Projects should be chosen by first seeking God's will, praying, reading Scripture, and becoming familiar with the community. We should ask, "Father, what do You want us to do?" We should be motivated by God's intentions, independent of the needs we see around us. It should be God who directs our service, rather than "felt need."[2] Felt need and God's direction will often merge, but we need to be careful that felt need is not the primary motivation for our action.

4. *Seed Projects should be thoughtfully planned.*

    - When Jesus spoke of "counting the cost" for sacrificial discipleship, He alluded to planning as a logical necessity for successful results.[3] Planning includes preparation, prayer, writing, implementation, and evaluation. Included in this chapter is a tool to plan a Seed Project, covering these steps:

        ☑ State the problem or need

        ☑ State God's intentions concerning that need

        ☑ Describe a ministry activity or project that expresses God's intentions

        ☑ State the area of need that will be met by the project

        ☑ List project steps, people to consult, resources needed, persons responsible, and completion date for each step

---

[2] *Felt need:* Any need that people consciously lack and desire; anything perceived by people as something they need. Jesus only did what the Father intended (John 5:19)—even when He ministered to people's felt needs.

[3] Luke 14:28

☑ Check the plan to see where various areas of need are addressed

☑ Check the plan to see where each Seed Project Characteristic is reflected—and have a reason for any not reflected

- Planning does not eliminate the leadership of the Holy Spirit, as some fear. Some pastors hesitate to plan their sermons, wanting not to squelch the Spirit's inspiration as they preach. In the same way, some local churches feel led to respond to a community need, but do not make plans. Yet, Scripture reminds us that we have to count the cost to build a tower, that generals count the size of the enemy army before engaging in battle, that the ant prepares for the winter by gathering food, and that the walls in Jerusalem were rebuilt by careful plans. Planning is important—and good planning requires the Spirit's guidance. We can help the beaten man on the Jericho road without stopping to plan, but we need to plan whenever we can!

5. *Seed Projects must be simple and short, small and uncomplicated.*

- Seed Projects should be simple and short. The projects themselves should take no more than one or two days, though planning and preparation take longer.

Small Mountains First!

My young grandson loves his grandfather and will do almost anything I ask him to do. I love to climb mountains. If I would ask him, "Do you want to climb a mountain with Grandpa?" he would say, "Oh, yes!"

But he would fall, scrape his hands and knees, get bruises, struggle, and not have a good time. The next time I would ask, "Do you want to climb a mountain with Grandpa?" he would say, "No, Grandpa—it's too hard." Why? I asked him to do something beyond his experience and ability.

It's the same with churches. Don't ask them to climb mountains before they learn to walk! They need to gain experience and confidence first.

- There are several benefits to small ministry projects. First, God honors and brings great results to faithful, small works— He increases by *multiplication*, not addition. Second, small projects prepare people to carry out larger projects. People grow in faith and ability as they attempt and complete small projects, and small projects allow people to fail without major consequences. (If large projects fail, people are discouraged and unwilling to try again, but small-project failures can teach helpful lessons.) Third, numerous small projects— together—can make a large impact on communities. The impact of small projects increases as people develop a *lifestyle* of ministry and service.

6. *Seed Projects are to be done with local resources.*

- Seed Projects begin by using local resources—resources that already exist in the community. They do not come from the outside, from the church's denominational headquarters or a resource agency like World Vision or the United Nations. The local resources do not always come only from the local church, however. The church is also a member of the community. If the church builds a bridge over a swampy community road, the whole community can and probably should provide labor or be involved in raising funds to buy construction supplies.

- Outside resources can be helpful, but *when* and *how* they are introduced is very important. The local church must be sacrificially investing its own resources in ministry *before* receiving outside resources. If outside resources come first, powerlessness and dependency are reinforced. Local initiative is stifled. People learn to look to man—not God—to meet their needs.

- Outside resources are best used when: (a) people have already demonstrated a willingness to sacrificially use their own resources; (b) outside resources are not substitutes for local resources; (c) outside resources produce a multiplication of local resources; and (d) people understand that God ultimately provides all resources.

7. *Seed Projects are directed toward those outside the church.*

- We should not express God's love only to other Christians. We serve community members because Jesus commanded us to love our neighbor as ourselves. Ministering to the needs of those inside the church is good and necessary, but Seed Projects are designed to help churches demonstrate God's love *outside* the church.

8. *Those who benefit from the Seed Projects should also participate in them, as possible.*

- When those who are being helped are involved in the process of planning and helping, they have the dignity of participating in their healing. Doing things for people who are capable of participating—but not involving them—is paternalism. In fact, we are foolish if we do not utilize their first-hand knowledge. People who participate in a ministry project also have a greater sense of ownership. They are more likely to maintain the completed project, improve it, make it useful, and develop further projects.

- Ultimately, to not involve those being helped robs them of the dignity God has given them. Perhaps a church has decided to repair a widow's home. She's not strong, she doesn't know carpentry, and she's poor. The church might think, "She can't

---

Salt, Anyone?

In our conferences I like to ask, "How many of you like salt?" Most raise their hands. "Okay," I say, "please do something for me. When you get home, fill a spoon with salt and eat it all." They cannot hide the look on their faces! "I thought you said you like salt!" I say. They say, "Yes, but not like that—it's too concentrated." The same is true for the church. We're too concentrated. We are salt for the world, not for the church! We need to come out of the salt shaker. We need to get the church into the community. We need to "unchurch" the churched!

Dignity

One of our staff accompanied churches that planned to fix a sagging roof for an ailing widow. Her mud-and-thatch home was beyond repair. The churches decided to build a new home for her of block and concrete. Our staff suggested to the leaders: "Change can be difficult for the elderly. Could she tell you where she wants the window?" They replied, "That's not necessary—she's pleased."

Locating materials was a long process, and the ailing widow died before her home could be built. Our staff member says: "I've always wondered . . . maybe she died sooner because she felt she was losing her home. We ministered to her with love, but we should have allowed her this dignity, too."

do anything—we need to do this for her." But we need to ask ourselves, "How can she be involved?" Maybe the church could provide food for workers, and she could prepare it. Or, she could bring out the water, tea, or coffee. We need to look creatively for ways that those being helped can participate. God created her in His image—with dignity and significance. We rob her of that when we exclude her. We need to be a part of her life and not leave her as a powerless observer—even if she can only heat the water or help us plan. This may complicate the work, but *not* including her is a loss to both the helpers and the helped. When we do *"pure and faultless"* religion, [4] we must not omit this element.

9. *An observable spiritual impact is built into the Seed Project where it is appropriate.*

- Planning for every Seed Project includes prayer, study, seeking God, and thanking Him. This is essential, but it does not make a *direct* spiritual impact on outsiders. A project would be classified as having a spiritual impact only if we plan to inform the beneficiaries about God's role

---

[4] James 1:27

while the project is being carried out. This could be done through a planned celebration, dedication service, plaque, sign, written note, spoken words, or public prayer.

- There should be a planned spiritual impact whenever possible. In each Seed Project plan, it is essential to ask if there should be a spiritual impact on the *community*. If so, it should be intentionally built in the plan. Otherwise, we can become busy with the project and unintentionally omit the spiritual impact.

- In some cases, it may not be best to have an intentional spiritual impact for observers.

10. A Seed Project is evaluated by Kingdom standards.

- Evaluation is important—by Kingdom standards. Here are some questions to ask:

  ☑ Did God multiply the resources? Did Kingdom Mathematics take place?

  ☑ Have people—other than those who are serving—been blessed or favorably impacted by the project?

  ☑ Was God's love evident? Were His intentions demonstrated?

  ☑ Did God receive honor and praise from the observers? Did He receive more credit than the people who did the project? When the project was finished, did onlookers say, "Aren't those wonderful people?" Or "What a wonderful God they have!" We must serve in such a way that people see our good works and praise our Father.[5]

  ☑ Can this be said of your service?

    The service that you perform is not only supplying the needs of God's people but is also overflowing in many expressions of thanks to God. Because of the service by

---

[5] Matthew 5:16

> *which you have proved yourselves, men will praise God*
> *for the obedience that accompanies your confession of*
> *the gospel of Christ, and for your generosity in sharing*
> *with them and with everyone else.*[6]

- If there is not a clear "Yes!" to one or more of these questions, the Seed Project has likely fallen short of Kingdom standards, even though it was a well-intended human effort.[7]

Ten Seed Project Characteristics may seem like a large number to use, but I am encouraged to see how easily they are remembered by small group members who use this simple method:

- Group members read the characteristics in unison, twice.
- Without looking at the list, they recite as many characteristics as possible, together.
- Without looking at the list, one group member states the first characteristic. The next person states the second characteristic. The next person says the third characteristic. They continue until all ten characteristics have been given.
- They then repeat the process, but in the *opposite* direction.

On the next two pages is an exercise. Use it to check your understanding of Seed Project Characteristics.

Compare your answers with those at the end of this chapter.

---

[6] 2 Corinthians 9:12-13

[7] Trainers in Brazil, whose trainees have successfully completed many Disciplines of Love and Seed Projects, teach another key characteristic of Seed Projects—that of *shared responsibility.* Each person's role is significant and unique in the Seed Project plan. Each must do his part. Each depends on the other. When the project is finished, everyone has succeeded.

[8] Luke 14:28-32

Exercise 1

Check Your Understanding
of Seed Project Characteristics

Instructions	Seed Project Characteristics
1. Check "Yes" or "No" to indicate if a project fits Seed Project Characteristics. 2. If "No," write the number of the missing characteristic in the "#" column.	1. Covered in prayer 2. Compassionate—not manipulative 3. Motivated by God's intentions 4. Thoughtfully planned 5. Simple and short 6. Done with local resources 7. Directed toward those outside the church 8. Those who benefit participate 9. Spiritual impact where appropriate 10. Evaluated by Kingdom standards

PROJECT	Yes	No	#
a. A day of games and food for community children as an evangelistic outreach.			
b. A picnic for hungry children motivated by a community needs survey			
c. Latrine repair at the home of a church member			
d. A government-sponsored literacy program which has been covered in prayer			
e. A community discussion about a literacy program—opened with a brief prayer			

Continued on the following page

PROJECT	Yes	No	#
f. A garbage cleanup that takes place the day after the decision to do the cleanup			
g. A community seminar on nutrition—the organizing committee serves so well that the community participants only need to attend			
h. Media coverage of a Seed Project in order to get publicity for the church			
i. Development and operation of a child-care center			
j. Community meeting to discuss the formation of a child-care center			
k. A tree-planting project with no reference to spiritual issues			

The Wisdom of a Planning Tool

It is wise to make plans, implied Jesus, to complete a tower or win a war. We would agree—we understand the wisdom of planning big projects. Even though a Seed Project is simple and small, its success *also* requires planning. Churches that carefully plan Seed Projects greatly increase their potential to do them well, honor the Lord, and grow in the ability and grace to serve.

Planning to serve is difficult for many churches. We use a Seed Project Planning Guide to answer their concerns.

- Churches have appreciated this planning tool because it keeps them focused on God's focus. God calls us into a "partnership." He is the leader—and we seek His wisdom and guidance. We make a plan and continually allow the Holy Spirit to direct and empower it.

- Churches appreciate this tool's simple step-by-step format, so they can plan and carry out successful projects. Some hear about a good idea and try to implement it without planning. They fail, not because the idea is bad but because logistics were not considered.

- Churches appreciate this tool because it helps them think about details, delegate work, and check responsibilities and progress at a glance.

My colleagues in Brazil are experienced trainers and practitioners who help churches plan and carry out Seed Projects. If church members resist planning, the trainers remind them that planning is only the beginning. *The end goal is a Seed Project that demonstrates God's love.* Secondly, they use more Scripture to teach about planning. I have included more Scriptures about planning at the end of this chapter.[9]

Using the Tool—Seed Project Planning Guide

I usually recommend that churches and small groups use the tool exactly as it is presented the first several times they plan and carry out Seed Projects. After they have become comfortable with the process, they can better adapt the tool to their contexts.

To introduce the tool, a shortened version is shown on the following pages. A realistic version, with room for more steps, is included at the end of this chapter. Here are several suggestions for learning to use it well:

- Look at the Seed Project Planning Guide and the instructions for each part of the guide.
- Next, study the story and sample planning guide.
- Read about training, implementing, and reporting.
- Work with your own church or small group to plan, implement, and report a Seed Project.

---

[9] Cleiton and Eleuza Oliveira, manuscript review (Brazil: 2003).

Following are instructions for each part of the tool:

1. Problem: As God leads, identify a problem that the project will address. Summarize it in a few words on *Line 1*.

2. God's intentions and ***3. Scripture:*** Discuss God's general intentions for this need, using Scripture as a guide. Choose one passage. Write these on *Lines 2 and 3*. *Example*: We should live in a clean and healthy environment. Leviticus 11:36.

4. Seed Project title: Decide on a small project that can be done with local resources to help meet the need you selected. Write a descriptive title on *Line 4* of the Planning Guide. *Examples:* Roof Repair or Game Day for Children.

5. Primary and ***6. Secondary impact area(s):*** Use the four areas of Luke 2:52. Identify *one* primary project impact (*Line 5*) and one or more secondary impact areas (*Line 6*). *Examples:*

- Seminar on God's intentions for husband-wife relationships— Wisdom (Secondary impact: Social)

- Garbage cleanup—Physical

- *Jesus* film—Spiritual

- Game day for children—Social (Secondary impact: Physical)

Steps: Discuss the steps to complete the project. Use a separate line for each step. List them in the order in which they will be done.

Persons or institutions to consult: List people or institutions to consult for each step. Write them on the line for that step.

Resources needed: Under this heading, list resources needed for each step. Write them on the line for the appropriate step.

Person(s) responsible: List the person or persons responsible to see that each step is carried out. List their names or their positions on the line for the appropriate step.

Action date(s): Under this column, write the date of completion for each step.

Seed Project Planning Guide

1. Problem: _____

2. God's intention: _____ 3. Scripture: _____

4. Seed Project title: _____

5. Primary impact area: _____ 6. Secondary impact area(s): _____

Steps	Persons or institutions to consult	Resources needed	Person(s) responsible	Action date(s)
1.				
2.				
ADD SPACE FOR ADDITIONAL STEPS AS NEEDED				

Checklists: Check to see if your plan is complete by writing the project step numbers below.

Planned Impact Areas	**Seed Project Characteristics**
Write "Primary" or "Secondary" to the <u>right</u> of the planned impact area. On the <u>left</u>, list the step numbers that relate to the planned impact area. ___ Wisdom _____ ___ Physical _____ ___ Spiritual _____ ___ Social _____	List the step numbers that fit each characteristic. There may be more than one number on each line. ___ Covered in prayer ___ Compassionate—not manipulative ___ Motivated by God's intentions ___ Thoughtfully planned ___ Simple and short ___ Done with local resources ___ Directed toward those outside the church ___ Those who benefit participate ___ Spiritual impact where appropriate ___ Evaluated by Kingdom standards

Planned Impact Areas List only the steps that have a planned impact on the project's recipients.

Seed Project Characteristics Consider all the steps, whether they affect recipients, planners, the church, or others.

Checklists

In the final section of the tool are two boxes. One box checks the plan's impact areas. The other checks the plan's characteristics.

Planned Impact Areas: On the right side of an impact area, write "Primary" or "Secondary." On the left side of the impact area, write the step numbers planned to impact the project's recipients.

Seed Project Characteristics: Write the step number(s) from the plan next to the appropriate characteristics. Ideally, each characteristic should be seen in at least one step number.

A Sample Plan from Africa

One of the best ways to learn how to do something is to watch someone—and then do it. We may not be able to work alongside these brothers and sisters, but we can do the next best thing. In our imaginations, we can listen to their conversations and watch them plan. We can observe their Seed Project Planning Guide and check their plan against the Checklist.

This plan was actually designed at a training conference in Africa, but the dialogue is fictional.

Musa, an African pastor and trainer, learned about Seed Projects at a training conference. Inspired, he visited a rural village church and taught Seed Projects. The church formed a Wholistic Ministry Committee and asked Enoch, a deacon, to serve as the chairman. Two other men and three women were also chosen to serve.

Enoch called the first meeting. "Our first task," he said, "is to discover what God wants us to do as a Seed Project to show His concern for our village." He broke into prayer: "Oh, Father, thank you for calling us together. Please guide our discussion. Lead us to a project that will show people how much You care about them." One by one, the others prayed, earnestly asking the Holy Spirit to show them what God wanted them to do. After the final "Amen," they sat quietly for a little while. It was a holy moment.

Enoch asked, "What are some of you sensing we are to do?" "Well," said David, "three things came to my mind." Enoch encouraged him to tell the group. "Okay," David said, "our village has been hit hard by AIDS; our children suffer with intestinal diseases; and sanitation is poor, especially in the market." Florence said, "I considered AIDS as I prayed. AIDS is devastating, but I don't think that's where God is asking us to start." "That's exactly what I was thinking," agreed Samuel.

Sarah said, "I can't stop thinking about the horrible time I had at the market this morning. It was worse than usual after the rain. There was filthy water in the roads, and the children were playing in it. There were mosquitoes, and there were flies all over the fruit, vegetables, and butchered chickens! It was disgusting!" Samuel said pensively, "Yes, I think there's a connection between the children's diseases and the lack of sanitation that David mentioned." "Well, we can't avoid going to the market!" said Deborah, always practical. "But it's hard to know what to do. I boil everything we eat, and we still get sick."

"Couldn't we just make the market a more sanitary place? I mean, isn't there a verse in the Bible that says something like "Cleanliness is next to Godliness"?[10] asked David. Enoch smiled, "It's not in the Bible. It's just a saying, but it's a good one. See if we can think of any Bible passages that show us what God thinks about cleanliness." Enoch could see that God was directing the conversation. Samuel said, "Well, we're supposed to take care of the land. That includes keeping it clean." "Excellent!" said Enoch. "Anything else?" "Yes, there are lots of verses about cleanliness in Leviticus!" said Sarah. The others looked at her with astonishment. "You read Leviticus?" they asked. "Not often. But I know it's always talking about things that are clean and unclean. No wonder I feel so uncomfortable in the market—God doesn't like it, either!" Sarah shuddered as she recalled her morning at the market.

"I think we're getting somewhere. Let's look at the Seed Project Planning Guide," suggested Enoch. "Line 2 is for God's intention.

---

[10] This is an American idiom, but it fits well. Other cultures have similar idioms.

I'll write, 'We should live in a clean environment.' Line 3 asks for a Scripture." "Look at Leviticus 11:36!" David said. He was leafing through Leviticus, surprised to see how much detail God gave to help His people be clean and healthy. "Wow! How did we go so far away from what God intended?" Enoch glanced at the verse and wrote "Leviticus 11:36" on Line 3. "This is good," said Enoch. "But we still don't know what we're going to do!" Deborah reminded. Enoch asked, "Well, what comes to your minds? Does anyone sense where God is leading us?"

Florence, who speaks readily about what she hears from God and rarely about other matters, said, "I think He wants us to build a public urinal at the market." The others were surprised. There were a few moments of silence. Florence is bashful and uncomfortable talking with people—especially men. Now she was saying God wanted them to build a public urinal! "You know," said Samuel, pensively. "That might be just the answer—and it might take care of some of the sanitation problems." Sarah jumped. *"Might?* It would!" Her thoughts went back to the market, "The filthy water . . . the flies . . ."

Enoch asked, "What should I list as the problem on Line 1? Samuel thought and said, "'Public urination at the market'—that's the cause of our sanitation and health issues." Enoch wrote it. "How about a title for Line 4?" Enoch asked. Deborah quickly said, "Just write 'Building of a public urinal.'" The others smiled at her practicality. "Fine," said Enoch, writing.

"Now," said Enoch, "what is the primary impact area on Line 5?" "Please tell me again what that means," said David. Enoch began: "We want to help people grow like Jesus—in wisdom, physically, spiritually, and socially. There's usually one area where we expect the project to make the biggest change. Which of these four areas would be most helped by our project?" "That's easy," said Deborah. "Physical." "And the secondary impact area?" asked Enoch. Samuel said, "I see a social impact—people working together on a public project." "And spiritual—people will see us thanking God in a time of public celebration," said Florence. Enoch wrote "Social + Spiritual" on Line 6. "Now, we're ready to work on the steps."

The group was animated. They talked about the steps and discussed which had to happen first. For each step, they asked, "Who do we consult? What do we need? Who do we know who can help? Who will be responsible? When will we finish?" Enoch wrote their decisions in the Planning Guide. Finally, they came to the last step. They looked approvingly at the plan. "We can do this!" said David. "With God's help!" reminded Florence.

"Wait!" said Enoch. "We still need to do the Checklists." The group reviewed the Checklists and prayed with great thanksgiving. Enoch picked up his papers and smiled. Step 1 was done. Tomorrow, he would make an appointment for the committee to visit the mayor.

Now, look at the Sample Plan from Africa here and on the following page and then fill out its Checklists. The answers are given at the end of the chapter, but please complete your analysis first.

Sample Plan—Africa

1. **Problem:** *Public urination at the market*

2. **God's intention:** *We should live in a clean environment.*

3. **Scripture:** *Leviticus 11:36*

4. **Seed Project title:** *Building of a public urinal*

5. **Primary impact area:** *Physical*

6. **Secondary impact area(s):** *Social + Spiritual*

Steps	Persons or institutions to consult	Resources needed	Person(s) responsible	Action date(s)
1. Prayer and decision - Begin using the Seed Project Planning Guide	God	Time, reflection	Project Committee	Day 1
2. Community leaders' input	Mayor and/or assemblymen	Appointment	Project Committee	Days 2-4
3. Develop questionnaire	Project Committee	Ideas	Project Committee	Day 5
4. Prayer	Church	Scheduled time	Project Committee	Day 5
5. Survey of interest	Community and Assemblymen	Questionnaire	Project Committee	Day 6
6. Develop construction design and plan	*Engineer for plans *Assemblymen for urinal location	Expertise Permission	Project leader and engineer	Day 8
7. Raise funds from church and community	Pastor and assemblymen	Time	Project Committee	Days 9-10
8. Procure materials	Project Committee	Cement blocks, sand, stones, cement, tools	Project Committee	Days 11-12
9. Announce date of construction	Project Committee	Posters	Project Committee	Day 15
10. Arrange for food	Church and Community women	Menu and Volunteers	Project Committee	Day 15
11. Prayer	Church	Time	Pastor	Day 15
12. Construction	Church and Community	Free weekend	Project Committee	Days 16-17
13. Celebration and thanksgiving	Pastor and Mayor	Invitations and scheduled time	Project Committee	Day 17
14. Evaluation and report	Project Committee	Reflection	Project Committee	Day 18
15. Prayer and planning for next Seed Project	Project Committee	Reflection	Project Committee	Day 25

<u>Note</u>: This is only a sample. Use different steps for your project.

Checklists

Check to see if the sample plan is complete by writing the project step numbers below. Several answers are provided. Follow the directions to discover the rest of the answers.

Planned Impact Areas	**Seed Project Characteristics**
Write "Primary" or "Secondary" to the <u>right</u> of the planned impact area.	List the step numbers that fit each characteristic. There may be more than one number on each line.
On the <u>left</u>, list the step numbers that relate to the planned impact area.	*1,4,11,15* Covered in prayer
____ Wisdom ____	_____ Compassionate—not manipulative
12 Physical *Primary*	_____ Motivated by God's intentions
13 Spiritual ____	_____ Thoughtfully planned
____ Social *Secondary*	_____ Simple and short
	_____ Done with local resources
	_____ Directed toward those outside the church
	_____ Those who benefit participate
	_____ Spiritual impact where appropriate
	_____ Evaluated by Kingdom standards

Planned Impact Areas List only the steps that have a planned impact on the project's recipients.

Seed Project Characteristics Consider all the steps, whether they affect recipients, planners, the church, or others.

Compare your answers with those at the end of the chapter.

Seed Project Planning and Implementation

Seed Projects are best planned in small groups. *Any* small group can plan and carry out a project that reflects God's love and concern for community people. Since the projects are simple and short, a large group may divide into even smaller groups.

Here are suggested steps for planning and implementation:

1. *Pray for guidance.* Small group participants ask the Spirit's direction as they select a problem to address.

2. *Use the Seed Project Planning Guide.* Small group members then design each step of the Seed Project as they fill out the form. They should not omit the Checklist—it is helpful.

   A blank Seed Project Planning Guide is included at the end of this chapter.

3. *Present the plan.* The team or its leaders then meet with others for review and evaluation.

4. *Implement.* This is important! Group members carry out their Seed Project plan.

5. *Report, evaluate, and look toward the future.*

   - *Report.* Two reporting styles are shown here. One is a simple form. The other is a narrative. The group can choose its own style—but there should be a report. Group members complete the report together and use it to encourage the church or larger group, as appropriate.

   - *Evaluate and move forward.* Participants pray, evaluate, and plan ways to continue to tangibly express God's love. They may use the questions in the Final Reflection section of this chapter. To grow in a lifestyle of service, they can use the long-range planning and evaluation tools in the next two chapters.

Seed Project Report

Group Data:

Name of Group _____

Church _____

Address _____

Contact Information _____

Name of Pastor _____

Seed Project title: _____ Scripture: _____

Location: Country: _____ City _____ City Section _____

Dates of project: _____ Year _____

Primary impact area: _____ Secondary impact area(s): _____

(List only those areas for which there was a planned emphasis.)

Answer the following questions. Use as much space as necessary.

1. Whose idea was the project?

2. What was done? (Give a concise description of the seed project.)

3. How long did the project take? To organize: ____ days. To do the project: ____ days.

4. Who participated?

5. How many people participated? _____

6. Who were the primary beneficiaries?

7. How did the beneficiaries participate?

8. What resources were needed? Where did you get them?

9. What resources were contributed by the people who were being helped?

10. What indication was there that God blessed the project?

Seed Project Reports

Notice how the following Seed Project accounts answer the same questions in a narrative style. They also communicate the life and potential of small, planned, simple demonstrations of God's love. I think the Mayor would say, "Well done, good and faithful servants."

Serving the Servants

❖ A group from a U.S. church wanted, in their own words, "to do something special beyond our church walls that would make God smile!" They decided "to honor, encourage, respect, and applaud" the young adults who work at a nursing home as cafeteria workers and nurse's aids. The workers were invited to a dinner and evening celebration in their honor at the home of one of the group members. The primary focus was social/physical. The secondary was spiritual. The Scripture used was Galatians 6:9. Warm letters of invitation were sent to fourteen workers, and twelve came. The evening began with an icebreaker, a simple exercise to help people get to know each other. A member of the planning team then thanked the workers for their service to the elderly and said that the team's plan was to serve *them* this evening. The church women cooked, and the men served the dinner and cleaned. After the meal, there was an informal sharing time. The guests and hosts each told a little about themselves, several team members spoke, and the Seed Project team leader read Scriptures encouraging the workers not to grow weary in doing good and to realize that each person is created in God's image for a special purpose. Each guest received a decorative bowl from Mexico, a houseplant, and an encouraging book. To end the evening, the workers stood in a circle and received a group blessing. The Seed Project team received several letters of thanks. One said: "It was wonderful to be appreciated. I'll never forget it. The book really made me think how much I can achieve."

Two other things are important to know: (1) A nursing home in Mexico was renovated as an indirect result of this project. (2) The group said: "We never would have done the Seed Project if we had not sat down to plan it. *The planning made the difference!*"

A Children's Shelter

❖ A church group designed a Seed Project to build and furnish a community children's shelter. The primary impact was physical. The secondary areas were social and spiritual. The idea came from home fellowship participants. It took a month to plan and two days to implement. The beneficiaries were fifteen children of needy families. Three men participated by providing materials, and three other men from the community helped with labor. The verse that inspired the work was Proverbs 1:23.

Before this initiative, the children wrote on the dirt floor during tutoring classes. People stood during Bible studies. The Seed Project provided a cement floor, table, and twelve plastic chairs. Church members learned how to mobilize, and they expressed joy in serving their neighbors. Principles of Kingdom Mathematics were visible— one man decided to donate chairs when he visited the project site; community people called relatives to come and enjoy the new space and activities. Every time church and community members meet at the shelter, there is prayer. God is honored and receives the credit.

Children's Day Celebration

❖ Children's Day was a Seed Project of one church. The primary impact was social, and the secondary was spiritual. It was one member's idea, who said: "In our country, the celebration of 'Carnival' is connected with many bad things. I'd like the children from this community to remember it as a day they experienced God's love." Planning took three weeks and included collective prayer. The activities took one day. The beneficiaries were forty-five children. Twenty adults helped. Psalm 2:11 made it clear that the event was an expression of God's care. The children enjoyed breakfast, recreation, lunch, games, and a devotional. The day finished with a musical service and celebration of birthdays. Much food was donated. Other food was bought with funds regularly collected to help community children. The immediate results were relationships between children from the community and the church. Resources were multiplied so much that a lunch was prepared for the church and neighbors the next day. God was honored, and His love was shared.

A Public Restroom

❖ A middle-class church had served its neighbors in a nearby slum for several years, encountering every kind of need. The terrible condition of a small outdoor restroom sensitized them to the living conditions of the slum-dwellers. The church members wondered, "What will their lives by like in the winter? How will they stay healthy, especially the children?" Hebrews 13:3 inspired them: *"Remember those who are mistreated as if you yourselves were suffering."* They donated their time and resources to rebuild the restroom. Construction workers offered one workday. Merchants provided discounts on materials. Enthusiastic community residents helped. Approximately fifteen adults and six children were beneficiaries. Another benefit was that church members better understood that God was using them to reconcile their neighbors with the environment, part of God's big agenda. Through it all, God was glorified.

Final Reflections

Here are several suggestions to help a church or small group evaluate a recently completed Seed Project:

1. In what ways were God's intentions for the community furthered? How did God work in the lives of the participants? How did God work in the community?

2. What lessons did you learn through the process of planning and implementing the Seed Project? About God? About yourselves? About the community? About God's Kingdom ?

3. What follow-up steps are necessary after the Seed Project? What are some areas where participants need further training? What do you think God wants you to do next?

The Relevance of Planning

The Relevance of Planning gives a strong endorsement for planning! It was written by a colleague whose church has embraced Seed Project planning and is at the forefront of community and national transformation. The church has a weekly attendance of 12,500 people. There are 1,200 cell groups, and each cell group must do at least one Seed Project a year. Most do more! The national government has asked church leaders to help draft government policies on sex education, pornography, alcohol and substance abuse, domestic relations, and immorality in public entertainment.

The Relevance of Planning*

The Lord had impressed our hearts as pastors of Kampala Pentecostal Church to impact our community and bring healing.

While we were struggling with the "how" to influence and bring healing to our community, God providentially brought this material our way. It provided a philosophical and theological understanding of what we were doing. It opened our eyes to how we could impact the community and bring healing.

The lesson on Seed Projects was one of the practical things we learned. Seed Projects have impacted the lives of the cell leaders at our church. Planning is not culturally African. Africans, culturally, do things as they come. But planning has become valuable to our leaders. They see that any Seed Project that is thoroughly planned bears tremendous results and leaves great community impact.

Planning has become extremely relevant because—not only is it helping us to bear good fruit with Seed Projects—but it is also helping our leaders plan their *own* lives. It is amazing to see what the people have learned as they plan for Seed Projects. It is transforming their own lives. Leaders have seen that planning is important for fruitful ministry and productive lives.

As leaders in Africa, we do not just want to do things that are cultural. We want to do things that are of God, that are relevant, and that bring transformation in the community. I want to encourage all my fellow African leaders—and church leaders everywhere—to embrace planning. It will increase our efficiency, productivity, and impact on the community where we have been called to serve.

*Rev. Franco Onaga, e-mail correspondence to Bob Moffitt (Kampala, Uganda, 2005).

In the next chapter, we will look at how to strategically plan a *series* of varied Seed Projects, serving the Mayor's agenda in ways that are both wide and deep.

Seed Project Planning Guide

1. Problem: _____

2. God's intention: _____ 3. Scripture: _____

4. Seed Project title: _____

5. Primary impact area: _____ 6. Secondary impact area(s): _____

Steps	Persons or institutions to consult	Resources needed	Person(s) responsible	Action date(s)
1.				
2.				
3.				
4.				
5.				
6.				
7.				
8.				
9.				
10.				
11.				
12.				
13.				
14.				
15.				
16.				
17.				
18.				
19.				
20.				

Checklists

Check to see if your plan is complete by writing the project step numbers below.

Planned Impact Areas	Seed Project Characteristics
Write "Primary" or "Secondary" to the *right* of the planned impact area. On the *left*, list the step numbers that relate to the planned impact area. ____ Wisdom _____ ____ Physical _____ ____ Spiritual _____ ____ Social _____	List the step numbers that fit each characteristic. There may be more than one number on each line. _____ Covered in prayer _____ Compassionate—not manipulative _____ Motivated by God's intentions _____ Thoughtfully planned _____ Simple and short _____ Done with local resources _____ Directed toward those outside the church _____ Those who benefit participate _____ Spiritual impact where appropriate _____ Evaluated by Kingdom standards

Planned Impact Areas   List only the steps that have a planned impact on the project's recipients.

Seed Project Characteristics   Consider all the steps, whether they affect recipients, planners, the church, or others.

Answers to Exercise 1

PROJECT	Yes	No	#
a. A day of games and food for community children as an evangelistic outreach		✓	#2
b. A picnic for hungry children motivated by a community needs survey		✓	#3
c. Latrine repair at the home of a church member		✓	#7
d. A government-sponsored literacy program which has been covered in prayer		✓	#6
e. A community discussion about a literacy program—opened with a brief prayer		✓	#1
f. A garbage cleanup that takes place the day after the decision to do the cleanup		✓	#4
g. A community seminar on nutrition—the organizing committee serves so well that the community participants only need to attend		✓	#8
h. Media coverage of a Seed Project in order to get publicity for the church		✓	#10
i. Development and operation of a child-care center		✓	#5
j. Community meeting to discuss the formation of a child-care center	✓		--
k. A tree-planting project with no reference to spiritual issues		✓	#9

- A "No" answer signifies that the project does not meet the Seed Project characteristics.

- The number next to the "No" identifies the missing Seed Project characteristic.

- If you do not understand the answer, carefully review the characteristics.

Seed Project Characteristics

1. Covered in prayer
2. Compassionate—not manipulative
3. Motivated by God's intentions
4. Thoughtfully planned
5. Simple and short
6. Done with local resources
7. Directed toward those outside the church
8. Those who benefit participate
9. Spiritual impact where appropriate
10. Evaluated by Kingdom standards

Answers to Exercise 2

Checklists

Check to see if the sample plan is complete by writing the project step numbers below.

Planned Impact Areas	Seed Project Characteristics
Write "Primary" or "Secondary" to the *right* of the planned impact area.	List the step numbers that fit each characteristic. There may be more than one number on each line.
On the *left*, list the step numbers that relate to the planned impact area.	*1,4,11,15* Covered in prayer
	12 Compassionate—not manipulative
___ Wisdom ___	*1* Motivated by God's intentions
12 Physical *Primary*	*1-15* Thoughtfully planned
13 Spiritual *Secondary*	*12* Simple and short
12,13 Social *Secondary*	*7,8,10* Done with local resources
	2,5,6,7,12 Directed toward those outside the church
	7,10,12,13 Those who benefit participate
	13 Spiritual impact where appropriate
	14 Evaluated by Kingdom standards

The Importance of Planning

God Makes Plans . . .

"In days of old I planned it; now I have brought it to pass." (Isaiah 37:26b)

"What I have planned, that will I do."   (Isaiah 46:11b)

"For I know the plans that I have for you," declares the Lord, "plans to prosper you and not to harm you, plans to give you hope and a future."
(Jeremiah 29:11)

In him we were also chosen . . . according to the plan of him who works out everything.   (Ephesians 1:11)

We Plan . . .

With God's Plans: *Set up the tabernacle according to the plan shown you on the mountain.*   (Exodus 26:30)

"All this," David said, "I have in writing from the hand of the Lord upon me, and he gave me understanding in all the details of the plan."
(1 Chronicles 28:19)

With Noble Intentions and Deeds: *But the noble man makes noble plans, and by noble deeds he stands.*   (Isaiah 32:8)

With Dedication: *Commit to the Lord whatever you do, and your plans will succeed.*   (Proverbs 16:3)

Justly: *The plans of the righteous are just.*   (Proverbs 12:5a)

For the Good: *But those who plan what is good find love and faithfulness.*
(Proverbs 14:22b)

Timely, Wisely: *Go to the ant, you sluggard; consider its ways and be wise! . . . it stores its provisions in summer and gathers its food at harvest.*   (Proverbs 6:6,8)

With Advise: *Plans fail for lack of counsel, but with many advisers they succeed.*   (Proverbs 15:22)

With Diligence: *The plans of the diligent lead to profit.*
(Proverbs 21:5a)

Firmly: *When I planned this, did I do it lightly? Or do I make my plans in a worldly manner so that in the same breath I say "Yes, yes" and "No, no"?*   (2 Corinthians 1:17)

Clearly: *Then the Lord replied: "Write down the revelation and make it plain on tablets so that a herald may run with it."*   (Habakkuk 2:2)

Planning for Community Transformation

14

One Seed Project does not make a large impact for the Kingdom of God. One person doing Discipline of Love exercises does not change the world. But imagine the impact if this were the lifestyle of every individual believer and every local church in a community!

Small Seeds—the Beginning of Community Transformation

If Jesus were Mayor, I believe He would encourage His people and His church to plant small seeds. He would multiply them—into trees, fruit, and forests. Forests! My colleague Darrow Miller tells of an Ethiopian agricultural worker who wanted to see transformation occur in his community through agriculture. The agricultural worker explained: "We are trying to help the farmers see the forest in the seed!"[1] Each small seed planted by the Ethiopian agricultural worker is the beginning of a forest. Each small demonstration of God's love planted by a servant of Christ is the beginning of community transformation.

In the beginning of this book, I asked a question to fuel your imagination: *What would happen if, next Monday morning at 9 a.m., everyone in your community started to live as God intends?*

I think the Mayor's agenda would be well-served! Now, I would like to rephrase the question into several more specific questions:

- *What would happen if, next Monday at 9 a.m., every believer in your community started to live a lifestyle of faithful, loving, obedient, godly service?*
- *What if every church in your community began to demonstrate God's love and concern to the unchurched?*
- *Would your community notice?*

---

[1] Conversation between Darrow L. Miller (Food for the Hungry International) and Harvest Foundation Board of Directors, March 2004.

I think so! At first, the people might not know what had changed. They would only know that they liked it. Maybe the media would ask. Maybe the people in the public square would notice. Maybe the authorities would discuss it.

In fact, these results have occurred where followers of Jesus have obediently loved their neighbors and carried out the Mayor's agenda. Listen to these two accounts of individual believers in Kenya who, convicted by God, gave faithful and loving service:

❖ A Christian woman from a slum community of Nairobi became aware of a mother who had just given birth at home. The birth had not gone properly. The new mother was ill and could not care for her baby. She had no family to help her. Hearing this, the Christan woman took the mother to the hospital, where she was kept and treated for one week. This "Good Samaritan" also cared for the newborn for that week.

❖ Winnie, another Christian woman from Nairobi, volunteered in her church's distribution of food and clothing to the desperately needy in two nearby slum communities. Wanting to be of further help, she visited many women to gather information. She found that the two communities were characterized by fragmented families, alcohol abuse, domestic violence, early marriages, rape, and teenage pregnancies. After considering ways to help the families, Winnie decided to teach the women tailoring skills that would bring them income. The "Tabitha Outreach" began, enrolling eight women who shared three donated sewing machines. Winnie's vision was that the women would "learn together, work together, pray together, and grow together." Several of the women placed their faith in Christ and began to look for ways to help others. They started to visit and pray for the sick, bring them food, and assist them with household chores. The women also obtained the use of a small piece of land and grew vegetables to give away to the needy.

---

[2] The source for the story marked by ❖ is listed in the Bibliography at the end of the book.

What would happen if *each* follower of Christ lived a lifestyle of faithful, obedient service, loving God and their neighbor? I believe that the world around them would notice—and be changed.

In the same way, when local churches consistently demonstrate God's love through small projects, one after another, communities are transformed. We have seen this in communities that have been served wholistically by local churches, some for a decade or two.

❖ Look at the activities carried out in one year by a single body of believers in Tegucigalpa, Honduras. Imagine the difference the church made with its faithful responses to the needs around them!

- Soccer league
- Medical league
- Childcare class
- Clothes for needy children
- Home dental care by dentists
- Dental cooperative
- Bedsheets for prisoners
- School supplies for prisoners children
- Preventative health seminar
- Distributing vitamins
- Providing garbage collection barrels on community streets
- Fasting one meal per week to give funds for the needy
- Painting speed bumps on street
- Visiting families of alcoholics
- Filling potholes in street
- Requesting a city garbage truck
- Building concrete stairs on a steep path

❖ In 1998 Harvest produced a video, *A Vision for Carapita,* about a church in a barrio of Caracas, Venezuela. There was an amazing story to be told!

Originally, the church was scorned by the community. People threw rocks and bottles and shot at it. There were ten lawsuits against it. The church's vision, said the pastor, was "to fast, have vigils, and have services in the church." Then, our staff in Venezuela showed the Carapita leaders a small book, a true story from the Dominican Republic. They saw that an entire barrio changed when a local church's vision changed! They realized that Carapita needed a larger vision—one that no longer ignored community needs.

Our staff and Carapita church leaders began to study together. The church gained a higher view of its purpose. Members began with small actions, like taking food baskets to people in the community. Their small acts grew into larger projects that touched the whole community. They distributed medicines and food. They worked with schools, presenting the Gospel and giving lectures on drug prevention. They maintained and repaired schools and dangerous walkways. They began "Project Carapita," a project of health, recreation, sports, and culture. They reached the youth with social activities and sports. They repaired basketball courts and organized tournaments—to build harmony, keep the youth active, and present them with a fresh view of Christ. Now, the church is seen a blessing to the community. Listen to these remarks:

Pastor: *People are going to see the church as an example. If the judge is a Christian, he practices justice. If the counselor is a Christian, it applies to his job in the community. If the government official is Christian, he works for the community.*

Leader 1: *This plan we have is to tell them about the real God—not the small God that we had before, but the big God. Little by little, we're winning over the community, so that daily they may walk with God.*

Leader 2: *The vision that the church has at this time is to present the Kingdom with social and spiritual work—identifying ourselves with the community, sharing with the community.*

Pastor: *With a new vision, we became a part of them. We worked beside them, helping. Now, there is total respect for the church. Now, they see the church as the solution—the church, a solution for Carapita!*

❖ In another instance, a pastor from a church in India taught Seed Projects to his youth group. The youth began their application with a survey of the physical and social needs within a hundred meters of their urban church. They then decided to focus on the children of families that lived on a train platform near the church. Each youth worked with one child. They shared meals and played games on the platform. The parents became curious and eventually became engaged in a literacy program. This little Seed Project grew to a four-year, church-wide involvement with the people living on the train platform.

Long-Range Planning for Balance and Integration

The Seed Projects that a church does in its community should communicate that God is concerned about all areas of life. Not only should there be *balance*, but several impact areas should be *integrated* into each Seed Project.

Integration means that the people served by Seed Projects are made aware of more than one area of God's concern. If a church sponsors a football game between a church team and a community team, the primary impact is in the *social* area. If the church serves refreshments, there is a secondary impact in the *physical* area. If the coach asks God to bless the game, there is a secondary impact in the *spiritual* area. If he reviews the rules of the game and mentions ways that God wants us to follow His rules for the "game of life," there is a secondary impact in the *wisdom* area. The unspoken message is that God cares about people socially, physically, spiritually, and in wisdom. While a football game might seem insignificant, the message is part of the big picture— that we have a relevant, loving God who involves Himself in all areas of life, day after day, for now and eternity.

Balance means that we plan for a variety of projects. Balance and integration work best together. Let me explain by asking you to think about this: If one group of unchurched people is ministered to by your church's dental clinic, they might say to themselves, "Churches care about teeth." If your church goes to a different neighborhood and hands out tracts, people might think, "Churches want us to say this prayer and believe like they do." In either case, people have a narrow understanding of God and His concerns. When ministry is balanced and integrated, God's people reflect the truth that He is concerned and involved in *all* of life.

❖ A Korean pastor and church members have been developing eyes for community needs and often respond with Seed Projects. Recently, they designed a plan for a new church building with areas for public use—a library, coffee bar, movie theater, seminar room, and gymnasium. They not only expressed their heart for their community, but are exhibiting the truth that God cares about all areas of life.

❖ Capotillo, a community in the Dominican Republic, had become infamous for drugs, crime, violence, and riots. But God began to transform Capotillo through a local church. Led by a pastor with a vision for the community, the congregation prayed and witnessed to the love of God. Drug addicts and criminals came to Christ. Their lives were changed, and they told others about Jesus. The congregation grew and purchased a garage to convert into a church building. To fund the purchase and help its neighbors, the church rented out spaces for secure parking at night. The church also helped people start small businesses, began a preschool, and opened a cafeteria as a family-friendly alternative to local bars and gang hangouts. The neighborhood, it is said, is becoming a model of Christian community development.

The Church as a Window

Picture this. There is a window, and it has four sections. Each section of the window represents one of the four areas of God's concern. Now, consider:

The church is the window through which the people of your community see God and His concerns for all areas of their lives!

What a responsibility! We need to wash our windows so our community can see the God who loves them!

Not only must the windows but clean, but we need to heed the warning: "Don't let even the smallest of local churches replace its windows with mirrors!"

Using the Tool—Window of Vision

This chapter introduces a tool that allows us to plan for integration and balance in community ministry for one year—or any selected period. The tool looks like a window, with four sections. I have included a sample and a blank Window of Vision.

- Each section of the window represents one of the four areas of God's concern expressed in Luke 2:52.

- The four sections help churches or small groups plan Seed Projects in all four areas. As we look at an extended time period, we can better plan to demonstrate and express the whole of God's concern for those He created and loves.

- As churches or small groups do long-range Seed Project planning, they also continue to encourage individual church members in lifestyles of love and service.

The tool facilitates planning at least two wisdom, two physical, two spiritual, and two social Seed Projects. It also plans for ongoing Disciplines of Love by individual church members.

Planning and Implementation

1. *Meet together.* Before the period of service begins, have church leaders spend time together, pray, and think about Seed Projects. Together, read *Wholistic DNA in a Local Church,* located at the end of this chapter.

2. *Begin to plan.* Identify at least two projects in each of the four primary impact areas. A primary impact area is determined by the *nature* of the project, as defined by one of the four growth areas of Luke 2:52. The impact is for recipients (not for the participants or for the church). A secondary impact includes all other Luke 2:52 areas that are intended to impact the recipients.

   Examples: Seminars (wisdom impact); garbage cleanup (physical impact); party for senior citizens (social impact); showing the *Jesus* film in a public place (spiritual impact).

3. *Assign tentative dates and project coordinators for each project.*
   If possible, assign a different coordinator for each project to
   help the church develop more leaders.

4. *Fill out the Window of Vision.* Write one-line descriptions
   of planned Seed Projects inside the "windows." Remember
   that your church is the window through which the people
   of your community see God, His love, and His intentions
   for all of life. Check to see that your Seed Projects—taken
   together—reflect His broad care and concern for the people
   of your community.

5. *Evaluate after each Seed Project.*
   • Report and evaluate each project.
   • Together, thank God for what He accomplished—even
     for the fruit you cannot see.
   • Ask the Lord to give you a vision for similar, ongoing
     outreach projects.
   • Each time you complete a Seed Project, review your
     Window of Vision. Ask the Lord for additional insight.
   • Review *Wholistic DNA in a Local Church.* Discuss how
     wholistic DNA is impacting your church.
   • Begin the next project!

6. *Continue to encourage service and move forward.* Encourage
   wholistic service through every church ministry. Encourage
   individuals to lifestyles of loving their neighbors. Finally,
   use the tools in the following chapter to evaluate your
   church's obedience as a living example of God's love to your
   community.

Sample

Window of Vision
Long-Range Planning for Seed Projects and Disciplines of Love

Time Period: <u>January - December</u>

Wisdom	Spiritual
❑ Youth seminar on dating (January)	❑ Weekend of door-to-door visitation and witness (February)
❑ Meeting with mayor to discuss community issues (May)	❑ Community drama on the Prodigal Son (June)
❑ Community meeting to discuss literacy (September)	❑ Youth concert (October)
❑ Disciplines of Love (Ongoing)	❑ Disciplines of Love (Ongoing)
Physical	**Social**
❑ Garbage clean-up (March)	❑ Football game—church vs. community (April)
❑ Lunch for children in the barrio (July)	❑ Children's "Olympics" at park (August)
❑ Repairing desks for local public school (November)	❑ Alternative New Year's celebration (December/January)
❑ Filling holes in street (Dates to be decided after talking with officials)	❑ Disciplines of Love (Ongoing)
❑ Disciplines of Love (Ongoing)	

This may be the only window through which the watching world will see and be touched by God's love!

Window of Vision
Long-Range Planning for Seed Projects and Disciplines of Love

Time Period: _____

Wisdom	Spiritual
❑	❑
❑	❑
❑	❑
❑ Disciplines of Love (Ongoing)	❑ Disciplines of Love (Ongoing)
Physical	**Social**
❑	❑
❑	❑
❑	❑
❑ Disciplines of Love (Ongoing)	❑ Disciplines of Love (Ongoing)

This may be the only window through which the watching world will see and be touched by God's love!

Transformation of Community *and* Church

I encourage pastors and leaders to plan for and evaluate the wholistic DNA of their churches—in order to have both a theology and lifestyle of service.

Interestingly, as agents of change, churches themselves are often transformed as they serve their communities:

❖ The pastor of a small Uganda church of fifty members received wholistic ministry training. He then led several of the men from his church as they constructed a badly needed well for the community. This was followed by much more community ministry—road improvements, a pedestrian walkway, a free health clinic for community children, a used clothing store, and a school for those who could not afford public school. As the church reached its community, another transformation was taking place. The community began to see the church in a more favorable light—as the representative of God that He intended it to be. Church attendance grew from fifty to over two-thousand within five years. Though it has grown, the church has not lost its vision to transform its community.

❖ A pastor in India leads a church of eighty-three people. Most community members live in poverty, unemployment is high, literacy is low, and crime is common. The pastor used to beg God for outside resources for economic development. As church leaders discovered wholistic ministry, however, they began to understand that their first duty is to seek God for opportunities to bring healing and blessing to individuals, families, and their community. Making sacrificial contributions, church members themselves established a medical clinic and created a fund for small business loans. The church's vision was indeed transformed.

The tool on the following pages can be used as church leaders meet, pray, plan, and evaluate their wholistic service to those outside the church.

Wholistic DNA in a Local Church

Use this tool to reflect, plan, and evaluate
wholistic DNA in your local church.

1. CONVICTION

- *Element*: The church leaders are thoroughly convinced that God requires His people to demonstrate His love to their neighbors. This is not a negotiable option, but God's will. They are also convinced that obedience produces fruit.

- *Planning*: How will the church express this conviction in the selected time period or the coming year? (Any time period may be used.)

- *Evaluation*: What have you and your church done to express this conviction?

2. REPENTANCE

- *Element*: The church leaders have seen the difference between their church's ministry and God's intentions. They lead their church to repentance— turning away from the church's past inaction and disobedience—and walking in the new direction. The church may want to hold a service or another symbolic commemoration of its repentance.

- *Planning*: How will the church discover its need, repent, and declare its decision?

- *Evaluation*: What have you and your church done to express this repentance?

3. COMMITMENT

- *Element*: The church leaders are willing to do whatever it takes to make wholistic ministry part of the church's DNA. They are willing to invest time and effort and to take risks for this conviction, regardless of the consequences.

- *Planning*: What will the church plan to do to further its commitment in this time period?

- *Evaluation*: What have you and your church done to express this commitment?

4. APPLICATION

- _Element_: The church leaders apply wholistic ministry through the actual ministry activity of the church, using the Discipline of Love, Seed Projects, or other expressions of God's love.

- _Planning_: What will the church do to apply its convictions?

- _Evaluation_: What have you and your church done to apply your convictions?

5. ONGOING TEACHING

- _Element_: The church leaders communicate this message of loving service everywhere possible. It is woven into sermons, Bible studies, liturgy, small groups, and mentoring.

- _Planning_: How and where will ongoing teaching take place during this time period?

- _Evaluation_: What have you and your church done to integrate ongoing teaching into the church?

6. ACCOUNTABILITY

- _Element_: The church leaders hold themselves and others individually and corporately responsible for service and application. Small groups likewise hold people accountable. The church uses tools to measure faithful and loving service.

- _Planning_: What will the church do in this time period to hold its leaders and members accountable for service?

- _Evaluation_: What have you and your church done to hold one another accountable for service?

7. ACKNOWLEDGEMENT

- _Element_: The church leaders acknowledge service activities in weekly gatherings, testimonies, church bulletins or newsletters, and small groups—in order to celebrate service, to affirm the centrality of loving God by loving our neighbor, and to proclaim it as a normal lifestyle for all followers of Christ.

- _Planning_: What will the church do in this time period to celebrate, affirm, and acknowledge its service ministry?

- _Evaluation_: What have you and your church done to allow and encourage acknowledgement?

In Conclusion

As we close the chapter on planning for long-range impact and community transformation, allow me to challenge you again—as individual and corporate followers of Jesus Christ—with the opening questions:

- *What would happen if, next Monday at 9 a.m., every believer in your community started to live a lifestyle of faithful, loving, obedient, godly service?*
- *What if every church in your community began to demonstrate God's love and concern to the unchurched?*
- *Would your community notice?*

Measuring Obedience
By Their Fruit You Will
Recognize Them

15

If you were to ask Christians what comes to their minds when they think of "fruit," most would tell you the "fruit of the Spirit" that Paul lists in Galatians 5:22-23—love, joy, peace, patience, kindness, goodness, faithfulness, gentleness, and self-control. They would tell you that this is a list of Christian character qualities that the Holy Spirit develops in us. Yet, the majority of New Testament references to fruit are not about character qualities, but behavior—fruitful actions. Matthew 7 records what Jesus taught:

> *"By their fruit you will recognize them. . . . every good tree bears good fruit, but a bad tree bears bad fruit. . . . by their fruit you will recognize them. Not everyone who says to me, 'Lord, Lord,' will enter the kingdom of heaven, but only he who does the will of my Father who is in heaven."* [1]

Good fruit is essential! Good fruit is the test that indicates whether our faith is artificial or real. It is the criteria Jesus uses to declare whether or not He knows us. It is also the summary of how God intends His people to live: *"So in everything, do to others what you would have them do to you, for this sums up the Law and the Prophets."* [2]

Good fruit is more than the immediately observable results. Good fruit involves doing all God wants us to do in faithful and loving obedience to Him, trusting Him for results. Mother Teresa expressed this powerfully: *"God has not called me to be successful. He has called me to be faithful."* [3] It is more important to evaluate if we are doing what God calls us to do than to measure observable results!

---

[1] Matthew 7:16-21 (selected)

[2] Matthew 7:12

[3] The original citation is unknown to me. This statement is commonly attributed to Mother Teresa at such sites as http://www.loveoffering.com/MotherTeresa.htm.

I do not deny that Scripture encourages us to work so there will be results. We are to sow generously so we might reap generously,[4] and we are promised the multiplication of our efforts—up to 100 times.[5] There is biblical support for measuring both the activity and the obedience. Yet, if we focus on measuring results, we run the risk David took. He was at war with the Philistines. As a general, he wanted to know the strength of his army, so he ordered a census of Israel's fighting men. His action demonstrated his reliance on the number of warriors available to protect the land, rather than on God. God severely punished David.[6]

Though it is acceptable to measure results numerically, perhaps the church of today needs to be cautious that looking at numbers— church attendance, conversions, baptisms, or churches planted— leads us away from a focus on the God who brings the harvest. It must also not take us away from our task of making disciples, where results are harder to measure and healthy fruit takes longer to grow.

One of our South American colleagues ran into this dilemma. She directed an English-language program at her church. People tended to measure its success by the number of students and teachers involved. She explained how she dealt with this issue:

> When I am asked about the growth of the English language program, I prefer to deal with the issue of quality. This is an outreach program through which nonbelievers come to know Jesus and learn about His concern for all areas of life. We disciple the people who decide to pass from death to life. I tell the teachers: "Let's do a quality work now that we are small so we can learn from experience and be prepared to handle more challenges when the program gets bigger. It will expand—you will see." This does not mean that our goals are not ambitious for quantitative growth, but we need to be careful at each step.[7]

---

[4] 2 Corinthians 9:6
[5] Matthew 19:29
[6] 1 Chronicles 21:1-7
[7] Ruth Concha, manuscript review (Peru: 2003).

An important principle is heard in her encouragement to the English teachers—and in the eleventh chapter of Hebrews. That principal is faithfulness. The writer of Hebrews said many of God's people did not see the results of their faithfulness. They did not have much to measure in their lifetimes! Yet, God honored those steadfast people who lived in faithful obedience to Him. God brings results in His time, not ours. Like the heroes whose faith is catalogued in Hebrews 11, we are called to be faithful, whether we see fruit or not. We are called to do quality work. Our responsibility is to remain in Christ, the vine; He will bring forth fruit. Jesus explained: *"I am the vine; you are the branches. If a man remains in me and I in him, he will bear much fruit."*[8] It is key to know that we are connected to the vine, doing what God calls us to do. Here is a very important truth:

It is far more important to measure that which helps us see if we are being obedient and faithful—than it is to measure the results of our obedience.

Biblical Stewardship and Accountability

Honest reflection and evaluation are essential parts of good stewardship. God placed us in His creation and made us stewards, or managers. He calls local church leaders to be good managers of His church. Good managers have goals and plans, which they implement, monitor, evaluate, and adjust. One of a church leader's tasks as a good manager is ongoing evaluation and adjustment of the church's ministry plans and goals. Only God knows the final results, but honest reflection and evaluation are essential parts of managing what God has entrusted to us.

Accountability is encouraged throughout Scripture. It is a key part of being in the body of Christ. We help each other meet God's intentions. The book of Proverbs says: *"As iron sharpens iron, so one man sharpens another."*[9] We encourage each other to fulfill God's

---

[8] John 15:5
[9] Proverbs 27:17

agenda. Hebrews says: *"And let us consider how we may spur one another on toward love and good deeds."*[10] God holds us accountable. The book of Hebrews reminds us that spiritual leaders *"must give an account."*[11] Accountability should be a purposeful and essential part of our lives.

Shortcomings of Common Methods

There are two common ways to evaluate the process and results of wholistic ministry, but neither completely fits our need to be accountable for faithfulness and obedience. Both methods have shortcomings:

- We could use numbers—objective, statistical, quantitative analysis. We could gather and analyze data on project results. Statistics give us indications of what took place, but they do not tell us if we have been faithful to God's intentions or if there has been fruit for the Kingdom. If we measure only immediate results, we fail to measure the long-term value of an activity.

- We could use subjective analysis. We could take ministry "snapshots." We could tell stories and look at motivations, God's intentions, values, and outcomes. We could reflect on the progress made in comparison to expected goals. But we may be too subjective to evaluate our own faithfulness.

Evaluation tools usually do not measure whether the *right activities* are being done—but only if the chosen activities are *being done right*. They do not usually indicate if the activities are being done for the *right reason*, in the *right spirit* of faithful obedience, with the *right amount of credit* given to God.

Simple Measuring Tools

Some project evaluation tools—with complex data-gathering, questionnaires, and forms—are far too demanding for local churches. However, local churches can easily use *simple* methods to evaluate individual and corporate faithfulness to the Mayor's agenda. Such tools need to meet four criteria:

---

[10] Hebrews 10:24
[11] Hebrews 13:17b

- *Readily understood.* Users should not need a seminar to use it.
- *Easily completed.* Users can recall the information, without hard-to-find statistics.
- *Simple and short.* It should not intimidate the user with volumes of paper.
- *Immediately useful.* It should help people see if they have met their goals and if they need to avoid future mistakes.

This chapter offers simple measuring tools for individuals, small groups, accountability partners, church leaders, or the church at large. The tools can be used by churches of any size or literacy level. They should be used frequently, until wholistic outreach is a ministry habit. Faithful evaluation supports faithful service!

After Evaluation—What?

Evaluation has a purpose. We evaluate, act, then evaluate again. This is what the Prodigal Son did, in Jesus' parable recorded in Luke 15. One day, the Prodigal Son *"came to his senses."*[12] He took account—his life was in shambles. Next, he decided what to do—to return to his father and ask to be treated like one of the servants. Finally, he carried out the decision. The Bible gives us several possible actions in response to evaluation:

- *Change our course:* Like the Prodigal Son, we can reflect on our current course and see errors. We can see why we are not reaching our goal—and adjust to do what God intends.
- *Continue in faithfulness:* If we examine our course and believe we are being faithful, our action is simply to continue—to please God and to give Him greater service. In another parable, Jesus told His listeners of the master's remark to a faithful servant: *"Well done, good and faithful servant! You have been faithful with a few things; I will put you in charge of many things. Come and share in your master's happiness!"*[13]

---

[12] Luke 15:17a
[13] Matthew 25:21

Measuring Individual Faithfulness in Service

The goal of individual service is to actively demonstrate God's love to others—and develop a lifestyle of service as we continue in the good works God has prepared for us.[14] This is the most basic evaluation of our faithfulness to His call. Here are two wonderful accounts of individual faithfulness in service:

❖   The first was humbly told by a colleague, a leader of a Christian organization in a restricted country in Southeast Asia. This gentleman has been working to help his nation's churches understand their need to demonstrate the love of Christ by reaching out to help their neighbors. One night, my colleague awakened at 4 a.m., sure that the Lord was telling him to pray for the Buddhist monks living in a monastery near his home. *Faithful to the Lord's direction,* he immediately prayed for the monks. Soon, he learned that the monks at this monastery lacked food. They depended on donations, but the donations had not been sufficient. My colleague decided to call on other Christians, asking for rice for the monks. Some said: "No, let them die and go to hell!" But he persisted. He asked others and was able to collect half a sack of rice, which he presented to the senior Buddhist monk. The monk was greatly surprised by his compassion and asked if his intent was to convert him to Christianity. "No," my colleague replied, "I simply want to be *faithful to obey the instructions of Jesus to love my neighbors."* Then he left. One week later, the second-to-senior monk came to him and said he would like to learn about Jesus. My friend told him the Good News. Then the monk left. Another week later, the same monk returned and said he needed a new set of clothes. "Why?" asked my friend. The monk replied, "I'm going to leave the monastery. I want to be a Christian." My colleague then prayed with the monk to begin a life in Christ. After several months, my colleague heard that the former monk had introduced twenty others to Christ, including three other monks.[15]

In this instance, my colleague was able to see some of the spiritual

---

[14] Ephesians 2:10

[15] Sources for stories marked by ❖ are listed in the Bibliography at the end of the book.

fruit of his obedient service, but that is not always the case. Nor was it his objective! His objective was faithfulness to do God's bidding and obey Jesus' command. He was faithful to truths revealed in Scripture and to the inner promptings of the Spirit. He was faithful to pray in the middle of the night and to gather rice. God multiplied the fruit of my colleague's faithful service, many times!

❖   A young man in the United States works as a stock clerk in a grocery store. He has a humble occupation, but his faithfulness makes him effective. Through his influence, store employees—with the approval and participation of the owner—meet together and pray to bless the people who come into the store. Further, the stock clerk asks the Holy Spirit to make him sensitive to customers who have needs that God wants to meet. Then, the young man is faithful. He greets the customers, engages them in friendly conversation, and asks if they have needs for which he can pray. They are often surprised—but tell him their needs. He prays, asking God to help them. I have heard that a number of people have been introduced to the Savior through this young man's faithfulness.

Stories and testimonies may help us begin to "measure" faithfulness. Following are other means to help individuals further evaluate faithfulness in service. They can be used within small groups, in mentoring, with accountability partners, or individually.

- *My Journal of Service.* Individuals can use this to review a weekly activity of service and to examine themselves for hindrances to growth. I have included a sample and a blank form. (Individuals should keep journal entries in one book; they may also e-mail journals to accountability partners.)

- *Mementos* are another way to record individual service. Individuals keep mementos from times of service—letters, pictures, poems, or personal reflections. These can be kept in a box, drawer, bulletin board, scrapbook, journal, or album. They encourage warm memories and future service. They help us tell others what God did—and base our lives on what He taught us.

SAMPLE

Week of ~June 2-9~ **My Journal of Service**

1. Write about something you did in the past week that helped you or another person grow closer to God's intentions. This should not be something you normally do, but something that "stretches" you and causes you to develop more in the image of Jesus, the Servant. Be specific. Include: what you did; why you did it; who was involved. Identify which of the four Luke 2:52 areas were addressed by your action.*

2. Briefly describe something you did that hindered growth in you or others. Ask God to help you correct it. (This does not necessarily relate to your service activity.)

*Note: This report may also be used to describe a Discipline of Love exercise.

My Journal Notes

1. I was out for my daily walk on Saturday. One of my elderly neighbors, Arnold, was working in his garden. I stopped to say "Hi." He told me that his wife was very ill and not expected to live. I could tell that he needed someone to share his grief. So, instead of going on my walk, I took time to listen and let him know of my concern. I told him I had lost my mother a year ago. I told him I would be praying for him, and I have.

The primary area of my action was social, but I trust God will use it to spiritually encourage my neighbor. I plan to ask if there is anything I can do to help.

2. At dinner one evening I was sharing my thoughts about one of the leaders in my church. What I said reflected how I feel, but the way I said it didn't reflect the love of 1 Corinthians 13. I need the Lord to help me guard my mouth.

----

* FOUR AREAS OF LUKE 2:52

Wisdom: Activity that helps to teach, explain, or clarify God's will in some area of life

Physical: Activity which contributes to a physical need or physical growth

Spiritual: Activity which contributes to a spiritual need or spiritual growth

Social: Activity which contributes to a social need or social growth

Week of _____ My Journal of Service

1. Write about something you did in the past week that helped you or another person grow closer to God's intentions. This should not be something you normally do, but something that "stretches" you and causes you to develop more in the image of Jesus, the Servant. Be specific. Include: what you did; why you did it; who was involved. Identify which of the four Luke 2:52 areas were addressed by your action.*

2. Briefly describe something you did that hindered growth in you or others. Ask God to help you correct it. (This does not necessarily relate to your service activity.)

*Note: This report may also be used to describe a Discipline of Love exercise.

My Journal Notes

----

* **FOUR AREAS OF LUKE 2:52**

Wisdom: Activity that helps to teach, explain, or clarify God's will in some area of life

Physical: Activity which contributes to a physical need or physical growth

Spiritual: Activity which contributes to a spiritual need or spiritual growth

Social: Activity which contributes to a social need or social growth

Measuring Corporate Faithfulness in Service

The goal of local church service is, likewise, to serve others with the love of God. Here are two accounts of obedient service:

❖ In Brazil, ten young people and their youth pastor decided to develop a drug-prevention program for schools. After discussion and prayer, they sensed God wanted them to design materials that showed how drugs harm people in each area of life—physical, social, spiritual, and wisdom—and then point to Jesus as the answer. They were obedient and persevering. Representing their church, they presented the program in local schools. They were well received. Subsequently, the program was made available to 6,000 churches for use in partnership with schools, and the youth pastor showed it to the director of the national agency for drug prevention, who endorsed it. The Brazilian government now produces the materials for use in church and school partnerships throughout the country!

❖ Members of several Tokyo churches decided to demonstrate God's love in their city. Young people from one of the churches went to a large train station with a sign: "If you want to talk, we want to listen." They knew their approach was counter to Japanese culture, but they sensed that the idea was from God and wanted to obey Him. They hung their sign, sat, and waited. Their faithfulness was rewarded. People came to talk. Some poured out stories of deep struggles they were having, and the young Christians listened and prayed for them. One young man asked why they were doing this, and they replied that it was because of Jesus' love. He left, later returned, asked to participate, and has since given his life to Christ.

As with individual service, *stories and testimonies* of corporate service help us begin to "measure" the faithful service of a local church or small group. Following are additional tools to help groups further evaluate faithfulness in service. The tools do not only evaluate outcomes, but *process*. They help us identify where God is calling us to demonstrate His love. They help us set measurable objectives. They help us report to our congregations—during church services, in mailings, or at small group meetings. They help church members praise God for community impact and pray for specific outreaches.

In summary, they reinforce the church's commitment to service.

- *Evaluation 1* is a window of service in the four areas. Page 1 is *monthly*. Page 2 is a *calendar summary*. I have included both a sample and a blank tool.

- *Evaluation 2* is a numerical analysis, designed in Korea for use after an extended wholistic ministry training program. It evaluates how broadly the lifestyle of service has spread within a local church.

- *Wholistic DNA in a Local Church* (in the previous chapter) can be used to evaluate how wholistic ministry is affecting the DNA of a local church.

- *Memorials.* A church can display mementos of service activities—framed letters, a picture with a brief story, or something that helps the church remember what God did through its outreach in the community. The church is not congratulating itself on its goodness, but rejoicing at what God has done through its efforts. A memorial provides an opportunity to tell stories of God's work when someone asks, "What is this?"[16] Here is what one church did:

❖ A church in the U.S. collected blankets and pillows for the homeless. Church members collected the items at church and also at a grocery store. A sign at the store said the blankets would be demonstrations of God's concern for the poor. Before the items were distributed, they were brought to the front of the church. It was filled with blankets and pillows! The church prayed a blessing over the items and the people who would use them. This was a *blanket-and-pillow memorial* of the church's service.

Lifestyle Tools

We are servants! It is my sincere prayer that the tools in Part Four—including the evaluation tools on the following pages—help you and your church maintain lifestyles of individual and corporate service that honor Christ and serve those He loves.

---

[16] Joshua 4:1-7

Month of *June*   **The Church as a Window**   **Evaluation 1**
           For local churches or small groups   **SAMPLE**
MONTHLY EVALUATION

Last month, how did the church equip its members to carry out God's agenda in the community?
* *Individual service activities were reported in small group meetings*
* *Volunteers were trained to visit widows in our community*
* *Pastor preached sermon on James 1:27 and had follow-up altar call*

Last month, what was one activity that church members planned and did to demonstrate God's love? *Visits & food for widows*

What took place under each of the planned impact areas?*

Use the chart below, or tell the story on the back of the evaluation.

Wisdom	Spiritual
We held a training session for volunteers who wanted to visit community widows.	*Indirect impact: We said we were bringing the baskets to express God's love and care.*
Physical	**Social**
Four small groups visited a widow or single mother and brought food baskets. One single mother was from our church. The other three lived in our community but were not associated with our church. The women expressed surprise and joy.	*Indirect impact: We visited a long time with each of them.*

* **FOUR AREAS OF LUKE 2:52**
Wisdom: Activity that helps to teach, explain, or clarify God's will in some area of life
Physical: Activity which contributes to a physical need or physical growth
Spiritual: Activity which contributes to a spiritual need or spiritual growth
Social: Activity which contributes to a social need or social growth

Month of _____ The Church as a Window   **Evaluation 1**
                                                    Continued

ANNUAL SUMMARY

Write projects completed each month.

January *New Year's party for neighborhood children (Social)*	July
February *Meeting with community leaders to discuss street garbage (Wisdom)*	August
March *Garbage clean-up party (Physical)*	September
April *Provided housing for refugee family (Physical)*	October
May *Music concert for community (Spiritual)*	November
June *Visitation of widows (Physical)*	December

Blank forms are provided on the following pages.

Month of _____ The Church as a Window \hfill **Evaluation 1**

For local churches or small groups \hfill SAMPLE

MONTHLY EVALUATION

Last month, how did the church equip its members to carry out God's agenda in the community?

Last month, what was one activity that church members *planned and did* to demonstrate God's love?

What took place under each of the planned impact areas?*
Use the chart below, or tell the story on the back of the evaluation.

Wisdom	Spiritual
Physical	**Social**

---

* FOUR AREAS OF LUKE 2:52
Wisdom: Activity that helps to teach, explain, or clarify God's will in some area of life
Physical: Activity which contributes to a physical need or physical growth
Spiritual: Activity which contributes to a spiritual need or spiritual growth
Social: Activity which contributes to a social need or social growth

Month of _____ The Church as a Window   **Evaluation 1**
                                                     Continued

ANNUAL SUMMARY

Write projects completed each month.

January	July
February	August
March	September
April	October
May	November
June	December

The evaluation form on the following pages was designed in Korea. It is to be used after a church has been trained in wholistic ministry and service. It evaluates how broadly the lifestyle of wholistic service has spread within a local church.

Time Period Covered _____   **Evaluation 2**

Health Survey
Wholistic Ministry in the Local Church*
(For use after Wholistic Ministry Training)

Select only the one best answer for each question.

Circle the number of the answer to each question—1, 2, 3, 4, 5, or 6.

Follow instructions after the survey to evaluate your church's wholistic ministry health.

I.   How often is the church's leadership involved in demonstrating Christ's love in the community through small actions of service?

1.   Never
2.   Occasionally
3.   Two or three times a year
4.   Monthly
5.   Weekly
6.   Regularly, as a lifestyle

II. What percentage of the small groups in the church engage in actions that demonstrate Christ's love to their neighbor at least four times per year?

1.   Fewer than 10% of the small groups
2.   10% or more   3. 30% or more   4. 50% or more
5.   70% or more   6. 85% or more

III. What percentage of the preaching includes a call for the people to specifically apply the message at the level of loving their neighbors as themselves?

1.   Fewer than 10% of the sermons
2.   10% or more   3. 30% or more   4. 50% or more
5.   70% or more   6. 85% or more

IV. What percentage of the congregation has participated in a Seed Project in the last year?

1.   Less than 5% of the congregation
2.   5% or more   3. 20% or more   4. 40% or more
5.   60% or more   6. 80% or more

* Developed in Korea after an extended wholistic ministry training program for local churches.

V. How has the church been serving as an example of wholistic ministry to other churches in the community?

   1. We have been living as an example of wholistic ministry.
   2. We have discussed some of our church's experiences with another church.
   3. We have related the church's testimony in a formal setting.
   4. We have held a workshop to present wholistic ministry to other churches.
   5. One other church has begun wholistic ministry training because of our church's example.
   6. More than one church has followed our church's example in wholistic ministry and training.

VI. What is your church's wholistic ministry influence on cross-cultural ministry, or discipling nations?

   1. We have been a living example for our church's missionaries.
   2. We have communicated the vision for wholistic ministry to cross-cultural workers.
   3. Individuals or groups within our church have engaged in at least one cross-cultural activity that demonstrates Christ's love.
   4. Our church has sent members on short-term teams to engage in wholistic community ministry in a cross-cultural setting.
   5. Our church has ongoing mentoring of missionaries in wholistic ministry.
   6. Our church has sent out at least one cross-cultural missionary with a wholistic view of ministry.

VII. Has wholistic ministry training been extended throughout the church—including youth and children?

   1. Less than 5% of our church people have been trained in wholistic ministry
   2. 5% or more   3. 20% or more   4. 40% or more
   5. 60% or more   6. 80% or more

VIII. What percentage of church leaders and members regularly practice the Discipline of Love?

   1. Less than 5% of the congregation
   2. 5% or more   3. 20% or more   4. 40% or more
   5. 60% or more   6. 80% or more

IX. How often do our church members do Seed Projects?
1. Our church members have done one Seed Project.
2. Our members have done two Seed Projects in the past year.
3. Our church does one Seed Project every three months.
4. Our church is involved in doing Seed Projects monthly.
5. Our church members do more than one Seed Project monthly.
6. Seed Projects in the community are ongoing and long-term ministries of our church.

X. How is the community outside the church being impacted by the wholistic community ministry of the church?
1. The church has made initial efforts to be of service to the community.
2. The church has identified at least one area of need in the community that the church can address.
3. The church is involved in ongoing, consistent action that demonstrates God's love for the people of the community.
4. Many in the community recognize the beneficial role of the church for the life of the community.
5. The community is looking to the church for assistance in addressing community needs.
6. The community is looking to the church for leadership in addressing community needs.

INSTRUCTIONS: Tally the numbers from each of the ten questions.

There should be one number (1, 2, 3, 4, 5, or 6) circled in each of the ten questions. Total the circled numbers. The highest possible score is 60—if #6 was circled in all ten questions. The lowest possible score is 0.

Remember that numbers do not perfectly describe what God is doing through your church, but they help you see how to further implement wholistic ministry and vision.

Compare your score with the scale on the following page to evaluate your church's current wholistic ministry focus.

Transformation and Faithfulness

Biblical transformation advances in our communities and nations as we faithfully and obediently do the works God created for us, individually and corporately. As accountable stewards, we plan, serve, and evaluate. Walking in step with God, we have a potential impact beyond our imaginations, *as if Jesus were Mayor.*

Answers to Evaluation 2

If your total score was . . .

0 – 10	Your church has not yet seen its God-given role in the community
11 - 20	Your church is awakening to its role in the community.
21 - 30	Your church is taking its first steps in blessing your community.
31 – 40	Your church—individually and corporately—is growing in its ability and practice to love its neighbor as itself.
41 – 50	Your church and its members provide a healthy ministry example for other churches.
51 – 60	Your church—individually and corporately—is ministering wholistically. You need to continue and influence other churches by your example.

Epilogue

If Jesus were Mayor, how would your community change?

It is a great question, isn't it? It has been fulfilling for me to share my thoughts with you. I trust it has been just as challenging for you to think of possible answers—and their implications.

Jesus as Mayor is one of many metaphors we could use as we look at God's intentions for the role of each church in the community where it ministers. This is a compelling and challenging picture! There is no question that God intends each local congregation of His disciples to be an embassy of His government—to both proclaim and advance His purposes.

As we close our conversation, I would like the privilege of asking our Father to help us see and do His will as we answer this question with our individual and corporate lives.

Father, thank You for my brothers and sisters. You have given me the honor of sharing these thoughts with them about Your bride and her purpose.

Allow Your Spirit to sift the wheat from the chaff of what I have written. May what remains from the sifting burn in our hearts until the flame consumes that which holds us back from intentionally, aggressively advancing Your agenda in the churches where we serve.

Father, fill us more completely with a passion to do Your will—first in our own lives and then within the churches we serve—until the splendor of Your present Kingdom draws the lost and broken of our communities into your healing light.

Flood our minds and hearts with the reality that Your Son—our Mayor—intends to restore all things. May we be so filled that we cannot hold back from sharing and giving ourselves wholly to advancing the Mayor's agenda.

May Your Kingdom come, may Your will be done on earth as it is in heaven!

In Jesus' name, Amen

Appendix

The Local Church and the Parachurch

The Local Church
and the Parachurch
How Should They Relate?

This discussion is a call to *all* who are engaged in the mission of Christ—especially those who lead local churches and parachurch ministries. This is not a treatise against the parachurch. I am the leader of a parachurch mission. Instead, it is a call for prayerful examination of God's strategy for the task He has given.

There is a flurry of activity in the mission and development world today, produced by an entity known as the parachurch. With the activity come questions. What is the parachurch? How should it relate to the ministry of the local church? As we examine the relationship between the parachurch and the local church, it is important to observe two key premises:

- The parachurch is not the same as the local church.
- The local church, according to Scripture, is *the* primary institution through which God intends to accomplish His agenda.

At times, both the local church and parachurch misunderstand the primacy of the local church. As a consequence, both risk operating in ways that decrease their impact—and may even impede God's intentions for His church. Though this is true around the world, I will focus especially on the relationship between the local church and parachurch in the Two-Thirds World.

Challenging Relationships in the Two-Thirds World

Individual local churches of the Two-Thirds World are often weaker in many ways than the parachurch organizations that operate in their communities. The parachurch ministries—usually funded and controlled from the West—may have larger budgets, staff, technical resources, and networks than local churches. This creates challenges for both:

- If local churches do not understand their biblically ordained role, they risk a diminished harvest and the blessings God intends for them. They must guard against being replaced in that role by well-meaning but more powerful parachurch organizations.

- If parachurch organizations do not recognize and respect the primacy of the local church, they risk impeding or even aborting the ultimate goal for which they were created—even when they greatly desire to see the Kingdom of God extended.

The local church is the principal institutional vehicle through which God intends to accomplish His agenda.

The Universal Church—Expressed as the Local Church

This is seen in Ephesians, where the Apostle Paul confirmed God's plan to use the church as the administrator of His grand agenda:

> *Although I am less than the least of all God's people, this grace was given me: to preach to the Gentiles the unsearchable riches of Christ, and to make plain to everyone the administration of this mystery, which for ages past was kept hidden in God, who created all things. His intent was that now, through the church, the manifold wisdom of God should be made known to the rulers and authorities in the heavenly realms, according to his eternal purpose which he accomplished in Christ Jesus our Lord.*[1]

Paul was speaking of the universal church.[2] In Paul's experience, the universal church carried out this agenda in the context of the

---

[1] Ephesians 3:8-11

[2] *Universal church*: Includes all Christians and their institutions or fellowships.

local church. The local church is the only institutional expression of the church described in the New Testament:

- The first time we see the church-in-action in Scripture, no distinction was made between the universal church and the local church. The universal expression of the church in Acts assumes there were local churches, known by their geographical locations—Ephesus, Corinth, Antioch, Lystra, Derbe, Jerusalem.

- Scripture introduced a local-church leadership structure of elders and other leaders who were to guide—and sacrificially serve—local expressions of the church.

- Only members of a localized expression of the church could gather regularly to worship and share the Lord's Table.

The Parachurch

The New Testament has no record of parachurch organizations.[3] This absence, though, does not invalidate the parachurch any more than the absence of Bible schools or seminaries in the New Testament invalidates their validity or usefulness today.

The parachurch is part of the church universal, but it must never take the place of the local church. The local church is the only institution with an implied New Testament ordination to extend the Kingdom of God.[4] Because the local church is the only institutional representative of the universal church in the New Testament, I believe it is appropriate to see it as the principal vehicle that God uses to extend His Kingdom. Throughout history, though, God has raised up vehicles other than the local church to accomplish His purposes. I believe the parachurch is one such vehicle.

There is early precedent for the parachurch. There were specialized

---

[3] *Parachurch*: By definition, parachurch organizations come "alongside" the church. They generally offer a more specialized ministry and have a narrower focus than the local church.

[4] Matthew 18:19-20; Matthew 16:18; Ephesians 3:8-11

ministries outside the local church in early centuries—hospitals, hostels, religious orders, and more. But parachurch roles and purposes change according to the needs of their times. Many of today's parachurch institutions are relatively recent inventions.

Defining Characteristics of the Local Church and the Parachurch

THE LOCAL CHURCH	THE PARACHURCH
The New Testament implies that it is a local expression of the universal church.	We assume that anything known as "parachurch" is Christian and institutional. It is not the same as the local church.
The New Testament says that God gave leaders to the church—apostles, prophets, evangelists, pastors, and teachers. Most of these serve the local church and equip its people for works of service.[5]	The parachurch is not mentioned in the New Testament, but this does not invalidate it. Neither were Bible schools or seminaries.
The local church is charged with the broad mandate to live under the reign of Christ, representing and extending the Kingdom of God.	The mission of the parachurch is part of—but narrower than—that of the local church. (A parachurch organization that does disaster relief has a narrower mission than the church, even if it has geographically wider activity.)
The local church is guided by elders, deacons, and local leaders in various capacities. It may also be under the accountability structure of a larger and formal association of local churches.	Parachurch leadership structure is similar to organizational models of the secular world. It is usually independent of local churches—and is often independent of formal associations of churches.

---

[5] Ephesians 4:11-12

It gathers regularly and intentionally to worship God through adoration, praise, prayer, Scripture, doctrinal instruction, guarding against false doctrine, encouragement and accountability in Christian living, giving of tithes and offerings, celebration of the Lord's Supper, baptism of new believers, ministry to the needy, and evangelism.	The parachurch may gather to worship, study, and pray, but primarily to gain His empowerment, wisdom, knowledge, and plan for the specific part of His agenda that it carries.
The local church gathers for regular worship and equipping, but scatters to advance God's broad agenda.	The parachurch gathers for worship and equipping. In most cases, it scatters for specific service and its specific role in the larger task of God's agenda.
Its role and purpose have not changed since Christ instituted it—and will not change until He returns.	Its role and purpose change according to the needs of the people, the times, the locale, the church—and the world.

How the Parachurch Came to Exist

The second half of the twentieth century saw a proliferation of independent evangelical, charismatic, and Pentecostal parachurch agencies—Campus Crusade for Christ, World Vision, Youth With A Mission (YWAM), Inter-Varsity, Navigators, Compassion, Young Life, Medical Ambassadors, Business Men's Fellowship, Focus on the Family, Food for the Hungry, and our own Harvest. There are many reasons for this explosion:

- Individuals or groups were touched by God to cover gaps that seem untended or poorly manned by the local church. Founders of parachurch ministries often have a passion to see God's intentions fulfilled in a specific area of ministry.

- The spirit of individualism—especially in the West— encourages individuals to act alone, if necessary, to reach a goal. This individualistic spirit prompts those with pioneering personalities to say: "If the local church is not doing this, then I'll do it—and I'll find others who will do it with me."

- People with a purpose want to get things done! The focused task of the parachurch often allows more efficiency than the broader mandate of a local church. Campus Crusade for Christ began with a vision for evangelism on the university campus. Founder Bill Bright was able to develop a focus and strategy without concerning himself with the multiple tasks of a local church.

- A parachurch organization often has better potential to gather skills and resources for a specific purpose. World Vision can locate funds and staff to respond to international emergencies more efficiently than a local church, cooperating churches, or perhaps even a national denomination.

- Parachurch organizations are less tied to history. They are positioned to avoid the politics, narrow theologies, lack of vision, and inertia of local churches with long histories. Their leaders do not have to graduate from a specific school or be ordained by a specific denomination. In one sense, parachurch organizations are like "new wine in *new* wineskins." Of course, those of us in parachurch ministries recognize that imperfection infects us as much as it does the local church.

The contemporary version of the parachurch is a relatively new modality of the universal church, with the following characteristics:

- A desire—even a passion—to see a specific part of God's agenda accomplished
- A willingness to cover the gaps not well tended by the local church
- A relatively more efficient focus on a particular aspect of Kingdom activity than local churches with a similar focus
- An ability to mobilize resources for the mission from a broader base than an individual local church
- Relative freedom from historical "wineskins"

Why has there been such a proliferation of parachurch ministries in the last one-hundred years? A key reason it that it is simply easier to accomplish some Kingdom tasks as parachurch than as local church!

Questions about Parachurch Ministry

Parachurch ministry may be an easier way to accomplish some aspects of our Lord's mandate, but there are overarching questions to consider as the church moves into its third millennium:

- Does parachurch ministry operate in a way that reflects God's primary means of extending His Kingdom?

  For example, is it more consistent with God's intentions that youth be reached by the local church or by a youth outreach ministry, such as Youth for Christ or Young Life?

- If local churches carried out the tasks addressed by parachurch ministries, would it be more effective—in the long term—for Christ's Kingdom?

> For example, would there be a long-term difference for the
> Kingdom if young people were evangelized and discipled within
> a local church, rather than a parachurch ministry?

These thoughts about *God's intentions* and *long-term effectiveness*
form the framework for other questions:

Question: If parachurch ministry is part of God's principal plan
for extending the Kingdom, why do we not see it in the
New Testament?

Question: Why is it difficult to identify biblical titles for those
who lead or work as staff in parachurch organizations?
Are they leaders, apostles, prophets, evangelists, bishops,
pastors, elders, or teachers?

Question: Are the tasks of a parachurch organization something
that a local church, or coalition of churches, can or
should be doing?

Question: Do parachurch successes accelerate the extension of the
Kingdom of God? Would the Kingdom be extended
further if more parachurch resources were used to
empower local church outreach, instead of direct
parachurch ministry?

Question: Do parachurch actions sometimes rob local churches
in the Two-Thirds World of the opportunity to be the
blessing, light, and salt God intends? Do parachurch
organizations respond too readily with outside resources?
Does this discourage local churches from reliance on
God, obedient sacrifice, and the use of local resources to
begin to meet needs?

Question: Do parachurch organizations have a greater tendency to
respond quickly to "felt need," rather than pause and
seek God's intentions in the midst of crisis?

Question: If parachurch ministry is part of God's principal
plan, why isn't the United States—with parachurch
organizations for almost every aspect of ministry—more
spiritually healthy than it is?

Question: Do parachurch ministries have a greater history of corrupting local people through overwhelming economic and technical advantages?

Leaders of local churches and parachurch organizations testify to the value of each form of ministry. I do, too. Yet, these questions raise enough issues to tell us we need to continue to look for God's strategy for the roles and interrelationships of the local church and the parachurch.

Roles and Relationships of Parachurch and Local Church

I'd like to pose a second series of questions, and this time I'd like to suggest possible responses. The answers I propose imply that there can be relationships between the local church and the parachurch that take advantage of the strengths of both—and respect the local church's role as God's principal instrument in the mission of the universal church:

Question: *Do parachurch efforts fill a legitimate place in the universal church?*

Answer: Yes, when parachurch organizations have specialized roles beyond the capacity of a local church or local churches working together, there is an important place in the universal church for their efforts. Many parachurch organizations have specialized roles that are difficult for local churches to fill. MAP provides medical supplies and community health consultation. Floresta specializes in reforestation. ECHO specializes in under-utilized plants. MAF provides missionary air transportation. World Vision can coordinate and support disaster relief on a large scale that would be difficult, if not impossible, for local churches. These are needed and valuable services in the work of the Kingdom. I praise the Lord for members of the universal church who have the vision, desire, and skills to address this part of God's agenda to restore *"all things."* [6]

---

[6] Colossians 1:20

Question: *How can the parachurch empower the local church, especially in its specialty?*

Answer: The parachurch can *equip* the local church.

- Train it in the tasks for which the parachurch has a mandate
- Build skills—such as problem-solving, nonformal education techniques, planning, or evaluation
- Assist it to develop its *own* vision—instead of urging it to adopt the parachurch's vision
- Offer consultation as the church implements new vision and skills

The parachurch can *encourage* the local church.

- Share a vision from God's Word regarding its specialized ministry
- Walk alongside to help if the local church runs into difficulties or stumbles in the implementation of its vision
- Offer a covenant relationship of prayer—sharing tasks and burdens
- Foster reciprocity, so the local church also ministers to the parachurch

The parachurch can *network* the local church.

- Link it with other local churches that have similar visions
- Network inexperienced local churches with experienced churches, for the purpose of training
- Introduce it to local government and business relationships
- Introduce it to other local or international organizations with skills and resources that could help local churches carry out their visions

Question: *Generally, how should a parachurch organization relate to a local church?*

Answer: Parachurch organizations should ask themselves: "Is what we do something that the local church can and should do?" If the answer is affirmative, then the parachurch should utilize its resources to equip and support local churches to fulfill the mandate. (*Example:* Young Life directors train church youth leaders in effective high school ministry in their communities, instead of initiating independent outreaches.)

Question: *How should local churches relate to parachurch organizations?*

Answer: Local churches can actively pursue relationships with parachurch ministries, especially through staff. Local churches should embrace, encourage, and minister to the parachurch staff. The local church can also offer accountability to parachurch staff. Local churches should actively explore ways to work in mutual partnership with parachurch organizations and staff, maximizing the appropriate roles of both. (*Example:* The director of the Campus Crusade ministry at a major university intentionally involves his unchurched students in his local church, where they are nurtured and encouraged in their faith, service, and ministry.)

Question: *If the local church is the principal institutional vehicle to extend the Kingdom of God, how should the local church and parachurch relate?*

Answer: Where the local church has the potential to carry out a part of Christ's mandate, it has the priority, right, and responsibility. In this case, the parachurch organization should invest its primary energy in encouraging and equipping the local church. While so engaged, the parachurch should submit to the leadership of the local church it is encouraging and equipping. When there are parts of the mandate the local church cannot carry out—for example, large scale disaster relief—the local church should delegate or encourage other forms of the church, such as the parachurch, to do so. Even then, the local church should offer oversight. The parachurch ministry should acknowledge its role in carrying out its specialized part of Christ's mandate as *supplemental* to that of the local church.

Local Church and Parachurch Interrelationships— Special Situations

Here is a third series of questions, which help us consider how the local church and the parachurch can work together in special situations:

Question: *How can the parachurch respond carefully when there is competition and denominational bias between local churches?*

Answer: The parachurch should seek churches that are open to work in unity, without receiving credit for their work. The parachurch works primarily with these churches, but strives to maintain good relations with the others.

Question: *How should a parachurch ministry respond if the local church is weak?*

Answer: In many instances, a parachurch ministry is called to an area where local churches are narrow in theology, lacking in morals or integrity, limited in training or ability, regard themselves as poor, or are otherwise not interested in incorporating the specialized vision of the parachurch organization. The parachurch ministry can engender vision, offer encouragement, and invest itself in churches that are interested. The local church is God's ordained instrument, and the Holy Spirit will direct the parachurch to local churches where the long-term purposes of God will be maximized. If a parachurch organization works in an area where there are no local churches to train in its specialization, it might collaborate with other area churches to plant another local church that would eventually do so.[7]

Question: *What can be done where there is no local church?*

Answer: There are still many areas of the world where the advance of the Kingdom of God requires an apostolic ministry. Rather than plant a church, the parachurch can equip and advise church-planting teams from nearby local churches to go into unchurched areas. The teams represent the local church, not the parachurch ministry. Parachurch assistants strengthen and coach—but do not direct—local church teams. They may offer specific input in their area of specialization. When local churches are scarce, Christian relief and development organizations are generally better prepared to respond to urgent human need. In such cases, local churches should encourage and support parachurch organizations in the extension of God's mercy. At the same time, the parachurch should seek to find local or near-local churches. If and when they are found, the churches—as a matter of policy—should be incorporated as much as possible into the mercy ministry of the parachurch.

Question: *How could the local church participate in large-scale operations like famine relief?*

Answer: The parachurch should inform local churches of plans and strategies for relief and seek creative ways that local churches can effectively collaborate and participate. The local church can also be prepared to minister after the famine, after the parachurch has filled its role. The parachurch organization must never be paternalistic.

---

[7] This does not refer to such mission specialties as aviation, but areas of activity that can readily be handled by local churches—such as evangelism, discipleship, community service, or youth work.

Question: *What if governments are more responsive to large, international organizations—than to small church-based groups?*

Answer: Parachurch organizations can use their experience and reputations to help local churches operate creatively, network, interface, and work with government organizations.

Other Considerations

The local church is intended to remain as long as there are people to disciple. Parachurch organizations come and go, depending on their particular mission. Many of their projects and activities stop when they leave. The parachurch has a focused mission, but the local church has a broad mandate. Over time, the local church is actually *better* equipped to minister to the whole of human need in a geographical area.

Parachurch ministries often rely on material and technical resources, while the local church—especially the local church in the Two-Thirds World—tends to rely more heavily on God, His miraculous intervention, and the sacrificial work of its members to meet the needs of its community.

Finally, there is greater potential for multiplying wholistic ministry through the local church because it has a broad mission, while the parachurch has a narrower, more specific mandate.

God's Perspective

God intends the local church to be the primary instrument to extend His Kingdom. If we know and believe that, then we must act in accordance with it—or we sin. Sin is the voluntary choice by individuals or institutions to act contrary to the will of God. Righteousness is the voluntary choice to submit to God's design.

Those of us in the parachurch community are pragmatic people. We want to do what is effective—what seems to work best. Because of our pragmatism, though, we run the risk of doing what seems right in our own eyes, but this is wrong. We need to think of the timeframe of the Kingdom of God, which encompasses *all* of history. Instead, we make five-year or ten-year plans, rarely looking beyond our own life spans.

Several years ago, I read *Tongues of Fire* by a British sociologist, David Martin. As I read his history of Pentecostalism in Latin America, I was struck that God had been working powerfully in Latin America the last hundred years, yet it has only been in recent generations that *we* have seen His hand. Many of the Gospel messengers to Latin America in the first part of the twentieth century died with little visible evidence that God was working. We now see that He honored their obedience to His call.

I often wonder if the long-term results of our efforts would change if we became more concerned about following God's intentions for the local church than our own pragmatism! No matter how slow it may seem to carry out ministry through the local church—and no matter how little we may know about how to do it—if the local church is God's principal choice for the advancement of the Kingdom, then the most strategic thing a parachurch ministry can do is empower the local church to take its role in God's scheme. It may be slower in the short term; but it will be a better, more effective, more complete strategy in the long term.

Our Testimony

I have the privilege of directing Harvest, a parachurch ministry. Our first five years fit the relief and development industry model of providing outside resources to demonstrate God's concern for physical and social needs. We worked in Latin American and Caribbean communities. Sometimes we worked with local churches, and sometimes with local parachurch ministries. In 1986 God made us keenly aware that some of our well intentioned efforts were bypassing the primacy of the local church. As a result, our work even corrupted a few local pastors who managed the projects we facilitated. It created jealousy and division over the control of resources we had channeled.

Our leadership clearly sensed God directing us to help churches look to God, not to us or to North American partners, for vision *and* resources. We did not clearly understand what God was saying, but we believed we had heard Him speak. Sensing a need, we began developing Bible studies with practical applications. These studies focused on God's wholistic agenda for the broken creation; His commands to demonstrate His love; the use of small, practical acts of service that were done with local resources; and the need to trust Him for a Kingdom harvest.

This strategy was not easy. It required patience and wisdom, but God was gracious. We began to see results, which encouraged us to continue learning what He intends. Almost two decades later, we know that our calling as a parachurch is not to do things *for* the local church, but to help it see and practice the implications of its primacy in the Kingdom. Now, the local churches we train do not begin community-ministry projects with outside resources, but with the resources at hand—no matter how few or small their resources or how much sacrifice is needed.

It is clear from our experience that the advance of the Kingdom is far wider—and personal and community transformation are far deeper—than under our initial strategy. The stories from individuals and churches throughout this book provide illustrations of this grace.

I praise God every time I encounter another parachurch organization that wants to equip, encourage, and network the local church to more effectively carry out the agenda of Jesus—*as if Jesus were Mayor* of the community in which it serves. Together, may we assist the entire church to have the impact and influence that God intends.

Glossary

Biblical wholism: A mindset that understands the world according to God's whole agenda, as revealed in Scripture.

Conservative branch of the Protestant church: Evangelicals, charismatics, Pentecostals, and other conservative faith traditions that believe, among other tenets, that the Bible is the authoritative Word of God and individual salvation is essential.

Culture: All of the ways of life that define who we are as individuals and as a society. Culture includes the behaviors, patterns, beliefs, thoughts, institutions, values, traditions, habits, practices, and characteristics that we pass along to the next generation. Culture defines how a society thinks and operates. If we want to transform a society, we do so by transforming its culture.

Fall: Man's rebellion against God and the consequences of this rebellion (Genesis 3).

Gnosticism: The Greek dichotomy between the spiritual realm, which is considered sacred, and the physical realm, which is considered evil.

Liberal branch of the Protestant church: Many mainline denominations, churches, and organizations with a strong emphasis on social issues, generally interpreting Scriptures less authoritatively than in conservative churches and placing less emphasis on individual spiritual salvation.

Local church: A fellowship of Christians who identify themselves as such. The principal and biblical expression of the universal church on earth. All area fellowships can be considered as that area's local church.

Mayor: The primary leader in a local community.

Nation: In the Old Testament, "nation" (mishpachah, in Hebrew) means a family group, tribe, or clan. The New Testament uses the Greek word ethnos, indicating a race, people, or ethnic group.

Naturalism: A system that sees the world as ultimately physical and limited, controlled by the blind operations of impersonal natural laws, time, and chance. Also known as secularism, secular humanism, or humanism.

Parachurch: An organization that comes alongside the church, generally offering a more specialized ministry and narrower focus than the local church.

Premise: A foundational principle, a basis for reasoning and action.

Society: A distinct group of people distinguished by their common institutions, relationships, and culture.

Transformation: A substantial change in nature and character. Biblical transformation brings people into alignment with God's intentions.

Two-Thirds World: Geographical areas in Asia, Africa, Latin America, and limited regions of Europe and North America, characterized by contexts of need and by unique worldviews and cultures. Sometimes called the Third World (a term based on economic and quality-of-life indicators). Two-Thirds World, however, better indicates the percentage of the world's population in those geographical areas.

Universal church: Includes all Christians and their institutions or fellowships.

Western: While *Western Hemisphere* is a geographical term relating to the Americas (North, Central, South), there is also a *Western mindset,* referring to cultures originally marked by Greek, Roman, and Judeo-Christian influence. In this sense, the *West* refers to the conditions of life that characterize the worldviews of North American and European cultures, including contexts of relative affluence.

Wholistic ministry: Ministry that reflects God's concerns for whole persons and the whole of creation.

Worldview: A set of assumptions, held consciously or unconsciously, about the basic make-up of the world and about how the world works.

Bibliography

Bible Texts Cited (Abbreviations)

Living Bible (LB). Wheaton IL: Tyndale House Publishers, 1979.

New International Version (NIV). Colorado Springs CO: International Bible Society, 1978, 1984.

New King James Version (NKJ). Nashville TN: Thomas Nelson, Inc., 1979, 1982.

New Living Translation (NLT). Wheaton IL: Tyndale House Publishers, 1986.

The King James Version (KJV).

The Message. Colorado Springs: Navpress, 1993.

Story Sources

Story sources are *from Harvest archives*, unless otherwise noted.

Sources are listed *in order of the story's appearance in the chapter*. Names may be repeated if the same contributor's stories appeared more than once. A number in parentheses indicates the number of consecutive stories for one contributor. Source listings are intentionally vague to protect contributors.

Chapter 2
Dennis Tongoi, 2003. Stefan Eicher, FHI, 2001. Mark Wilson, FHI, November 2002. Cleiton and Eleuza Oliveira. Mary Tyler and Scott Allen, FHI, 2000. Ric Nisimiuk, 2001. Bob Moffitt.

Chapter 4
Bob Moffitt, undated. Guerino St. Simon, 1997. Ruth Concha, 2004. "Arturo's Story," Wholistic Ministry course, Disciple Nations Alliance, Internet.

Chapter 5
Demere Seyoum, FHI/Ethiopia, published paper, 2001.

Chapter 7
R. Beckham. John P. Wood, February 2004. Jon Sanborn, March 2004. Bob Moffitt and Jack Tesch, 1984; Cleiton and Eleuza Oliveira, 2003. Simon Nziramakenga; Pastor G.F. Muzala, 2003. Ric Nesimiuk.

Chapter 8
Ric Nesimiuk, 2002. John P. Wood, 2003. Simon Nziramakenga. Dennis Tongoi, 2003. Scott Allen, 2001. Cleiton and Eleuza Oliveira. Simon Nziramakenga. B. Hedlund, 2002. R. Beckham.

Part Three Prelude
Pastor Franco Onaga, 2003. Videotape from a global cell church meeting in Hong Kong, 2003.

Chapter 9
Bob Moffitt, 2003. Guerino St. Simon, 2004. Simon Nziramakenga, 2002. Cleiton and Eleuza Oliveira. *A Vision for Carapita*, Xiomara Suarez. 1998. Bob Moffitt, 1980s. Tom Polsin, 2003. Karla Tesch, 2004. Stephen Langa.

Chapter 10
Bob Moffitt, 1986. Joel Hauser, Nehemiah Center. Archives, 1980s. Chris Ampadu, 2002. Pyone Kyi, 2000. John P. Wood, 2002. Cleiton and Eleuza Oliveira, 2001. John P. Wood, 2002. Bob Moffitt, 1980s, John P. Wood, 2002. Bob Moffitt, Pastor S. P. Ratnakar, 2005.

Chapter 11
Bob Moffitt. Pastor Franco Onaga, 2003. Bob Moffitt, John P. Wood, 2002. John P. Wood, 2002, 2004(2). Andre Mwitwa, 2004.

Part Four Prelude
Bob Moffitt, 1980s. *Atuka,* video, 1996. Dr. Benjamin, 1989.

Chapter 12
Sample exercise sources: Linda Morris. Chris Ampadu. Karla Tesch. John P. Wood. Karla Tesch. Cleiton and Eleuza Oliveira. Linda Morris. Bob Moffitt. Chris Ampadu. Cleiton and Eleuza Oliveira. Chris Ampadu. Ric Nesimiuk.
Quiz exercise sources: Chris Ampadu. Linda Morris. John P. Wood. Karla Tesch. John P. Wood. Alex Fearon. Bob Moffitt.

Chapter 13
Chris Ampadu. Baptist pastor at Bangkok conference. Cleiton and Eleuza Oliveira. Tom Polsin (2). Cleiton and Eleuza Oliveira (6). Tom Polsin.

Chapter 14
Pastor Meshak Okumu, 2005. Karobia Njogu A., 2005. Alex Fearon, early 1990s. *A Vision for Carapita*, 1996. Pastor from mainline church in Maharashtra, India. Pastor Sohn Hoon, 2005. Ricci Paulino, 2005. Scott Allen, Disciple Nations Alliance, 2005. Stefan Eicher, Food for the Hungry, 2005.

Chapter 15
Aung _____, 2004. Bob Moffitt, 2005. Cleiton and Eleuza Oliveira, 2005. Bob Moffitt, 2005. Tom Polsin, 2004.

Works Cited

A Vision for Carapita. Phoenix: Harvest Foundation, 1997. Videocassette.

Atuka. Phoenix: Harvest Foundation, 1996. Videocassette.

Arizona Republic, "Thousands of deaths unsolved in Guatemala," 2 March 2004.

Barna, George. *A Fish out of Water.* Nashville TN: Integrity Publishers, 2002.

Barna Research Online. "Beliefs: General Religious—Faith Groups (2002)." Available from http://www.barna.org/cgi-bin/PageCategory.asp? CategoryID=2. Internet.

Barna Research Institute, "A Biblical Worldview Has a Radical Effect on a Person's Life," 1 December 2003. Available from http:// www.barna.org/FlexPage.aspx?Page=BarnaUpdate&BarnaUpdate ID=154. Internet.

Blackaby, Henry T. and Claude V. King. *Experiencing God.* Nashville: LifeWay Press, 1990.

Bloesch, Donald G. *The Reform of the Church.* Grand Rapids MI: William B. Eerdmans, 1970.

Boyd-MacMillan, Ronald. "The Cry of Iraq's Church." Available from http://www.charismamag.com/articledisplay.pl?ArticleID=7852. Internet.

Branco, Alex. "Business Men's Fellowship – India." Available from http:// bmfindia.org/mission.htm and http://bmfindia.org/whatis.htm. Internet.

Brown, Daniel A. *The Other Side of Pastoral Ministry.* Secunderabad, India: OM Books, 1999. Originally published in the U.S. by Zondervan.

Burnett, David G. *The Healing of the Nations: The Biblical Basis of the Mission of God.* Carlisle U.K.: Paternoster Press, Biblical Classics Library, revised edition, 1996.

Cahill, Thomas. *The Gifts of the Jews.* New York NY: Anchor Books, 1998.

Cahill, Thomas. *How the Irish Saved Civilization.* New York NY: Anchor Books, 1996.

Carlson, Raymond G., Cyril E. Homer, and D.V. Hurst. *The Assemblies of God in Mission.* Springfield MO: Gospel Publishing House, 1970.

Chambers, Oswald. *My Utmost for His Highest: An Updated Edition in Today's Language*, ed. James G. Reimann. Grand Rapids MI: Discovery House Publishers, 1935, revised 1992.

Chambers, Oswald. *My Utmost Devotional Bible.* Nashville TN: Thomas Nelson, 1992.

China Prayer Watch, Volume 11, Number 1. January-June, 2004.

Colson, Charles. *BreakPoint.* 22 March, 2004, quoting Hugh Hewitt.

Concha, Ruth. Manuscript review. Peru: 2003.

Crossman, Meg. Manuscript review. Arizona: 2003.

F. Davidson, A.M. Stibbs, and E.F. Kevan (eds). *The New Bible Commentary.* Grand Rapids MI: Eerdmans, 1968.

Disciple Nations Alliance. *Wholistic Ministry.* Phoenix: Food for the Hungry International and Harvest Foundation, 2002. Online course. Available from http://www.disciplenations.org. Internet.

Farah, Charles. "America's Pentecostals: What They Believe." *Christianity Today,* 16 October, 1987.

Graelein, Frank E. *The Expositor's Bible Commentary.* Volume 11. Grand Rapids MI: Zondervan, 1978.

Grant, George, *The Micah Mandate.* Chicago: Moody Press, 1995. Quoted in Disciple Nations Alliance. *Wholistic Ministry.* Phoenix: Food for the Hungry International and Harvest Foundation, 2002. Available from http://www.disciple-nations.org. Internet.

Hall, David W. (ed), "Earlier Paradigms for Welfare Reform: The Reformation Period." In *Welfare Reformed: A Compassionate Approach.* Phillipsburg NJ: Presbyterian & Reformed Publishing and Franklin TN: Legacy Communications, 1994. Co-publishers.

Hahn, Scott. *The Splendor of the Church.* St. Joseph Communications, Inc., undated. Videocassette.

Hannah, Ian. Monasticism. London: Allen and Unwin, 1924. Quoted in Pierson, Paul. "Missions and Community Development: A Historical Perspective." In *Christian Relief and Development: Developing Workers for Effective Ministry*, ed. Edgar J. Elliston. Dallas: Word Publishing, 1989.

Hepzi Joy, R.J. *History and Development of Education of Women in Kerala (1819-1947).* Kannammoola, Thiruvananthapuram, India: Seminary Publications, K.U.T. Seminary, 1995.

Holmes III, Urban. quoted in Ruben and Shawcheck, *A Guide to Prayer for Ministers and Other Servants.* Nashville TN: The Upper Room, 1983.

Homan, Ben. Food for the Hungry informational letter, Phoenix, 2001.

Lapin, Rabbi Daniel. "Equal Earthquakes with Unequal Results." 15 January, 2004. Available from http://www.tothesource.org/1_15_2004/1_15_2004.htm. Internet.

Lewis, Robert. *The Church of Irresistible Influence.* Grand Rapids MI: Zondervan, 2001.

Lord, Ellen. "Poverty prevalent in Haiti," *The Cincinnati Post.* 3 June 2000. Available from http://www.cincypost.com/news/2000/2haiti060300.html. Internet.

Mahan, Clarence. Review of *How the Irish Saved Civilization,* by Thomas Cahill. In AIS Bulletin, April 1997. Available from www.irises.org/ais810.htm. Internet.

Mangalwadi, Ruth and Vishal. *The Legacy of William Carey.* Illinois: Crossway Books, 1999.

Mangalwadi, Ruth and Vishal. *William Carey: A Tribute by an Indian Woman.* New Delhi: Nivedit Good Books Distributors Private Limited, 1993.

Mangalwadi, Vishal. *Truth and Social Reform.* London: Nivedit Good Books Distributors Pvt. Ltd., 1985. Note: This work was not cited but is recommended reading.

McLaughlin, Bishop Vaughn, Potter's House Christian Fellowship, www.pottershouse.org. Internet

Miller, Darrow L. *Discipling Nations: The Power of Truth to Transform Cultures.* Seattle: YWAM Publishing, 2001.

Miller, Darrow L., Bob Moffitt, and Scott D. Allen. *God's Remarkable Plan for the Nations.* Phoenix: Food for the Hungry International, 2004.

Mother Teresa. Available from http://www.loveoffering.com/MotherTeresa.htm. Internet.

Newton, Joseph Fort. "Social Saviors." *Union Life,* July/August 1990.

Nouwen, Henri. quoted in Ruben P. Job and Norman Shawchuck, *A Guide to Prayer for Ministers and Other Servants* (The Upper Room, 1983), p. 68.

Oden, Thomas C. "Two Thousand Years of Caring for the Poor." *Stewardship Journal*, Spring 1993.

Oliveira, Cleiton and Eleuza. Manuscript review. Brazil: 2003.

Pierson, Paul. "Missions and Community Development: A Historical Perspective." In *Christian Relief and Development: Developing Workers for Effective Ministry*, ed. Edgar J. Elliston. Dallas: Word Publishing, 1989.

Ro, Bong Rin. "The Perspectives of Church History from New Testament Times to 1960." In *In Word and Deed: Evangelism and Social Respnsibility*, ed. Bruce Nichols. Grand Rapids: Eerdmans, 1985.

Scottsdale Tribune. "1 billion pledged to rebuild Haiti." 21 July 2004.

Sider, Ronald J. "An Inseparable Partnership." In *One-Sided Christianity?* Grand Rapids MI: Zondervan, 1993.

Sine, Tom (ed). *The Church in Response to Human Need.* Monrovia CA: Missions Advanced Research and Communication Center, 1983.

Snyder, Howard A. *The Community of the King.* Downers Grove IL: Inter-Varsity Press, 1977.

Southern Baptist Church, "The Baptist Faith and Message, Section XV." Available from http://www.sbc.net/bfm/bfm2000.asp#xv. Internet.

Spittler, Russell P. "Children of the Twentieth Century." In *The Quiet Revolution,* ed. Robin Keeley. Grand Rapids MI: Eerdmans, 1985.

St. Francis of Assisi. QuotationReference.com. Available from http://www. quotationreference.com/quotefinder.php?byax=1&strt=1&subj= St.+Francis+of+Assisi. Internet.

Stark, Rodney. *The Rise of Christianity.* San Francisco: HarperCollins Publishers, 1997.

Stephens, Randall J. "Assessing the Roots of Pentecostalism: A Historiographic Essay." Available from http://are.as.wvu.edu/ pentroot.htm. Internet.

Stott, John. *Involvement: Being a Responsible Christian in a Non-Christian Society.* Old Tappan NJ: Fleming H. Revell, 1984, 1985.

Transparency International. *Corruption Perceptions Index 2002.* Available from http://www.transparency.org. Internet.

U.S. Department of State. *Background Notes: Haiti, March 1998.* Available from http://www.state.fov/www/background_notes/haiti-0398. bgn.html. Document on line. Internet.

Warren, Rick. *The Purpose Driven Life.* Michigan: Zondervan, 2002.

Warren, Rick. *The Purpose Driven Church.* Michigan: Zondervan, 1995.

Willard, Dallas. *The Divine Conspiracy.* New York: HarperSanFrancisco, 1998.

Wright, Alex. Review of *How the Irish Saved Civilization* by Thomas Cahill. 24 December 2003. Available from http://www.agwright. com/blog/archives/000802.html. Internet.

Wright, Christopher J. H. *Deuteronomy: New International Biblical Commentary—Old Testament,* Volume 4. Peabody MA: Hendrickson Publishers, 1996.

Additional Resources for Wholistic Ministry

Written for the Local Church—Internationally

Bush, Luis K (ed). *A Unifying Vision of the Church's Mission*. Thailand: 2004 Forum for World Evangelization, 2004.

Yamamori, Tetsunao y C. Rene Padilla (eds). *The Local Church, Agent of Transformation: An Ecclesiology for Integral Mission*. Buenos Aires, Argentina: Ediciones Kairos, 2004.

Written for the Local Church in North America

Allen, Roland. *The Spontaneous Expansion of the Church*. Grand Rapids MI: Eerdmans, 1962.

Clegg, Tom and Warren Bird. *Lost in America: How You and Your Church Can Impact the World Next Door*. Loveland CO: Group Publishing, Inc., 2001.

Dennison, Jack. *City Reaching: On the Road to Community Transformation*. Pasadena CA: William Carey Library, 1999.

Gibbs, Edie. *In Name Only: Tackling the Problem of Nominal Christianity*. Wheaton IL: Victor Books, 1994.

Hunter, Kent. *Discover Your Windows: Lining up with God's Vision*. Nashille TN: Abingdon Press, 2002.

Mallory, Sue. *The Equipping Church*. Grand Rapids MI: Zondervan/ Leadership Network, Inc., 2001.

McManus, Erwin Raphael. *An Unstoppable Force: Daring to Become the Church GOD had in Mind*. Loveland CO: Group Publishing, 2001.

Rusaw, Rick and Eric Swanson. *The Externally Focused Church*. Loveland CO: Group Publishing, Inc., 2004.

Schwarz, Christian and Christoph Schalk. *Natural Church Development*. St. Charles IL: ChurchSmart Resources, 1998.

Sjogren, Steve. *Conspiracy of Kindness: A Refreshing New Approach to Sharing the Love of Jesus with Others*. Ann Arbor MI: Servant Publications, 1993.

Sider, Ron, Philip Olson, and Heidi Rolland Unruh. *Churches that Make a Difference: Reaching Your Community with Good News and Good Works*. Grand Rapids MI: Baker Books, 2002.

About the Authors

Bob Moffitt is an experienced teacher and organizational strategist. His work is based on these primary convictions:

- The Gospel must be both proclaimed and demonstrated.
- The local church is God's principal vehicle to demonstrate His love in our broken world.
- Demonstration of God's love must be individual *and* corporate.

Bob is founder and president of Harvest, which trains local church leaders in wholistic ministry—especially pastors and church leaders in the Two-Thirds World. Harvest develops wholistic training materials and conferences. Since 1981, Bob has conducted conferences for thousands of local church leaders in over thirty countries.

God has given Bob rich experiences that have shaped this work:

- Peace Corps service in Malawi, Africa
- Graduate studies in Israel, Switzerland, and the U.S.
- Mobilization of Christians—founding and directing Partners Inc.; the Hunger Corps of Food for the Hungry; and Harvest
- Ph.D. in Adult Education and Community Development

Bob serves his local church as an elder and missions chairman. He and his wife Judy have three adult children and grandchildren.

Karla Tesch has served as Harvest's editor since 1983. Her education, interests, and experience have made *If Jesus Were Mayor* a delightful challenge. Nothing, though, has qualified her as much as her life-long experience with a wide range of local churches—from social action to evangelical, from liturgical to charismatic. She has learned from each and has long believed that spiritual and social ministry are not opposites. *If Jesus Were Mayor* is her message, too.

Karla and her husband Jack are active in their church and community. They have two adult children and a growing family circle.